ATHEISM:
A GUIDE FOR THE PERPLEXED

ATHEISM:
A GUIDE FOR THE PERPLEXED

KERRY WALTERS

continuum

The Continuum International Publishing Group Inc
80 Maiden Lane, New York, NY 10038

The Continuum International Publishing Group Ltd
The Tower Building, 11 York Road, London SE1 7NX

www.continuumbooks.com

Library of Congress Cataloging-in-Publication Data
A catalog record for this book is available from the Library of Congress.

ISBN: 978-0-8264-4326-7 (hardcover)
ISBN: 978-0-8264-2493-8 (paperback)

Typeset by Newgen Imaging Systems Pvt Ltd, Chennai, India
Printed in the United States of America

For Fred Mahan
A lifelong seeker of truth

CONTENTS

WHAT THIS BOOK ISN'T AND WHAT IT IS

After Buddha was dead, his shadow was still shown for centuries in a cave—a tremendous, gruesome shadow. God is dead; but given the way of men, there may still be caves for thousands of years in which his shadow will be shown.

Friedrich Nietzsche, The Gay Science

A deluded patient runs into a doctor's office. "Doc!" he shouts, panic-stricken. "I think I'm dead!" The doctor tries to persuade him that he's in fact very much alive, but the patient won't listen. Finally the exasperated doctor says, "Look, dead guys don't bleed, right?" "Right," agrees the patient. "Okay then," replies the doctor. "Let's just see if *you* bleed." He takes a needle and jabs it into the patient's thumb. The patient stares at the blood beading up and shakes his head in disbelief. "Holy cow!" he says. "I was wrong. Dead men *do* bleed!"

In the eyes of many, disputants in the seemingly endless debate about God's existence frequently come across like the patient in this joke. Intractably set in their beliefs, atheists and theists too often seem more intent on scoring forensic points at one another's expense than carefully following where the evidence leads them. Each side appears so utterly convinced of the correctness of its own position and the absurdity of the other that it's difficult to see what, if anything, either would allow as legitimate counterarguments. Like the patient too convinced he's dead to see evidence to the contrary, many of the loudest voices in the debate about God refuse to accept the possibility that anyone who disagrees with them deserves to be taken seriously in even the slightest way.

The already acrimonious debate has morphed into a cultural slugfest in recent years with the rise of religious fundamentalism on the one hand and the so-called New Atheism on the other. Fundamentalist Muslims issue fatwas that condemn Enlightenment values and condone violence against nonbelievers. Christian fundamentalists just as loudly condemn all opinions and behavior that fail to accord with their closed worldview. Fed up with such intolerance, especially since the terrorist attacks of 9/11, champions of atheism react by indiscriminately decrying religious belief as absurd, fanatical, and violence-prone. The angry militancy on both sides encourages a take-no-prisoners style of debate that increasingly sacrifices civility and rational discourse for the sake of making global denunciations. It doesn't help that the debate is frequently egged on by revenue-hungry publishers eager to cater to the public's delight in a good row.

Thus Sam Harris, Richard Dawkins, and Christopher Hitchens, the best-known atheists today and leaders of the New Atheist movement, thunder that "preposterous" religious faith "allows otherwise normal human beings to reap the fruits of madness and consider them holy" (Harris 2004, p. 73); that religious education of any kind is tantamount to "child abuse" (Dawkins 2006, p. 315); and that "religion poisons everything" (Hitchens 2007, p. 13). Theistic champions are scarcely less pugnacious. Alister McGrath (McGrath 2007, pp. xii, xi) dismisses Dawkins' best-selling *The God Delusion* as a "half-baked" presentation of "tired, weak and recycled arguments" and Roy Abraham Varghese (Varghese 2007, pp. xxiii, xxii), insisting that popularizers of atheism view themselves "not simply as scribes, but as high priests," charges that their exegesis is often "patently dishonest."

The angry mutual denunciations that characterize the recent debate have gotten so out of hand that one perceptive commentator concludes that "the blustering televangelists, and the atheists who rant about the evils of religion, are little more than carnival barkers. They are in show business, and those in show business know complexity does not sell . . . They banter back and forth in predictable sound bites [and] trade absurdity for absurdity" (Hedges 2008, p. 32). Unfortunately, this is not an inaccurate appraisal. The God debate in general, and rational defenses of atheism in particular, have a long and honorable pedigree. But of late the conversation has been hijacked by high profile militant fundamentalists and celebrity atheists.

The attack-dog style adopted by the big-name adversaries in the debate about God's existence not only tends to generate more heat than light. It also, sadly, models a particular tone and method subsequently

2

adopted by thousands of readers, viewers, and auditors of the public debate. Even a quick scan of the hundreds of blogs devoted to the atheist/theist tussle reveals a shockingly high level of rancor and name-calling and an equally chilling scarcity of rational examination of arguments. Believing and disbelieving bloggers gleefully condemn each other's moral character, intelligence, motivations, and political leanings in terms whose militancy allow for no real discussion.

The heat generated by the question of God's existence isn't surprising. The topic, after all, is one in which most people on both sides are emotionally and intellectually invested, and it's not hard to understand how disagreement can quickly roll over into polemical sniping. For the genuine theist, faith in a loving, powerful, and perfect God is the nucleus which holds all her other beliefs in place and provides her with a deep sense of meaning. Having that belief called into question—much less derided as morally and intellectually bankrupt—can be excruciatingly threatening. For the genuine atheist, an equally strong commitment to reason and naturalism—a commitment which serves as her intellectual center of gravity and source of meaning—makes belief in God both irrational and dangerous. She's not merely intellectually frustrated by God-belief. Given the sorry history of religious persecution in general and the recent surge of fundamentalism in particular, she may even feel personally threatened by it. In such a climate, it's hard for her to adopt a live-and-let-live attitude towards theists.

But the disputants' deep personal investment in the God debate does more than explain the militancy and intractability of either side. It also points to the real need to think as clearly and fairly as possible about the issue. Put simply, the stakes are too high to settle for conclusions based more on vehement dislike of the other side than on sensitive and rigorous thinking. Granted, some good arguments can be found in both atheism proponents and their theistic adversaries. But ferreting them out from the thicket of polemic that surrounds them is both wearisome and disheartening. For the general reader trying to make some sense of the debate, it can all be frustratingly perplexing. So it's important to take a step back from the polemical battles long enough to sound out the strengths and weaknesses of the pertinent arguments.

In this book, I try to do just that in examining the case for atheism. I've written especially for three classes of readers: (1) those who, although perhaps entertained by the pyrotechnics of the current popular debate, are ultimately intellectually dissatisfied by its generally polemical approach; (2) those who have dipped into the non-polemical, philosophically technical defenses of atheism, been puzzled by the formalistic (and typically incomprehensible to the person untrained in symbolic logic) ways in which the arguments are presented, and seek a rigorous alternative written in plain language; and (3) those looking for an even-handed and representative exploration of the atheist position which goes beyond quick summaries and actually analyzes representative arguments and counterarguments drawn from the analytic and Continental philosophical traditions as well as contemporary biological and physical science.

My hope is that this book also will be of service to readers who already may have made a choice for either atheism or theism, but who (unlike their militant counterparts) realize that both sides have something to learn from one another. Commitment, after all, isn't dogmatism. The universe is a big place, and it's folly to presume that one's own perspective maps all its corners in a perfectly adequate way. French philosopher Simone Weil once wrote that atheist challenges can serve as a "purification" of religion (Weil 1952, p. 168). By the same token, a good understanding of theism can keep atheists honest. Too frequently, especially these days, atheists tilt against theistic windmills that God-believers long ago abandoned. So fruitful conversation between proponents of atheism and proponents of theism is always possible. If nothing else, each position serves as a useful check on the other's excesses. More positively, open-minded dialogue may reveal that atheists and theists, despite their disagreement about the reality of God, hold more in common than extremists on either side are willing to admit. True believers may feel no need of this clarification, but thinking persons do.

The atheists getting most of the press these days, the New Atheists (more on them in the next chapter), have focused a great deal of their attention (and rancor) on institutional religions and fundamentalist doctrine. The enthusiasm with which the New Atheists' bestsellers are read testifies to the contempt in which religious fundamentalism is held by wide segments of North Americans and Europeans, and this in itself is a phenomenon worth noticing. But the approach also has been roundly criticized on two separate counts. In the first place, detractors argue, condemnations of the intolerance and outright violence that institutionalized religions can breed are perfectly justified, but they don't speak one way or another about whether there is a God. Religion is an anthropological and psychological phenomenon, but questions about God's existence are metaphysical. Second, highlighting the absurdity of fundamentalist beliefs and practices and then triumphantly announcing that God-belief has thereby been demolished is straw-manning of the worst sort. Serious challenges to theism should properly focus on its strongest, most central arguments, not the outlandish claims of fringe extremists that most reasonable people, theist and atheist alike, already reject.

The New Atheists to whom these criticisms are directed defend their approach, and some of their responses are examined in later chapters. But to lay a few of my cards on the table, I confess that my sympathies in this regard are with the critics. Accordingly, to invoke the distinction famously made by Pascal, the arguments analyzed here deal more with the "God of the philosophers" than the "God of Abraham, Isaac, and Jacob." My working assumption is that atheism stands or falls on how strong a philosophical case its defenders can offer, not on how clever they are at pointing out inconsistencies in scriptural texts, vivisecting popular folk beliefs, or revisiting the depredations of organized religion. There may be a place for such exercises, but this book isn't one of them.

Chapter 1 explores a few crucial preliminaries. Perplexities in defining the words "atheism" and "theism" are discussed, the argument over which side in the debate has the burden of proof is examined, and a sketch of the history of atheism is offered. We'll discover that even though there are scattered forerunners stretching back to ancient Greece, atheism as we most commonly use the term today is a quite modern phenomenon.

Atheism isn't simply a rejection of God's existence. Although it may sound strange, disbelief in God is only one aspect, and not necessarily the central one, in the reflective atheist's way of thinking about reality. Chapter 2 discusses the naturalistic worldview that typically grounds the atheist's disbelief. While atheism proper doesn't really arrive on the historical stage until the seventeenth century, naturalism has a long and honorable lineage, dating from the pre-Socratic philosophers. In exploring the naturalism that typically underpins modern atheism, we'll spend some time thinking about worldviews in general and whether they necessarily beg the question when it comes to first principles. This in turn leads to an examination of the rather common charge that atheism is as much a "faith" as the theism it rejects.

An endorsement of naturalism doesn't necessarily rule out the possibility of a God. So-called methodological naturalists, for example, can with perfect consistency embrace either theism or agnosticism. So atheists typically go a step further by (1) rebutting traditional arguments for God's existence, and (2) offering positive arguments against God's existence. Chapters 3 and 4 examine both traditional and contemporary versions of the strongest of these arguments. Chapter 3 examines atheistic rebuttals of ontological, cosmological, and design arguments. Chapter 4 explores positive arguments based on divine hiddenness, the incoherence of divine attributes, the meaninglessness of religious language, and the problem of evil.

I've mentioned that I agree with the claim that there's no necessary connection between the beliefs and practices of religious institutions and the existence of God. While it's true that organized religion historically has encouraged much intolerance and violence, it's also the case that (1) religions have no monopoly on such things, and (2) religions have also enriched cultures when it comes to humanitarianism, architecture, literature, the musical and visual arts, and so on. Still, if the atheist is correct in her denial of God's existence, the obvious perplexity is why religions exist in the first place. Chapter 5 explores some naturalistic explanations of religion and God-belief offered by biologists, psychologists, anthropologists, and philosophers.

One standard criticism of atheism is that the denial of God opens the door for moral nihilism. The atheist retort is that while a loss of faith in God *can* lead to ethical libertinism, there's no necessity that it *must*. Chapter 6 explores the atheist case for a godless morality by (1) examining the counter-claim that it's actually theism, not atheism, that breeds moral chaos; (2) analyzing atheist claims that morality based on divine commands is either normatively unpredictable or logically incoherent; and (3) taking a look at some of the naturalistic foundations and principles that atheists have suggested for humanistic rules of conduct.

Most people want their lives to mean something. The meaning for which theists yearn is intimately bound up with their belief in God. For them, God's existence guarantees physical orderliness and spiritual purposefulness in the universe, and offers personal fulfillment in this life and the next. The intuition behind this, so deeply engrained by history as to seem self-evident, is that the only meaning worth having is cosmic meaning. But as we'll see in Chapter 7, atheists deny that this notion of overarching purposefulness is necessary for a fulfilled life. One's life, they argue, can be quite meaningful even in the absence of cosmic purpose. In fact, some atheists argue that the reality of anything like the purposefulness theists desire would inhibit and impoverish human opportunities for meaning.

Chapter 8 examines whether it makes any sense to talk about a godless spirituality. Some atheists argue that psychological experiences such as awe, wonder, gratitude and love, which religious traditions try to explain by appeals to God, remain emotionally, conceptually, and morally important even after belief in God vanishes. Dismissing them as irrationalities or trivialities, or refusing to take them seriously because of their traditional association with religious and mystical experience, seems foolishly reductive. Regardless of how much we come to know about the physical workings of the universe, the sheer mysteriousness of why there's something rather than nothing remains—or, at least in the mind of many (although not all) atheists, should remain. So the key question examined in this chapter is how this sense of mystery can be appreciated from an atheist perspective. In exploring the case for an atheist spirituality, I suggest that the mystery-of-being experience might be common ground for a fruitful atheist/theist dialogue.

Obviously this book is intended to be read as a whole from start to finish. But each chapter may also be read separately without losing too much meaning. Thus, readers who are particularly interested in some chapter topics more than others and who wish to go straight to them should be able to do so without any difficulty. My primary goal throughout has been to make this as reader-friendly a book as possible.

A final word. Although many atheists today come across as the dogmatic true believer lampooned in the joke which launched these introductory remarks, my suspicion is that most thinking nonbelievers are more temperate. For many of them, the sense of liberation that a rejection of religious faith can bring is always shadowed, sometimes just barely and sometimes quite bleakly, by the realization that their position calls for levels of intellectual honesty and moral courage that are sometimes hard to bear. Theistic belief may indeed be merely a cultural habit that has no basis in reality. But it's a longstanding one to which most of us in the West, for all our contemporary indifference to institutionalized religion, have been bred.

It's difficult, even today, not to feel the same sense of ambivalent nostalgia expressed a century and a half ago in Matthew Arnold's "Dover Beach":

> The Sea of Faith
> Was once, too, at the full, and round earth's shore
> Lay like the folds of a bright girdle furl'd.
> But now I only hear
> Its melancholy, long, withdrawing roar,
> Retreating, to the breath
> Of the night-wind, down the vast edges drear
> And naked shingles of the world. (Arnold 1961, p. 162)

Arnold goes on to say that the new land revealed by the Sea of Faith's retreat is "like a land of dreams," diverse, beautiful, and new. But at the same time, he warns that the very novelty that stirs up wonder and excitement also reveals a "darkling plain" where God's palpable absence throws traditional certitude, peace, and succor in doubt. Arnold's reminder of the distressing sense of dislocation that can arise from a personal and cultural loss of faith in God is not only an astute psychological observation. It's also a judicious caution both to overly-cerebral atheists who think that the choice for or against God is a purely intellectual one, and to militant atheists whose disdain for theists inhibits the empathy that's essential for dialogue.

CHAPTER 1

WHAT IS ATHEISM?

To you I'm an atheist; to God, I'm the Loyal Opposition.
          Woody Allen, "Stardust Memories"

It is only a common prejudice that induces us to believe that atheism is a most fearful state.
          Pierre Bayle, "On Comets"

Most people just naturally assume that an atheist is someone who doesn't believe in God. This is a decent enough common sense definition, but it's not very helpful if the point is to analyze philosophical arguments for and against atheism. The trouble with the common sense definition is that it's too broad. It doesn't help us distinguish between different levels of nonbelief in God. It doesn't give us any idea of whether there's more than one variety of atheism. And it doesn't tell us anything about the sort of God the atheist doesn't believe in.

So in this chapter, we'll clear the stage for later ones by distinguishing atheism from other varieties of nonbelief, looking at some of the motivations for nonbelief, examining the relationship between atheism and theism, exploring the question of the burden of proof in the debate between believers and atheists, and taking a quick look at the development of atheism in Western thought. For readers anxious to dive straight into the particulars of the disagreement between believers and atheists, this preliminary discussion may seem dry. But in this debate, as in so many others, a great deal of potential confusion can be forestalled by getting clear on just what it is that's being debated. So patience here, as elsewhere, is a virtue.

REQUIEM AETERNAM DEO

In one of his most gripping and famous parables, Friedrich Nietzsche tells the story of the "madman" who wandered through the streets "in the bright morning hours" holding up a lighted lantern and repeatedly crying "I seek God! I seek God!" Townspeople laughed, mockingly asking him whether God was hiding or had gotten lost somewhere in the cosmos. Finally losing patience at their gibes, the madman shouts out that *he'll* tell the people where God is. *"We have killed him*—you and I. All of us are his murderers." And then he forced his way into a nearby church and struck up a requiem for the late deity, insisting that churches had now become "the tombs and sepulchers of God" (Nietzsche 1974, pp. 181, 182).

For Nietzsche, the "murder" instruments wielded against God were twofold: cultural indifference to traditional religious beliefs on the one hand, and outright skeptical hostility to them on the other. The indifference was the product of an age so preoccupied with pursuing the bottom line that it had no time for other-worldly concerns; the hostility sprang from embracing the alternative scientific worldview defended by Darwin, among others. Although Nietzsche was under no illusions about the difficulty of the transition—it's one thing to forgo intellectual allegiance to the notion of a God, he insisted, but quite another to shake off emotional reliance on it— he was hopeful that his "madman" was prophetic of a new world in which humans, rejecting God, became god-like through their repudiation. "There has never been a greater deed," he wrote, "and whoever is born after us—for the sake of this deed he will belong to a higher history than all history hitherto" (p. 181).

Obviously, Nietzsche's hopes for a godless future haven't panned out. People all over the world still believe in a divine being or beings, even though concepts of God vary from religion to religion and even from person to person within the same religious tradition. But Nietzsche wasn't entirely mistaken, either, because between 500 million and 750 million people today do *not* accept the existence of God. In the global line-up of beliefs about God, this impressively puts nonbelief in fourth place after Christianity (2 billion), Islam (1.2 billion), and Hinduism (900 million). There are twice as many nonbelievers as Buddhists and 41 times as many as Jews. And even though some kind of God-belief is still by far the majority opinion, religion has lost much of its hold on popular culture in many societies. So even though modern secularization may not actually have murdered God, it certainly has made many traditional features of God-belief appear quaint and implausible.

Generally speaking, erosion of God-belief is more evident in nations that are healthier (and have lower birth rates), wealthier, better educated, and democratic. Recent surveys indicate, for example, that well over half of all Swedes, Danes, Norwegians, Japanese, South Koreans, Czechs, and French don't believe in God. Nonbelievers in Estonia, Germany, Russia, Hungary, the Netherlands, Britain, and Belgium hover around the 50 percent mark. By contrast, God-belief in Asia, Africa, and the Middle East is alive and well. The only obvious exceptions to this correlation are relatively poor Vietnam, which reports an astounding 81 percent nonbelief rate (although this may be inflated because of Vietnam's official status as an atheist nation), and the affluent United States, which reports a mere 3 to 9 percent nonbelief rate (Zuckerman 2007).

Revealingly, self-reports of nonbelief in God change pretty drastically if respondents are specifically asked whether they identify themselves as "atheists." One study showed, for example, that only 10 percent of Norwegians, 19 percent of French, and 20 percent of Czechs are willing to accept the title (Greeley 2003). One commentator (Zuckerman 2007, p. 47) speculates that this is because the "designation 'atheist' is stigmatized in many societies," and doubtless this is part of the explanation. The word "atheism" until quite recently has been used mainly as an insult. But it also indicates that "atheism" oughtn't to be thought of as synonymous with "nonbelief," and this in turn means that there's more than one way to not believe in God.

VARIETIES OF NONBELIEF

Atheism, of course, is only one class of nonbelief in God. Moreover, there are several subsets of atheism proper. So it's possible for someone to be a nonbeliever without also being an atheist. But all atheists are necessarily nonbelievers.

In the broadest sense, nonbelief includes,

1. Unbelief, an agnostic suspension of belief that either denies there are good grounds one way or the other for God-belief, or holds that arguments on either side are equally strong.

2. Overt disbelief or atheism, which can be further subdivided into (a) positive atheism, an active disbelief in God and (b) negative atheism, the absence of belief in God. All positive atheists are necessarily negative atheists, but the converse doesn't hold. Both positive and negative atheism may be further subdivided into (i) militant and (ii) moderate varieties. Militant atheists, such as physicist Steven Weinberg, tend to think that God-belief is not only erroneous but pernicious. "I am all in favor of a dialogue between science and religion," writes Weinberg, "but not a constructive dialogue," and asserts that he'd like to make it impossible for all intelligent people to be religious (Weinberg 2003, p. 40). Moderate atheists agree that God-belief is unjustifiable, but see nothing inherently pernicious in it. What leads to excess, they argue, is intolerant dogmatism and extremism, and these are qualities of ideologies in general, religious or nonreligious. Thus atheist philosopher Julian Baggini, while sympathetic to the militant's position, ultimately concludes that it's "healthier to at least admit the possibility that there is something in what [religious people] believe than to simply stamp my foot and curse their stupidity" (Baggini 2003, p. 104).
3. Finally, both atheism and agnosticism may be (a) practical, a (frequently uncritical) working assumption of nonbelief that undergirds one's worldview and everyday living; or (b) philosophical, a reflective, intellectually justified nonbelief. Obviously any given nonbeliever's position may be both practical and philosophical.

Not surprisingly, philosophical atheists put a high premium on reason, insisting that a rejection of God-belief must be based on the same judicious scrutiny of available evidence and arguments called for in examining any claim. But in fact, most people who consider themselves nonbelievers of one kind or another probably have arrived at their positions through less than rigorously logical routes.[1]

Some, for example, may have grown up in nonreligious families, and because of their early enculturation are simply indifferent to religion. Their atheism or agnosticism isn't based on rational arguments so much as the fact that belief was never a live possibility for them to begin with. John Stuart Mill, raised in an utterly secular family and describing himself as "one of the very few examples of [someone] who has not thrown off religious belief, but [instead] never had it" (Mill 1924, p. 36), falls into this category. Nonbelief born from familial indifference doesn't preclude the possibility of consciously grounding it with rational arguments later, and Mill certainly went on to do precisely this. So it's entirely possible for a culturally-absorbed nonbelief to become a deliberative, consciously-chosen, philosophical nonbelief. But as the influence of traditional religious beliefs continues to decline in secularized societies, nonbelief of the enculturated indifference variety is likely to increase.

Other people may disbelieve in God because they endured unhappy religious experiences as children or because an especially traumatic incident in which God didn't answer their prayers persuaded them of God's nonexistence. Literary and autobiographical accounts of childhoods blighted by religiously fanatic parents attest to the fact that many nonbelievers reject God because of what atheist Richard Dawkins doesn't hesitate to call the "child abuse" of early religious training. (We'll explore his reasons in Chapter 6.) Edmund Gosse's 1907 autobiography *Father and Son* or Ayaan Hirsi Ali's searing recent memoir *Infidel* attest to the vehemence with which young victims of zealotry can be physically battered into rebelling against God-belief later in life. Other negative experiences may be less overtly brutal but still psychologically traumatic. An acquaintance of mine once confessed that she lost her belief in God when, as a child, the God whom she implored to fix the wrist she'd just broken in a fall from a tree bitterly disappointed her by failing to come through. Similarly, the fifth-century BCE Diagoras of Melos apparently became an atheist after praying unsuccessfully to the gods for the return of a lost manuscript (Thrower 2000, p. 32).

Of course, the psychological trauma that can slay God-belief need not be generated by events in which the nonbeliever is directly involved. Many people have had their faith shattered by natural disasters or egregious acts of inhumanity in which they personally suffer no harm. The great Lisbon earthquake of 1755 which killed upwards of 100,000 persons, hundreds of them women and children attending mass in the city's dozens of churches, shattered many a faith in a wise and benevolent deity. Eli Wiesel, in his autobiographical novel *Night*, tells the story of an Auschwitz inmate who, his faith destroyed by the horrors of Auschwitz, despairingly shouts out during the execution of a fellow prisoner that it is God who dangles from the gibbet (Wiesel 1982, p. 62).

As in the case of nonbelief from indifference, rational defenses for trauma-induced nonbelief may be, and frequently are, constructed later on. But the fact that the initial impetus is sparked by a painful experience usually adds a particular poignancy to subsequent arguments not found in more abstractly philosophical discussions.

Some nonbelievers claim they doubt or reject the existence of God because they possess generally skeptical temperaments. Nietzsche, for example, called himself a "natural atheist," although it's not entirely clear what he meant by the term. Others may find religious ritualism so disagreeable that they migrate from aesthetic repulsion to actual nonbelief. Still others may find the moral hypocrisy of some religious leaders distasteful enough to wash their hands of religion altogether. Finally, in all honesty, still others may be nonbelievers for much the same reasons that they're also politically apathetic or culturally illiterate or couch potatoes: intellectual and imaginative shallowness.

The point is that nonbelievers can and do arrive at their positions by way of any number of meandering and sometimes intersecting paths. That's why, when nonbelievers *do* begin to construct philosophical arguments for their position, it's important that they not confuse psychological, biographical, or environmental *causes* with objective, evidential *reasons*. It's one thing to disbelieve in God because of unanswered prayers, overbearingly pious parents, or a skeptical temperament. It's another to justify this by providing rationally grounded reasons for it. The former explains (perhaps) why one holds a particular belief, but does nothing in the way of providing grounds for it. Only reasons can do that.

One would think that the distinction between causes and reasons is an obvious one, but it's so frequently blurred in debates about God's existence that it's worth mentioning. Disputes about God are rarely (I'm tempted to say "never") the dispassionately rational affairs that philosophers like to imagine them. For most people—including philosophers—they dredge up deep feelings of anger, insecurity, resentment, confidence, betrayal, and gratitude. They reanimate the pain or joy of past experiences and color the hopes and fears we invest in the future. Even those people who grew up in religiously indifferent households have probably formed some positive or negative religious associations simply by living in societies where God-belief is the broader norm. It's not surprising, then, that what may be emotionally powerful causes of our beliefs about God are frequently confused with the reasons for those beliefs about God. The wonder is that we manage to disentangle them as well as we do.

There are two more common kinds of nonbelief which are especially interesting because they're not what they appear to be. The first might be called de facto nonbelief, and the second de facto belief.

Although he doesn't actually use the term, de facto nonbelief was a special concern for the nineteenth-century philosopher Soren Kierkegaard. To his mind, it's a form of self-duplicity indulged in by complacent people who claim to believe in God but whose manner of living and scale of priorities suggest otherwise. If one believes in the existence of God, says Kierkegaard, then consistency demands that one also necessarily believes that nothing is more real than God. (As we'll see in Chapter 4, this claim isn't unlike one of the steps in the ontological argument for the existence of God.) God's being relies on nothing, whereas the being of everything else is totally dependent for both origin and continuation on God. It follows that one's belief in God should be the nucleus around which all other beliefs revolve, and that the believer's subjective relationship to his God-belief should be more intense (a "passionate inwardness," says Kierkegaard) than his relationship with any of his other beliefs. In other words, genuine belief in God should outweigh all others in centrality and intensity because the authentic believer holds nothing to be more real than God.

In practice, though, many believers—most of them, suspects Kierkegaard—don't give God-belief pride of place. Their belief is marginal, although occasionally leaping to center stage in foxhole moments of crisis or ostentatiously invoked in solemn tones when it's self-servingly expedient to do so. Their daily existence, their interpersonal relationships, their self-identity and their working assumptions about the world are for the most part untouched by their compartmentalized God-belief. The belief remains impersonally abstract. It's a pseudo-belief rather than a genuine one, and its holder is actually a de facto nonbeliever rather than the believer he thinks he is. The position is more subtle than garden variety hypocrisy, but it's just as ancient. The author of the Christian Book of Revelation roundly condemns "tepidity" in the faithful, a characteristic strikingly similar to de facto nonbelief (Rev 3: 15–16).

Kierkegaard's insistence that a person's God-belief must be his absolute center of gravity may be too uncompromising. Perhaps it makes more sense to think of religious conviction in terms of gradations, with lesser degrees of intensity not necessarily being inauthentic simply because they fall on the lower end of the scale. But Kierkegaard's general point is still intriguing. If nothing else, it's a reminder that, for many, God-belief is more habit than conviction.[2]

A de facto nonbeliever is someone who deceives himself into thinking he's a believer when he's not. Although not quite as common, a de facto believer is a person who deceives himself into thinking he's a nonbeliever, when in fact he *does* believe. Again, this isn't hypocrisy so much as self-deception.

There are two kinds of de facto believers. One is the self-proclaimed nonbeliever who, thinking she's repudiated God's existence, nonetheless clings to a vision of reality which carries most or all of the characteristics it would if God existed—for example, some version of personal immortality, deep purposefulness, cosmic benignity and even benevolence, and so on. One frequently finds this sort of de facto believer among liberal religionists (some Unitarian-Universalists, for example) who intellectually doubt or even deny the existence of a deity but feel great nostalgia for traditional religious values, beliefs, and assurances.

The other type of de facto believer is the God-rebel, a person so outraged by innocent suffering in the world that she angrily condemns the God she holds responsible for it, and confuses her moral condemnation of God for a rejection of God's existence. The give-away is the high level of rage and betrayal the de facto believer hangs onto even after she persuades herself that she no longer believes in God. Philosophically, she may indeed have embraced nonbelief. But practically, things are otherwise. One doesn't react so strongly to an abstract and false concept. One doesn't rage against someone or something whose reality one doesn't accept. Ivan Karamazov's fury against a God he claims not to believe in is perhaps the most obvious fictional illustration of the de facto believer.

THEISM AND ATHEISM

At this point, the reader may be wondering why I've taken so much time to distinguish between different varieties of nonbelief. Surely atheism can be defined adequately as disbelief in God or gods, regardless of whether that disbelief is practical or theoretical, emotional or intellectual, fiercely or distantly held.

Not quite. Although "atheism" is generically used to designate nonbelief in any kind of deity, the word really denotes the rejection of a very specific variety of God-belief, the kind that's known as "theism." When a-*theists* deny the existence of a God, therefore, their skepticism is directed at the *theistic* God, and their arguments, focused as they are on the theistic understanding of God, may not necessarily extend to all other concepts of deity. One contemporary atheist, acknowledging the specificity of the word "atheism," tries to salvage it as a generic term by distinguishing between what he calls "broad" atheism, nonbelief in all kinds of gods, and "narrow" atheism, nonbelief in the theistic God in particular (Martin 1990, pp. 464–5). This distinction allows us to use the word "atheism" in the popular sense while still distinguishing it from the more precise one. But it may be less confusing in the long run to use the more general "nonbelief" as a repudiation of nontheistic gods, and reserve "atheism" for the denial of the theistic one.

The broader point is that nonbelief is always relative to the type of God-belief it repudiates. Theoretical physicists may dream of a "general theory of everything," but it's unlikely that there will ever be a "general theory of nonbelief." This is an important methodological principle for the atheist to keep in mind. It cautions him against the hasty assumption that rebutting arguments for the existence of a theistic deity effectively casts doubts on the existence of any god.

The God whose existence atheists reject is the deity worshipped by modern adherents of the three "Religions of the Book": Judaism, Christianity, and Islam. These three monotheistic faith traditions share one sacred text (the Hebrew Bible) and Christianity and Islam claim additional ones (the New Testament and the Qur'an) that the faithful believe to be tradition-specific revelations. These texts, together with centuries of folk belief and theological speculation, have shaped the idea that comes to mind for well over half of the world's believers when they hear the word "God." Naturally there's a certain degree of flexibility within each tradition's understanding of the deity, and both laypersons and theologians endlessly debate divine properties. But the three Religions of the Book, for all their distinctive doctrinal differences, display remarkable agreement in their general conception of the Divine. Each of them proclaims what's come to be known as "the God of classical theism," with "classical" here intended as a synonym for religious orthodoxy as well as a reference to the Platonic and Aristotelian philosophical traditions which heavily influenced all three monotheisms.

What are the characteristics commonly attributed to this God? Richard Swinburne, one of the most influential Christian theologians of our day, writes that the God of traditional theism is "a person without a body (i.e. a spirit), present everywhere, the creator and sustainer of the universe, a free agent, able to do everything (i.e. omnipotent), knowing all things, perfectly good, a source of moral obligation, immutable, eternal, a necessary being, holy, and worthy of worship" (Swinburne 1977, p. 2).

The first thing to be noted about this list is that it's difficult to know exactly what to make of the specific properties assigned to the theistic God. Take Swinburne's first attribute, the one which theists take to be the most important: God is "a person," but one who is pure spirit. Immediately, problems arise. Everything that we know about personhood flows from our awareness of ourselves and other humans, and this means that our understanding of personhood is inseparably wrapped up with embodiment. We can imagine someone losing several limbs without thereby ceasing to be a person—think, for example, of the tragic protagonist in Dalton Trumbo's anti-war novel *Johnny Got His Gun*—because we associate personhood with mental functions such as consciousness, self-awareness, and so on. But it's difficult for us to imagine other than in a foggy way either *what* an utterly bodiless person would be like or *how* he could be in the first place. Without the body that contributes to my sense of identity by distinguishing me from everything I'm not, how could I remain a "person"? How could I have any of the mental functions associated with personhood without a brain? How could any of the modes of knowing that feed my consciousness—ways all inseparably connected to my five senses—continue in the absence of my body?

So whatever is meant by the claim that God is a nonphysical "person" can't be identical to what's meant when we say that a human is a person. The same goes for the other characteristics ascribed to God that seem to have human correlates: freedom, goodness, knowing, and so on. The best we can do is to interpret the divine qualities analogically, understanding that the properties ascribed to an infinite God are similar to but not identical with their finite human correlates. "This way of using words," argued Thomas Aquinas, one of the most influential defenders of the analogical method, "lies somewhere between pure equivocation and simple univocity, for the word is used neither in the same sense, as with univocal usage, nor in totally different senses, as with equivocation" (Thomas Aquinas 1980, 1a.q13.aa5–6). There's no universal agreement among theists, either in Aquinas' day or since, about the adequacy of analogical descriptions of God. But they are regularly invoked by theists, laypersons and theologians alike.

According to this way of thinking, calling God "a person" suggests that God possesses something analogous to the "personal" characteristics we associate with humans. Since God is without body, these must be functionally like, but not identical to, the human mental functions outlined earlier.

But in addition to possessing self-awareness, intelligence, and freedom, Swinburne says that God is also immutable, eternal, and necessary—that is, dependent for existence upon nothing other than himself. It's here that an analogous understanding of divine person-hood begins to get messy. Human persons are capable of intense emotions and error. We alter our opinions either by adding new or rejecting old knowledge. Moreover, we're mortal, and this means that our manner of existing is contingent. There's no necessity for us to be. We could just as easily not-be. We are, in short, mutable, temporal, and contingent, and all of that is implicated in what it means to be a human person. What possible similarity could there be between these qualities and divine immutability, eternity, and necessity? If God is immutable, he doesn't change—which means he doesn't emote or alter his opinions. If God is eternal, he's not mortal. If God is necessary, he cannot not-be. These qualities seem to be negations rather than analogues of human ones. And if so, what sense does it make to call God "personal"?[3]

I hope I've said enough to suggest that the theistic notion of God as personal is both complicated and perplexing. It's a topic we'll return to in Chapter 4. But overriding the conceptual perplexities of ascribing personal characteristics to God is the psychological importance for monotheists to believe that the God they worship is personally interested in them, personally accessible through prayer and contemplation, and most of all personally concerned about their well-being. In this sense, "personal" connotes intimacy and connect-edness: the theistic God is personal because humans are capable of entering into an intimate inter*personal* relationship with him.

In addition to "personal" qualities, both those that connote intimacy and those that seem perplexing when conjoined with immutability, the theistic God, as Swinburne says, is also omni-attributed: all-knowing, all-good, and all-powerful. Human persons are finite, and so their abilities to know, to be virtuous, and to exert influence are necessarily limited. But since God is constrained by neither time nor place nor body, God's analogous exercise of the functions of knowing, doing good, and empowering must be unconstrained as well. God is capable of knowing past, present, and future. God is capable of doing anything that's logically possible—or, according to some theists, anything at all, logically possible or otherwise. God is supremely benevolent, incapable (or inherently unwilling, depending on which theologian one reads) of not being good.

The theistic God is also believed to be the creator and sustainer of everything that is. His presence may be traced within the created order by natural theologians, similar to the way art critics can discern identifying styles of painters in their work. But the theistic God is distinct from the created order because he is beyond time (eternal), and the created order is, of course, temporal. Distinct as he is from the created order, God nonetheless directs (without manipulating) and sustains events within it, either by setting in motion natural laws through which his intentions trickle down to all levels of creation or through occasional miraculous interventions (this latter possibility follows from his omnipotence).

God's influence in the created order is both physical and moral. His intelligence establishes natural laws and his goodness ordains moral ones, thus infusing orderliness and value into creation. Both are signatures of his divine nature, and both are also gifts that the all-good Creator wishes to bestow on humans. It's precisely this majestic omnipotence, setting him apart from everything else, which constitutes the holiness Swinburne ascribes to God. Finally, God's graciousness in creating the universe and everything in it properly solicits our gratitude and worship.

In subsequent chapters, each one of these divine qualities will be called into question by atheists on the grounds of coherency and consistency. My purpose here has been to sketch the framework within which an atheist must work if she wishes to deny the existence of the God some three billion people believe in . Her specific arguments against the theistic deity may stretch to target nontheistic concepts of the divine as well. But there's no guarantee that they will.

Consider, for example, the God of deism. Popular in the Enlighten-ment as an alternative to "supernaturalist" religions, deism—frequently called "rational religion" by its adherents—defended the concept of an impersonal God who created the universe and the laws of nature, but who has no immediate involvement in the created order. This notion of God as First Cause is impervious to many of the standard atheistic objections to the theistic God. Since the deistic God is impersonal, for example, one doesn't have to worry about the coherency of nonembodied personhood or analogous qualities. If one objects to God-belief on either of these two grounds, as atheists frequently do (we'll explore the objections in Chapter 4), the God of deism may remain untouched.

The pantheistic God may be similarly resistant to standard atheist criticisms. There are many varieties of pantheism, but all of them defend the general claim that God is identical to the universe. This usually means that God is just as impersonal for the pantheist as for the deist. But it also means that the pantheist, unlike the theist, thinks there's no distinction between God the creator and the created order. So standard atheistic objections to theistic arguments for a creator God (such as the ones we'll examine in Chapter 3) may be beside the point.

As we'll see in Chapter 4, one of the strongest atheist objections to God is based on what's called the problem of evil or the suffering of innocents. The theistic God, recall, is omni-attributed—that is, is all-knowing, all-good, and all-powerful. But if this is so, why do bad things happen to good people? Such misfortunes seem incompatible with the existence of a God knowledgeable enough to foresee them, good enough to want to prevent them, and powerful enough to do so. So either God doesn't exist, or he's radically different from the standard theistic understanding of him—a possibility which, most atheists assume, is unacceptable to the committed theist.

This is a strong argument and, if the testimony of ex-believers can be trusted, is the rock against which much faith has foundered. But it's only relevant in the context of belief in an omni-attributed theistic God. If one accepts the notion of a malevolent God, one who can't foresee future events with absolute certainty, or one who's less than all-powerful—if, in short, one believes in a God who either isn't omni-attributed at all or is only partially omni-attributed—then the atheistic objection to God based on the problem of unmerited suffering is beside the point.

An example of such a concept of God is defended by process theologians such as Charles Hartshorne (1983). For them, God, just like the natural order, is in the process of becoming. In fact, the evolution of the two is mutually dependent. God, then, is powerful, but not supremely so. At any given point in time, God's power to foresee (and change) the future is limited by present contingencies.

So not even God can prevent bad things from happening to good people. When faced with unmerited suffering, God, like humans, can only observe and grieve.

Once again, then, standard atheistic arguments don't necessarily stretch far enough to include all notions of God. It may be that there are good rebuttals of nontheistic models of God such as those found in deism, pantheism, and process theology. But these would have to be rebuttals relative to the kind of God being rejected.

BURDENS OF PROOF

This chapter is devoted to preliminaries, the fundamental ones being the claims that, (1) there are different forms of nonbelief, (2) these forms are relative to the gods whose existence they repudiate, and (3) atheism, one type of nonbelief, is relative to the theistic God. There's one more preliminary that we ought to examine briefly. It has to do with the burden of proof.

Atheists and theists squabble about which of their positions should be the presumptive or default one. Theists frequently claim that since atheism is the minority opinion, the burden of proof should be on nonbelievers. Atheists counter by saying that because theists typically endorse positions that run contrary to ordinary experience of the world, the burden of proof properly falls on them.

A more sophisticated version of the atheist position is Antony Flew's well-known "presumption of atheism" argument. Flew wants his "presumption of atheism" position to be understood along the lines of the law's "presumption of innocence" default: just as defendants are presumed innocent until proven guilty, so God should be supposed not to exist until proven to do so. The onus of proof is on he who asserts, and the more outrageous the claim, the weightier the onus. Given that the theist's assertion of God's existence runs counter both to everything the sciences tell us about the nature of reality as well as our everyday experience, it is his responsibility—not the atheist's, who merely denies rather than positively asserts—to convince us.

It is by reference to this inescapable demand for grounds that the presumption of atheism is justified. If it is to be established that there is a God, then we have to have good grounds for believing that this is indeed so. Until or unless some such grounds are produced we have literally no reason at all for believing (Flew 1976, p. 22).

Philosopher Michael Scriven agrees that atheism is the proper default position in the debate between believers and nonbelievers. According to him, the proper alternative in the absence of evidence isn't suspension of belief, but rather active disbelief. If theists want to be taken seriously, the burden is theirs to supply compelling evidence—something which Scriven thinks they haven't as yet done, or can (Scriven 1966, p. 103).

By way of contrast, theistic philosopher Alvin Plantinga argues that disbelief isn't the default position at all. He contends that God-belief, far from being implausibly outlandish and hence carrying the burden of proof, is in fact a properly "basic belief." A basic belief is one that is not inferred from any other belief, but which instead is so fundamental that other beliefs are inferred from it. Plantinga's position, which is frequently referred to as "Reformed epistemology," has evolved over the years. In its latest manifestation, the basic belief in God is warranted because of the presence of a cognitive faculty which Plantinga, following John Calvin, calls a *sensus divinitatis.* This faculty, when properly operating, provides an immediate and palpable awareness of God. The fact that not everyone has God-belief as one of his or her basic beliefs is attributable to sin's corruption of the *sensus divinitatis.* So nonbelief, concludes Plantinga, is actually a moral and epistemic malfunction. The "healthy" or normal state of affairs—the default position—is belief (Plantinga 1999; 2000).

The debate about burden of proof is more often a forensic tactic than a substantive methodological point, and it can even become a red herring that shanghais the entire conversation. Common sense dictates that every person who asserts an opinion has the burden of defending that opinion. This means marshalling the strongest appropriate evidence and arguments as well as responding to criticisms and objections. While it's reasonable to presume that opinions which run contrary to experience and intuition require proportionately greater amounts of evidence, it's also reasonable to presume that mere denials of assertions count for little unless backed up by positive arguments and explanations. It's of little value simply to say,

"I disagree with your position; you haven't made your case," and leave it at that. Such pronouncements evade the responsibility to explain the grounds of the disagreement.

Moreover, it's simply not true that the atheist position is always one of denial rather than assertion. This certainly isn't the case with positive atheism, although it might be with negative atheism. The positive atheist actively asserts the nonexistence of God. This is taking a definite position, and as such reasonably calls for some defense. As we'll see in the next chapter, both atheism and theism ultimately rest on quite different worldviews that make specific and strong assertions about the nature of reality. These assertions are always implicit in any debate between believers and nonbelievers, thereby calling into question Flew's claim that the atheist merely denies and hence carries no burden of proof.

At the end of the day, the presumption that there's a genuine default position when it comes to the God debate is a fruitless conceit. The atheist obviously believes his/her denial of God is the more rational, intuitive, and "natural" position. The theist thinks the same about her/his affirmation of God. Neither is likely to accept the other's opinion as the default position, which suggests that the same arguments that need to be invoked in defense of either atheism or theism would also be required to establish that the burden of proof falls more heavily on one than the other. In other words, debates about default positions are always question-begging. So it seems more economical for both the atheist and the theist to cease worrying about which one carries the heaviest burden of proof and to get on with making the best case for their positions that they can. The goal, after all, isn't to score points in a debate, although this is something that apologists on both sides often forget.

FROM ADEVISM TO ATHEISM[4]

Philosopher Alfred North Whitehead may or may not have been correct when he surmised that "the progress of religion is defined by the denunciation of the gods," (Whitehead 1933, p. 19), but it *does* seem that denunciation of gods is a marker of the direction recent western philosophy has gone. It's not too much to say that atheism as a fully articulated position is a modern invention, appearing some-time in the seventeenth century (Hyman 2007). There were only a handful of nonbelievers in the Hellenic and Hellenistic eras, and none of note has come down to us from the medieval and early renaissance periods.

Pre-modern nonbelievers for the most part didn't deny the existence of God so much as denounced the deities of popular belief and folk religion. The nineteenth-century orientalist Max Muller called this denial of folk gods "adevism" (from the Sanskrit *deva* = deity). All atheists are adevists, but not all adevists are atheists.

The pre-Socratic philosopher Xenophanes (570–480 BCE), for example, famously satirized religious belief. "Mortals suppose that the gods are born as they themselves are, and that they wear man's clothing and have human voice and body." Thus "Ethiopians make their gods black and snub-nosed, Tracians red-haired and with blue eyes." But this is ridiculous, continues Xenophanes. "If cattle or lions had hands, so as to paint with their hands and produce works of art as men do, they would paint their gods and give them bodies in form like their own—horses like horses, cattle like cattle" (Nahm 1964, p. 84). Yet his disdain for anthropomorphized deities doesn't mean that Xenophanes is an atheist. There is a God, he declares: "God is one, supreme among gods and men, and not like mortals in body or in mind" (p. 85). A bit less than a century after Xenophanes' death, the Athenian Socrates would be sentenced to death in 399 BCE on charges that included "impiety," when it's clear that what he was trying to do was to cast doubt on the same anthropomorphic inventions that Xenophanes had taken on.

Socrates' contemporary Protagoras (ca 490–420 BCE), the leading Sophist philosopher of his day, was an agnostic adevist. He confessed to disbelief when it came to the folk religion of his day, and apparently denied that the soul was likely anything other than the operations of the senses. But "as to the gods," he wrote, "I have no means of knowing either that they exist or that they do not exist. For many are the obstacles that impede knowledge, both the obscurity of the question and the shortness of human life" (Nahm 1964, pp. 228–9). According to tradition, pronouncements like this led to Protagoras' persecution. His book on the gods (which opened with the passage cited above) was condemned and publicly burned and he was exiled from Athens.

Perhaps the clearest example of a strict disbeliever in gods to emerge from the Hellenic period is the skeptic Carneades of Cyrene (213–129 BCE). He's a fascinating figure whose criticisms of religious belief sound compellingly modern. He denied that the universe was the product of a divine plan, and hypothesized that belief in gods evolved from the awe and fright inspired by natural phenomena. (He was quick to point out, however, that even if his supposition was true, understanding the origin of a belief sheds no light on the truth of that belief—a topic we'll return to when we examine theories about the origins of religions in Chapter 5). He pointed out that the attribution of individual qualities to an unlimited God is problematic, because qualities by definition limit. And he concluded that the better part of reason was to deny divine existence[5] (Thrower 2000, pp. 39–42).

Western nonbelief seems to have disappeared (or, more likely, gone underground) for nearly a millennium, finally to reemerge, although somewhat timidly, in the seventeenth century with the rise of modern science. Francis Bacon (1561–1626) writes of skeptics in his essay "On Atheism" (1597), and Pierre Bayle (1647–1706) strove mightily to convince his contemporaries that celestial events such as comets were natural phenomena that had no need of miraculous explanations. Both men claimed to be believers. But their emphases on nonsupernatural causation pushed God into the background and prepared the way for the materialism and overt rejection of God-belief that characterizes so much of the eighteenth-century Enlightenment.

Two transitional figures that bridged the gap between the seventeenth-century's discovery of empirical science and the eighteenth-century's full blown atheism are Thomas Hobbes (1588–1679) and Jean Meslier (1664–1729). Like Bacon and Bayle, Hobbes never publicly defended atheism, although (unlike Bacon and Bayle), he probably disbelieved in God. Hobbes offered the first fully articulated defense of materialism which left no room at all for God except, perhaps, as a distant First Cause: "that which has no body is no part of the universe: and because the universe is all, that which is no part of it is nothing, and consequently nowhere" (Hobbes 1904, p. 497). Like Carneades before him, Hobbes also offered an account of religious belief that stripped it of any hint of supernaturalism by reducing it to superstition, ignorance of causes, fear, and "taking of things casual for prognostics" (p. 73).

Meslier, who served, remarkably, as a parish priest for 40 years, repudiated belief even in God as First Cause. For him, all concepts of God, but especially Christianity's, were not only false but pernicious in that the religion institutions they inspired generally cooperated with secular powers to oppress the poor. Although it's frequently attributed to Voltaire, Meslier is the actual author of the famous opinion that all the nobles in the world ought to be strangled with the guts of all the priests. It appeared in a book-length defense of atheism he wrote but kept secret during his lifetime and which was published only posthumously. When it did appear, however, his *Testament* rocked France and inspired non-atheist but anti-clerical thinkers such as Voltaire as well as militantly atheistic ones such as Denis Diderot (1713–1784) and Baron d'Holbach (1723–1789). These men and their fellow skeptics wrote articles, books, and the famous multi-volumed *Encyclopedie* defending a naturalistic world-view based exclusively on a rational analysis of the physical world, the mind, and human behavior. They had no need of a "God of the gaps" to fill in empty spaces in human knowledge because they were confident that reason was ultimately capable of explaining everything. In quick order this "enlightened" way of thinking spread to Britain, Germany, and even the American colonies. "Atheist" remained a term of insult in common parlance, but skepticism, ranging from deism to atheism, was more widespread than in any previous historical period. It is in this period that atheism as a direct assault against supernatural Christianity came into its own.[6]

David Hume (1711–1776) was one of the Enlightenment thinkers who absorbed the French example of skepticism. (Hume claimed that he'd never met an atheist until dining with d'Holbach, and was then astonished to learn he was in the company of no fewer than 17 of them [Thrower 2000, p. 106].) Possibly Britain's greatest philosopher, Hume held his religious cards close to his chest, never actually declaring himself an atheist. He may in fact have been a believer of sorts, most likely a deist. But he denied personal immortality, declared that miracles violated both reason and experience, followed in the footsteps of Carneades and Hobbes by writing a natural history of religion, and most importantly wrote *Dialogues Concerning Natural Religion,* published a year after his death. In that book, Hume rigorously argued against the rationality of religious belief, in the process savaging traditional arguments for the existence of God that we'll examine in detail in Chapter 3. The influence of the *Dialogues* can scarcely be exaggerated. Every effort after Hume to offer rational arguments for the existence of God or philosophical defenses of religious belief in general must respond to his objections.

Atheism in the Enlightenment was born from the fact that the rise of the empirical sciences convinced many thinkers that God was either an unnecessary hypothesis when it came to understanding the world and hence best jettisoned or, if retained, was reckoned as the unobtrusively distant cause of the universe. There was also an element of hardy dislike, especially in France, of what was seen as "priestcraft": the deliberate encouragement of superstition, fear, and obedience to church and state. These sensibilities carried over into the nineteenth century and influenced thinkers as diverse as Ludwig Feuerbach (1804–1872), Karl Marx (1818–1883), Friedrich Nietzsche (1844–1900), and Sigmund Freud (1856–1939). But just as Hume was the single greatest influence on atheism to emerge from the eighteenth century, so Charles Darwin (1809–1882) undoubtedly played that role in the nineteenth. Ironically, Darwin—like Hume—may not have been an atheist (although he certainly rejected the Christian God). But his theory of natural selection threw a spanner into God-belief that caused more damage than anything the Enlightenment atheists did.

Up to the 1859 publication of Darwin's *The Origin of Species*, religious believers could manage an accommodation—even though a somewhat strained one—with the Enlightenment's discovery that the natural order had no need of God in its day-to-day operations. This was accomplished by conceding that God worked his will distantly through orderly and uniform natural laws, but nonetheless hanging onto the conviction that God was the creator of the universe, that humans were made in his likeness, and that there was a divinely-ordained purposefulness to reality. Natural selection called these remnants of faith into question by arguing that an examination of the development of species revealed no semblance of overarching design or purposefulness, and that there was no good reason to suppose that humans are a privileged family that somehow stands apart from the accidental transmutations that shape all species. The immediate uproar over Darwin's theory focused on his insinuation that humans had a non-divine origin. But a much deeper anxiety was generated by the realization that if humans weren't created directly by God, there was no reason to think that the universe had purpose or, for that matter, that God even existed. It was a shattering blow to religious belief and a leap forward for proponents of atheism.[7]

Twentieth-century atheism recognized the Darwinian breakthrough as a serious obstacle to religious belief because it helped to flesh out the increasingly complex and comprehensive naturalistic worldview presented by the sciences. But strictly philosophical examinations of atheism tended to flow from two distinct camps: Anglo-American analysis and Continental existentialism. The figurehead for the first camp was unquestionably Bertrand Russell (1872–1970), who in dozens of papers and lectures criticized God-belief and religion-based ethics. Russell's defense of atheism, while courageously honest, was neither original nor terribly profound, and for the most part repeated arguments made familiar by Enlightenment thinkers such as Hume. But it is unlikely that any other philosopher writing on atheism has enjoyed his popularity and influence.

A stronger Anglo-American challenge to God-belief came from logical positivists such as A. J. Ayer (1910–1989) and a number of philosophers of language who argued that discourse about God, being neither empirically verifiable nor self-evident, is therefore meaningless. (We'll examine some of their arguments in Chapter 4.) Although the philosophical conversation has moved beyond the language debate, its legacy has been an increasingly rigorous testing of logical consistency and coherency in religious claims by academic philosophers such as John Hick (1922–), Antony Flew (1923–), Kai Nielsen (1926–), Michael Martin (1932–), and Quentin Smith (1952–).

While twentieth-century Anglo-American atheism was heavily influenced by the natural sciences and linguistic philosophy, atheism on the Continent was much less so. Taking their cues more from Nietzsche and Marx than Darwin and Russell, members of the so-called atheistic existentialism school—notably, Jean-Paul Sartre (1905–1980), Simone de Beauvoir (1908–1986), and Albert Camus (1913–1960)—based their denial of God on their appraisal of the universe as absurdly pointless as well as the conviction that human freedom would be compromised by the existence of a deity who designed the universe and everything in it. (We'll examine these two points in some detail in Chapter 7.)

The most recent wave of Western atheism has been dubbed the "New Atheism," and its leading spokespersons the "New Atheists" (Wolf 2006). The most influential New Atheists are two Englishmen and two Americans: Richard Dawkins (1941–), Daniel Dennett (1942–), Christopher Hitchens (1949–), and Sam Harris (1967–).

The New Atheists have been astoundingly successful at popularizing atheism as an alternative to religious belief. Their books are best-sellers on both sides of the Atlantic, and all four men appear frequently in the media. Doubtlessly because they are popularizers, however, they have frequently been criticized for a lack of depth.

With the exception of Dennett, none of them are trained philosophers. None of them, even Dennett, displays the familiarity with theological literature which their Enlightenment and Victorian forebears did. For the most part, they by-pass philosophical defenses of atheism in favor of scientifically-based ones, drawing especially from physics and evolutionary biology.

The New Atheism movement is noted for its militant and colorfully polemic condemnation of all religious belief. Its defenders have a tendency, as one critic has said, to create a number of unjustified "shrinkages" by refusing to distinguish between fundamentalist and liberal religions (Haught 2008, p. 38). The vehemence with which the New Atheists attack religious belief is traceable in no small part to their frustration at the recent surge in Christian and Muslim fundamentalism as well as religion-inspired violence. It remains to be seen what the long-term influence of the New Atheists will be. But for the foreseeable future, theirs are the main voices in Western atheism.[8]

NOTES

[1] Steven Weinberg (2001) rather astoundingly denies that these sorts of nonbelievers deserve to be called "atheists" because they haven't carefully thought through their position.

[2] Daniel Dennett perceptively notes that there are also people "who consider themselves believers [but who] actually just believe in the *concept* of God . . . Notice that they *don't* believe in *belief* in God! . . . They do think that their concept of God is so much better than other concepts of God that they should devote themselves to spreading the Word. But they don't believe in God in the strong sense" (Dennett 1996, p. 216).

[3] There is, of course, an entire tradition in theology, called "negative" or "apophatic" (from the Greek *apophanai* = "to say no"), which argues that the only possible way to understand God is by describing what he is not. What's left over after all non-divine, anthropomorphic qualities are peeled away is a deity who can be experienced mystically, perhaps, but who is fundamentally incomprehensible. The first systematic treatment of the apophatic way was written by the sixth century Dionysius the Areopagite. Recently, postmodern theologians have rediscovered apophasis. See, for example, Marion (1995) and Bulhof and ten Kate (2000).

[4] No one is more aware than I of how sketchy this historical overview of atheism is. More thorough historical treatments may be found in Bury (1913), Thrower (2000), and Hecht (2003). Gaskin (1988) offers a convenient compendium of historical atheist voices, as does Joshi (2000). Jacoby (2004) offers a good survey of unbelief on the American scene.

[5] For more on ancient nonbelief, see Thrower (1979).

[6] Two excellent histories of Enlightenment nonbelief are Lecky (1955) and Buckley (1987).

[7] For more on nineteenth-century European atheism, see Miller (1963), Irvine (1956), and Wilson (1999).

[8] In addition to the New Atheist primary sources listed in the "Introduction," the reader may also find some of the ever-growing theological criticism of them interesting. Much of it is written in a rather screechy evangelical voice. More reasoned treatments include McGrath (2007), Beattie (2007), Day (2008), and Haught (2008).

CHAPTER 2

THE ATHEIST WORLDVIEW

The clash of civilizations in the world today is not between socialism and capitalism, or Islam and the West . . . but between the spirit of the Scientific Revolution . . . and those persons north, east, south, and west who define themselves by the authority of holy books, tradition, or prophets.
          Chet Raymo, When God Is Gone, Everything Is Holy

British philosopher Antony Flew, one of the most perceptive atheists of the late twentieth century, underwent an intellectual conversion in 2004. Believing that honest thinkers must always "follow the argument wherever it leads," Flew moved from an overt denial of God's existence to a rather cerebral version of deism. The move was prompted by his conclusion that the existence and complexity of the universe as well as the origin of life are inexplicable in the absence of a divine Creator. Flew is clear that the God he now believes in isn't theistic, and that he in no way can be called a Christian. Instead, his deity is an intelligent but impersonal First Cause (a notion of God more fully explored in the next chapter).

Predictably, Flew's conversion has dismayed his erstwhile fellow atheists. Responses have ranged from reasoned rebuttals to rather hysterical charges that Flew is in his dotage. In response, Flew defends himself by posing a somewhat barbed challenge to his former fellow atheists: "What would have to occur or to have occurred to constitute for you a reason to at least consider the existence of a superior Mind?" (Flew 2007, p. 88).

At first glance, this seems a perfectly reasonable question, not the least because atheists and theists have been asking similar ones of each other for centuries. *What would it take for you to believe in God?*

What would it take to shatter your belief in God? The assumption behind these questions is that changing one's mind merely means adding or subtracting beliefs—reaching a tipping point, as it were—and that if one can simply pile up or take away enough of them, the scales will move one way or the other.

There are some situations which this rather mechanical understanding of decision-making fits. If I'm sizing up a job applicant, I'm likely to reach a point in ticking off the information on her resume at which my uncertainty about her qualifications rolls over into approval or disapproval. If I'm in the market for a new car, I read consumer reports and tote up pros and cons of different models until I finally reach a tipping point and make my choice. In both cases, what it takes to decide are enough facts to enable me to say yea or nay.

But when it comes to God-belief, the question, popular as it is, is misplaced. Atheism—at least a reflective, thoughtful atheism—isn't embraced by refuting an argument for God's existence or rejected because of a single "religious" experience. This is because the atheist's denial of God's existence is but one strand—although an absolutely integral one—in a much more complex web of belief that, taken as a whole, constitutes a full-fledged worldview. Worldviews are basic ways of looking at reality, cognitive and emotional lenses through which we apprehend and relate to the world around us. They aren't built out of a simple accumulation of facts, nor can they typically be easily dismantled, precisely because what we accept as factual and reject as illusory is in large part determined by our worldview perspective.

The worldview through which the thoughtful atheist examines the world around him is "naturalism." By contrast, the theist's worldview is "supernaturalism." For atheists and theists to change their minds about God would mean that they'd have to either completely throw over their respective worldviews, or so seriously modify them that they come to look through very different lenses indeed. The first task is well-nigh impossible, and the second extremely difficult. This isn't to deny that atheists occasionally become theists and theists sometimes do lose their faith and embrace atheism. It's only to say that merely fiddling with a belief here or a belief there within the framework of their old worldviews isn't likely to lead to the change of mind that Flew is asking about. An atheist operating from a naturalistic worldview probably can't in all honesty imagine what Flew wants him to—that is, a reason to take God-belief seriously—because his worldview doesn't allow for even the possibility of such a thing. (He may contrive a reason for the sake of the argument, of course, but it will only be pretending.) Even if God Almighty were to appear before him and announce Himself, the atheist would probably chalk the experience up to a psychotic episode—that is, would explain it in terms of his basic naturalistic orientation. By the same token, a convinced theist who reads experience through the worldview of supernaturalism is unlikely to be able to come up with a hypothetical that would demolish his belief in God. He could always chalk up a sudden bout of apostasy to a sinful failure of faith. Physicist Chet Raymo is quite correct to see the conflict between these two worldviews as fundamental.

In this chapter we'll explore the contours of the naturalism which grounds atheism, contrast it with the supernaturalism alternative, and examine the question of whether there's any way for the two to declare a detente. As we'll discover, some atheists believe that they can co-exist while others vehemently disagree. But before that, we need to examine the nature of worldviews a bit more closely.

WHAT IS A WORLDVIEW?

The German word for worldview, *Weltanschauung*, literally means "looking at the world." As mentioned earlier, a worldview is a core of basic assumptions, beliefs, values, and commitments about reality that colors the way we think about the world and the things in it (including ourselves), how we relate to others, and what kinds of hopes or fears we have about the future. Personal factors as well as cultural ones coalesce to form worldviews. The fact that I'm born in a particular place and time, with a specific ethnicity, gender, and social position, all contribute to my way of looking at the world. But so does my psychological temperament and physical health, my personal experiences and memories, and my private talents and weaknesses.

Although everyone looks at the world through a set of basic beliefs and commitments, it's not necessarily the case that the core is deliberately examined or articulated. Quite frequently, the worldview serves as the important but unnoticed backdrop against which our lives transpire (or, to remain loyal to the word itself, the lens through which we view the world). At moments of crisis or intense confusion we may remove the lens or it may be shaken off us long enough for us to examine it. But for the most part, with most people, it's simply taken for granted.

Worldviews may be imagined as a set of concentric circles. The innermost circle is the core, containing all the root beliefs that give the worldview its particular character. The outwardly expanding circles are peripheral beliefs. The former are axiomatic, simply accepted as givens. When they are consciously articulated, they aren't typically argued *for* so much as argued *from*. They are neither explanations, theory, nor method, but instead serve as the crucible from which one's understanding of reality and self-identity, ethical values, political positions, evaluative standards, and so on are all generated. The peripheral beliefs that cluster around them may be confirmed, modified, or rejected by appeals to logic, experience, or consistency. But the core axioms themselves are taken as self-evident. Moreover, the selection of what will count as a cause for modification or rejection is itself shaded by them. There is, then, a certain inevitable circularity at play here. Worldviews color our way of thinking about the world, and our thinking about the world confirms our worldviews.

To what extent peripheral belief change can affect core beliefs is an open question. The usual flow seems to be outward: core beliefs influence the nature of our peripheral beliefs. W. V. Quine, who tended to use the expression "web of belief" rather than "worldview," argued that beliefs on the outer edges of the web can be modified or even abandoned with no or only minor alterations to the core (Quine and Ullian 1978). But if we apply the analysis of scientific revolutions offered by Thomas Kuhn to worldviews, it may be that exposure to countervailing ideas and values eventually can so undermine the outer integrity of a worldview that its holders must question the inner core. In this case, the flow would be inward: disruption of peripheral beliefs can lead to deep reflection on what has been taken up to that point as axiomatic. Of course, there's no necessity that this occur. Auxiliary explanations loyal to the core commitments frequently can be spun that account for countervailing evidence. But this strategy, if pursued too far, results in a heaviness at the edges that unbalances the entire worldview (Kuhn 1996).

Regardless of how worldview modification transpires, one thing seems to be clear: given the interconnectedness of the beliefs that make up our worldviews, they must be examined in a body rather than singly. Any given hypothesis or claim rests upon a complex foundation of background assumptions—the worldview's core beliefs—and these must be taken into consideration. Consequently, there is no single crucial experiment or test that can be invoked to settle the issue between two competing worldviews. A challenged peripheral belief can usually be modified or dropped in response to challenges without damaging the core assumptions. And what that means is that a variety of competing hypotheses can be compatible with the available evidence.[1]

One final word about worldviews before we examine naturalism. I said earlier that most of us probably have never articulated to ourselves or others the core beliefs that make up the nucleus of our worldviews. But one way of inferring what they are is through the observation of behavior. Practice will often reveal genuine core beliefs, even if they can't easily be spoken by their holders. Recall the discussion in the previous chapter about de facto belief and de facto nonbelief. If asked, a person who's a de facto nonbeliever will insist that she is religious, that she accepts the existence of a deity, and so on. But her practice, which makes no room in her daily life, moral decision-making, or fundamental loyalties for any religious-tinted considerations whatsoever, gives the lie to both her own self-understanding and how she identifies herself to others.

NATURALISM

The worldview that undergirds atheism is one whose deepest core belief is that the natural world is all there is. The theoretical model generated by that core belief is sometimes called "materialism," but a better label, for reasons we'll see shortly, is "naturalism."

Naturalism in the atheist sense needs to be distinguished from what's often called "scientific" or "methodological" naturalism. The latter is the basic investigative principle of the sciences: only those explanations for phenomena which can be scientifically tested should be sought or accepted, and this automatically precludes any hypothesis that rests its case in part or in whole on "occult"—non-natural—postulates. Scientific testability in turn is defined by the hypothetical-deductive method, which consists of observing natural phenomena, formulating a hypothetical explanation for them, predicting future occurrences based on the hypothesis, and testing the accuracy of the prediction. The conclusions arrived at are always susceptible to further scrutiny, revision, or rejection. The mark of a good scientific conclusion, in fact, is that it remains testable and hence falsifiable. A dogmatic hypothesis is a bad hypothesis. On the other hand, a hypothesis which is so squishy that it claims to accommodate any number of exceptions is also dubious. Likewise, statements about the world based on subjective or intuitive appeals that are beyond confirmation are inappropriate objects of scientific scrutiny. They may in fact be true, the methodological naturalist will allow. But they can't be scientifically tested[2] (Fales 2007, pp. 123–4).

Methodological naturalism is the standard operating procedure of working scientists. One need not be an atheist to employ it. In fact, a good case could be made for the claim that methodological naturalism of a sort is the working assumption of the person in the street who goes to physicians instead of faith healers when ill or consults the Weather Channel rather than a ouiji board when planning a picnic. The person who believes that natural explanations for his illness are better than occult ones may believe in God. So may the working scientist who endorses methodological naturalism (although the percentages here are lower[3]). Both may even pray, attend public worship services, and so on. But if they do, they must find some way to square their religious faith with their methodological naturalism. (We'll return to this issue shortly.)

Not all methodological naturalists, then, are atheists. But all atheists are both methodological and what might be called "onto-logical" naturalists. They don't just insist that scientific hypotheses must be kept free of occult explanations. They argue that scientific explanations are legitimate because there is nothing in reality that can't be understood ultimately in material, physico-chemical, natural-istic terms. For the ontological naturalist, there is nothing apart from nature, and nature is self-originating, self-explanatory, and without overall purpose. Some naturalists are ruthlessly reductionistic (they're sometimes called "strict" or "scientistic" naturalists[4]), believing that all phenomena, including mental states, are nothing more than physical states. But others argue for an "emergent" naturalism which recognizes that certain emergent complex phenomena such as mental states can't be totally explained in terms of lower levels of complexity. Instead, they require explanations appropriate to their level—but explanations which are nonetheless naturalistic.

Both reductionistic and emergent naturalists are monists who hold that naturalistic explanations can and should be applied across the board (although not necessarily in a reductionistic way) in order to develop integrative generalizations. Atheist Paul Kurtz calls such an enterprise "coduction." "Contrasted with induction and deduction," he writes, "this means that we coduce explanations that cut across scientific disciplines in order to develop a more comprehensive cosmic outlook." At the very least, naturalists "need to make every effort to develop a 'synoptic perspective'."[5] (Kurtz 2007, pp. 28–9).

This being said, it's been noted by more than one philosopher that even though we live in an age in which naturalism is the going paradigm (especially among scientists and philosophers), there's remarkably little precision about just what is meant by either the word "naturalism" or "nature." Naturalists are generally good at providing negative descriptions of their position—thus Kai Nielsen says that "naturalism denies that there are any spiritual or supernatural realities . . . . There are no supernatural realities transcendent to the world"—but not so good at positive descriptions—naturalism "is the view that anything that exists is ultimately composed of physical components" (Nielsen 1997, p. 402; Goetz and Taliaferro 2008, p. 9). What remains murky is how to understand "physical," beyond the stipulative claim that it's the opposite of "spiritual." What is the nature of nature? How do we identify what's natural and what's not? What standards can we invoke that aren't circular? These are the sorts of questions which prompted Roy Wood Sellars to characterize naturalism as "vague" and "general," a tendency rather than a clear belief (Sellars 1922, p. vii). Philosopher Barry Stroud expresses this ambiguity well by comparing the word "naturalism" to "World Peace."

> Almost everyone swears allegiance to it, and is willing to march under its banner. But disputes can still break out about what it is appropriate or acceptable to do in the name of that slogan. And like world peace, once you start specifying concretely exactly what it involves and how to achieve it, it becomes increasingly difficult to reach and to sustain a consistent and exclusive 'naturalism'. There is pressure on the one hand to include more and more within your conception of 'nature', so it loses its definiteness and restrictiveness. Or, if the conception is kept fixed and restrictive, there is pressure on the other hand to distort or even to deny the very phenomena that a naturalistic study . . . is supposed to explain (Stroud 2004, p. 22).

THE CLASH WITH SUPERNATURALISM

Naturalism can be described as the belief that the natural world is a closed system: nothing exists outside of it, so nothing influences it from without. By contrast, supernaturalists embrace a worldview whose deepest core belief is that reality is dualistically open, divisible into natural and supernatural realms that interact in one way or another. They agree for the most part with the naturalist's description of the physical world, but disagree with the claim that there's nothing apart from nature. In addition to nature, there is an irreducible realm of spiritual reality which isn't bound by physical laws, and this realm infuses the physical world with a deep meaning and purposefulness. The most obvious example of the supernatural is God, who exists as pure spirit outside space and time. But humans also participate in the supernatural insofar as they possess nonmaterial souls capable of surviving the death of their physical bodies. Moreover, the existence of both God and soul is knowable, although not by the methods employed in the sciences. Spiritual disciplines such as prayer, meditation, and fasting free the mind of material distractions and make it more receptive to the possibility of an encounter with spirit. In addition, experiences such as private revelations are valued for the insights into spirit they can provide. This isn't to say that the supernaturalist will accept at face value reports of private religious illumination, but only that she's more willing than the naturalist to take them seriously. Finally, the supernaturalist usually believes that fundamental truths about the realm of spirit are available in the sacred scriptures of her faith tradition.

Exactly how the natural and the supernatural interact with one another, and where the borders of one ends and the other begins, is something of a mystery. A traditional theist is likely to claim that God is separate from creation but perfectly willing to influence it from time to time through miraculous intervention. A pantheist, on the other hand, will argue for a much more immanent concept of spirit, claiming that divine intelligence is present throughout every aspect of creation. Regardless of the relationship between matter and spirit, supernaturalists ultimately conclude that the material realm is less real than the spiritual one, dependent on the spiritual one (that is, that God regulates, either immediately or distantly, the physical world), and displays, for those who know how to spot them, tokens of the divine Artist's attributes. These tokens include beauty, intelligence, goodness, and order.

A supernaturalist is quite likely to find the questions the naturalist asks both fascinating and important. But he finds additional ones that the naturalist dismisses as meaningless or unanswerable equally if not more important. Think back to Antony Flew's move from atheism to deism. Flew writes that there are three questions which he found increasingly inescapable—Why does nature obey laws? How did conscious, puprposeful life arise from matter? Why is there anything at all instead of nothing?—and that the more he thought about them, the more persuaded he became that they could only be answered by postulating an intelligent Designer (Flew 2007, p. 89). For Flew the deist, and certainly for theists, these questions simply can't be avoided. They cry out for answers. But a naturalist finds nothing necessarily compelling about them, and likely looks upon them irritably as obfuscations. *Why does nature obey laws?* Who knows? It's enough that it does. *How did conscious life arise from matter?* Whatever the answer, it's necessarily one that fits into a naturalistic framework. Don't make it out to be a spiritual mystery. *Why is there something rather than nothing?* How is such a question even to be understood, much less answered? Stick to puzzles that are solvable.

The difference between the naturalist and supernaturalist worldviews has been interestingly conveyed by two sets of metaphors, one proposed by Daniel Harbour and the other by Daniel Dennett. Harbour contends that naturalism is "Spartan" while supernaturalism is "baroque." A Spartan worldview makes "the minimal number of assumptions."A baroque worldview, on the other hand, is "richly embellished, coming complete with a set of beliefs about what exists, why those things exist, how they came to exist, and so on." The former's small number of working assumptions leaves room for continuous exploration and revision. The latter's heavy baggage "forbids revision of the basic assumptions" (Harbour 2001, pp. 10–11).

Dennett, while probably agreeing with Harbour's Spartan/baroque distinction, takes a different tack by focusing on the difference in causal flow offered by the two worldviews. According to Dennett, supernaturalism presumes that the origin of the universe, the direction in which it's moving, and any meaning discernible in it all flow from divine will. God has a plan and this plan serves as both blueprint and engine for the course of cosmic history. This is a "skyhook" way of thinking: attributing everything to a from-the-bottom-down heavenly or supernatural cause under the assumption (or delusion, Dennett thinks) that spirit directs matter in a way science cannot fathom. Naturalism, on the other hand, adopts a "crane" lifting-from-the-bottom-up understanding of the world. There's no need to appeal to mysterious "final causes," as Aristotle might say, to explain the world. The impersonal laws of nature, discovered by observing the physical world rather than spinning top-heavy theologies, are sufficient explanations (Dennett 1995, pp. 73–80).

Harbour, Dennett, and all other atheists obviously favor the Spartan, craned worldview of naturalism. They think that the baroque skyhooked one of supernaturalism is not only false but dangerously so because, as mathematician David Shotwell says, "if you admit the supernatural into your calculations, anything goes" (Shotwell 2003, p. 49). The thought experiment he uses to illustrate his point is a perfect example of the baroque busyness of supernaturalism deplored by Harbour. As a "rival hypothesis" to scientific physicalist accounts of matter, says Shotwell,

> Let us assume that each subatomic particle is inhabited by a ghostly little gremlin. Each gremlin maintains the existence of its particle by a continuous creative act and is in instantaneous tele-pathic communication with all of the others. By this means they cooperate to produce the universe and its lawful behavior. (p. 49)

The gremlin hypothesis, continues Shotwell, offers an explanation for "everything that exists and every event that occurs"—and it can also conveniently clear up the puzzle about why evil exists in a universe created by a benevolent God (more of this puzzle in Chapter 4). All we have to do is posit that the gremlins "are mischievous and, in some respects, malevolent" (p. 49). But of course this is all absurd, as Shotwell intends it to be in order to imply that more conventional skyhook explanations are equally so. Neither the gremlin nor the God hypothesis is needed to explain the behavior of subatomic particles. In fact, they're positive obstacles to understanding it.

Obviously, the atheist assumption that naturalism is the better—and, indeed, the only rational—way of thinking about reality is denied by supernaturalists. Surprisingly, though, straightforward theistic efforts to grapple with the challenge of naturalism have been remarkably sparse. Catholic theologian John Haught admits that the typical response of Christian thinkers to naturalism has been to ignore it and blithely continue writing about God as if the modern scientific understanding of the world didn't exist (Haught 2000, p. 28).

Sometimes, particularly with fundamentalist theists, the claims of naturalism are ignored because they're dogmatically denied. But such denial is not only bizarre when it entails outlandish beliefs such as those preached by Young Earth advocates or creationists, it's also remarkably inconsistent. As astronomer Owen Gingerich (himself a theist) points out, the very people who "take in stride the modern technology of cell phones, laser scanners, airplanes, and atomic bombs" refuse to accept "the implications of the science" that invented them. This is a paradox, he concludes, that deserves sober reflection (Gingerich 2006. p. 11).

Less crudely, theists can also sidestep the naturalist challenge not by explicitly denying it but by bracketing it so that its claims are kept radically separate from the claims of supernaturalism. This separatism is generally based on the claim that science and religion deal with two different sorts of problems. Science is concerned with questions about physical or natural causes, and religion is more concerned with the ultimate meaning of things. So long as science and religion stick to their respective concerns, there's no need for a clash over which perspective is sounder. The two are separate but equal.[6]

But the problems this approach creates are obvious. Bracketing can be a disguised form of denial that shoves the naturalist challenge to the sidelines and makes it easy to ignore. That this is frequently the practical consequence is revealed by the fact that very few theists, as Haught noted, are well acquainted with what the scientific community has to say about the natural world. If they were, they might be less confident in their beliefs. Finally, the separate-but-equal thesis doesn't offer a compelling justification for the bifurcated view of knowledge it endorses (divided between scientific and religious discourses) nor the apparent diminution of God's sovereignty which its pigeonholing of religion suggests.

Ironically, the most influential defender of a separate-but-equal understanding of naturalism and supernaturalism is an atheist: the late paleontologist Stephen Jay Gould. He calls his thesis NOMA: Non-Overlapping Magisteria. (*Magisterium*, of course, is Latin for "authority.") According to Gould, the naturalist claims of science and the supernaturalist claims of religion are based upon two different kinds of authority, both equally legitimate. Trouble arises when one authority encroaches or overlaps onto the other. But when kept in their separate spheres, difficulties disappear.

The *lack of conflict* between science and religion arises from a *lack of overlap* between their respective domains of professional expertise—science in the empirical constitution of the universe, and religion in the search for proper ethical values and the spiritual meaning of our lives. (Gould 2003, p. 193)

Gould points out that science and religion aren't the only two magisteria or "domains of teaching authority." There's also the magisterium of art, for example. Nor does he draw the neat and well-defined border between the two that some theists would wish. He concedes that the two frequently "bump up" against one another, "interdigitating in wondrously complex ways along their joint border" (p. 196). But for all that, maintains Gould, the distinction between the two is still fairly clear: science asks "what is the universe made of (fact) and why does it work this way (theory)," while religion focuses on "questions of moral meaning and value" (p. 195).

The on-going historical clash between science and religion is usually more complex than the individual battles fought in it suggest, because the particular issues that trigger spats always reflect the more global disagreements between naturalist and supernaturalist worldviews. One of the most obvious points of contention has to do with authority. The naturalist insists that reason and empirical knowledge exert the ultimate authority. The supernaturalist counters that inspiration and faith are also important authorities in understanding the world.

Gould is well aware of this more fundamental disagreement about authority, and NOMA is intended to address it. Allowing two compatible but separate authorities, each with their own proper domains, allows for a "mutual humility" that encourages conversation between theists and atheists. This humility stems from the fact that NOMA reins in both science and religion from treading on one another's turf. "If religion can no longer dictate the nature of factual conclusions residing properly within the magisterium of science, then scientists cannot claim higher insight into moral truth from any superior knowledge of the world's empirical constitution" (p. 201).

Apparently the National Academy of Sciences agrees. In a 1998 statement, the Academy declared that the "root" of the worldview conflict is a "misunderstanding of the critical difference between religious and scientific ways of knowing." Religion seeks to answer questions about cosmic and personal purposefulness, while "science is a way of knowing about the natural world" and limits itself to natural cause explanations. "Whether God exists or not is a question about which science is neutral" (National Academy of Sciences 1998, p. 58).

Some atheists may be able to live with Gould's NOMA model by telling themselves that since religion is illusory anyway, it's to the good that its authority is contained by sharply delineating it from the sciences. But others find Gould's argument both false and bewildering. Richard Dawkins is one of them. In one of his more generous moments, he describes NOMA as "bending over backwards to positively supine lengths" to placate religionists, and dismisses it as a "Neville Chamberlain" kind of accommodationism (Dawkins 2006, pp. 55, 67). In a less generous mood, he alternates between opining that Gould "couldn't possibly have meant" what he said in defense of NOMA, suggesting either confusion or dishonesty on Gould's part (Dawkins 2006, p. 57), and decrying NOMA as "a cowardly flabbiness of the intellect" (Dawkins 2003, p. 205).

But when one cuts through his histrionics, Dawkins' fundamental objection to NOMA is worth heeding. He argues that Gould's drawing of impermeable (even if interdigitating) borders between science and religion is an inaccurate description. Science and religion constantly influence one another; it's unrealistic that things could be otherwise. Religion appeals to facts in its efforts to explain why the universe has deep, divinely-ordained meaning. Science appeals to value in its efforts to monitor its goals, prioritize its agendas, and watchdog its treatment of human and animal experimental subjects. The boundary between his two magisteria is more porous than Gould allows.

Even worse, according to Dawkins, is religion's inevitable drive to absorb science.

[I]t is completely unrealistic to claim . . . that religion keeps itself away from science's turf, restricting itself to morals and values. A universe with a supernatural presence would be a fundamentally and qualitatively different kind of universe from one without. The difference is, inescapably, a scientific difference. Religions make existence claims, and this means scientific claims.[7] (Dawkins 2003, p. 208)

It's worth pointing out that even a few theists agree with Dawkins' observation that religion makes existence claims, and that therefore it necessarily steps on science's toes. But unlike Dawkins, they applaud this, seeing it as a more reasonable understanding of the relationship between the two. Anglican theologian Alister McGrath offers an alternative to NOMA which he calls POMA: Partially Over-lapping Magisteria. He argues that science and religion interpenetrate in the subject matter they investigate and the methods they use, and that recognizing this opens up exciting "possibilities of cross-fertilization" (McGrath 2007, p. 19). McGrath fails, however, to give even a semi-specific account of what he means by "partial" overlap. And for Dawkins and many other atheists, POMA is even less acceptable than NOMA. Recognizing either is allowing the camel's nose in the tent: the moment one concedes that there is a supernatural dimension to reality, the worldview of naturalism comes crashing down and science becomes something quite different from what naturalists conceive it to be.

In point of fact, though, Gould's NOMA may not be the threat that atheists like Dawkins suppose. A close examination of it reveals that Gould is doing little else than invoking a species of the fact/value distinction made famous by David Hume.[8] Although Gould uses the word "religion" to describe one of his separate-but-equal magisteria, what he means is more along the line of ethical values than belief in the supernatural. "Nature just is," writes Gould. "We cannot use nature for our moral instruction." Therefore, "I will . . . construe as fundamentally religious (literally, binding us together) all moral discourse on principles that might activate the ideal of universal fellowship among people" (Gould 1999, pp. 195, 62). This is a definition of religion which some supernaturalists and all theists might find necessary but certainly not sufficient. It makes no place for God and could just as easily be applied to secular humanism.

If any one should be concerned about Gould's NOMA, in fact, it's the theist. Dawkins fears that Gould's model, if accepted, would change the very way in which we look at the universe, flipping us from a naturalist to a supernaturalist worldview. There's some merit in this concern. But what Gould more likely has done is to pay lip service to "religion" while stripping it of any real importance. He tells us, after all, there is no intrinsic meaning or purpose to nature, and he insists that this is a *fact* established by the magisterium of science rather than simply a matter of interpretation or speculation (pp. 178–9). This, along with his curiously anemic definition of religion, necessarily means that religious claims cannot but be vague and quite ignorable epiphenomena, and that the only real game in town is the solid scientific magisterium. This clearly isn't what Gould intended, but it's a fair interpretation of what he actually said. It's also an understanding of religion that a naturalist can live with.

THE UNIVERSE IS JUST THERE

In a famous 1948 BBC radio debate between Jesuit priest F. C. Copleston and atheist Bertrand Russell, one of the topics of conversation was the contingency argument for God's existence. (We'll examine this argument in the next chapter.) Copleston tried to get Russell to admit that the universe must have some sufficient reason for being, and that this reason can only be the existence of a divine Creator. Russell replied by saying that he didn't see why the universe should have a reason for being. Copleston parried by asking if, therefore, Russell supposed the universe to be "gratuitious," and Russell's reply has become quite famous: "Well, the word 'gratuitous' suggests that it might be something else; I should say that the universe is just there, and that's all" (Russell and Copleston 1964, p. 175).

Russell's response to Copleston perfectly encapsulates the naturalist position: the universe is just what it is, and there's no point in looking outside it for explanations or answers as to *why* it's the way it is. Dawkins reminds us, and Russell would certainly agree, that "not every English sentence beginning with the word 'why' is a legitimate question . . . . Some questions simply do not deserve an answer" (Dawkins 2006, p. 56). Trying to get in back of nature, somehow to lift the veil and see the "why," is a long-standing temptation in the West, and it can hardly be denied that it served as an impetus for the rise of modern science. But as the naturalist sees it, supposing that the answer to the "why" must be supernatural is a foolish temptation encouraged by centuries of superstition. There is no veil to lift. The universe just is, a brute fact that needs no reason outside itself to account for its being.

The point may be put in a slightly different way: the search for a foundation must stop somewhere, and for the naturalist, the physical universe is a much better place to stop than a mysterious God. As we saw at the beginning of this chapter, every worldview is circular to the extent that it presupposes certain basic beliefs and then interprets facts about the world by appealing to those beliefs. The rock-bottom belief of naturalism is that any explanation about the world must come from within the world because the world is all there is. If that means dismissing certain "why" questions as undeserving of an answer, so be it.

But even allowing that certain "why" questions such as the three that nudged Flew toward deism persist, and granting that all world-views are circular to one degree or another, the atheist contends that his worldview is still a better account of reality than supernaturalism. Any worldview generates a description of the way things are. As such, it's reasonable to suppose that competing worldviews may be judged by the same standards that have been tried and proven effective in the examination of any pair of conflicting descriptions. These standards include simplicity, coherency, intelligibility, and testability.

In all four, the atheist believes that naturalism bests supernaturalism. As Harbour pointed out, the supernatural worldview is baroque, cluttered with all sorts of spiritual entities—not the least of which is God—for which there simply isn't any evidence, whereas naturalism accepts only those claims which can be empirically verified or logically defended. The messier the worldview, the more opportunity for error, and naturalism is much less messy than supernaturalism. Moreover, naturalism is the more coherent of the two, precisely because it isn't saddled with the burden of relating two completely different substances, matter and spirit, to one another. In addition, naturalism is intelligible while supernaturalism isn't. Naturalism has an explanation for causes in comparison to which supernatural explanations come across like Shotwell's gremlins: fascinating and fun to speculate about, perhaps, but ultimately implausible. Finally, the claims of naturalism are publicly testable, and testable moreover in a way that definitely allows for the possibility of rejecting some and verifying the truth of others.

But what possible test is there for rejecting a religious claim? What faith tradition can't absorb challenges to its claims simply by appealing to mystery and God's inexplicable will? As New Atheist Sam Harris notes, "faith is nothing more than the license religious people give one another to keep believing when reasons fail" (Harris 2006. p. 67). All of this, says biologist E. O. Wilson, makes the naturalistic worldview "superior" to the religious one, and he specifically applauds "its repeated triumphs in explaining and controlling the physical world; its self-correcting nature . . . ; its readiness to examine all subjects sacred and profane; and [its capability] of explaining traditional religion by the mechanistic models of evolutionary biology" (Wilson 1978, p. 201).

In all fairness, however, it may be the case that naturalism isn't quite as spartanly efficient as its defenders suppose. The two most successful physical "theories of everything" going today, general relativity and quantum mechanics, are incompatible with one another. Moreover, philosopher of science Nancy Cartwright argues that the entire concept of natural law upon which the sciences rest may need re-thinking. We don't live in an elegantly uniform universe where the same physical laws apply neatly across the board. Instead, our world is "dappled" or patchworked. Science can perceive (or perhaps contrive) pockets of order in the natural world by cobbling together any number of different scientific theories. But no single one of them is sovereign (Cartwright 2008). Considerations such as these suggest that naturalism may have a certain baroque messiness to it that either must be uneasily tolerated or which invites (and perhaps demands) reexamination of basic naturalist assumptions about matter, causation, and physical laws.

IS NATURALISM A RELIGION?

A frequently heard challenge is that naturalism has the status of a religion among its defenders. It's not entirely clear what's meant by the claim, although one suspects that a "you have your own religion, so why do you begrudge me mine?" tactic is probably in play. The point seems to be that the naturalist's conviction that nature is all there is itself is an expression of faith with its own tradition, dogmas, blindspots, and intolerances. After all, the truth of the naturalist perspective is no more "provable" than that of supernaturalism. Opting for it, then, must involve a leap of faith.

"Faith," of course, is a difficult word to define. Its meanings run a gamut from the maximal of religious faith (which itself is open to any number of interpretations: is it intellectual acquiescence to certain unverifiable propositions? trust and hope in things unseen? a particular kind of lifestyle? an openness to being?) to the minimal of confidence in inductive generalizations (the assurance, for example, that the sun will rise in the east tomorrow morning). All understandings of faith include some degree of believing without full proof. The question is at what point believing without full proof becomes irrational.

In what sense could naturalism be a faith? In the first place, it clearly isn't a religious faith, if by that we mean a system of beliefs that accepts the existence of a supernatural God. Instead, it's a self-consciously secular worldview. But, second, we've already noted that all worldviews inevitably include some fundamental beliefs that either are not provable or are justified circularly, and so bootstrapping from first principles is a necessity. Naturalism is no exception to this rule, but neither is supernaturalism or any other systematic perspective. What counts are the inferences that one makes from these axiomatic first principles and how well they make sense of experience. As Chet Raymo observes, "Every explanatory system refers back upon itself. [But] it is the timbre of the web and the way the web makes empirical verification possible that give us confidence that we are doing something right" (Raymo 2008, p. 32). So if what makes naturalism a faith in the eyes of its critics is its acceptance of certain unprovable core beliefs, then the charge is true but rather trivial. Finally, of course naturalists place rational trust in inductive generalizations about the nature of reality and the occurrence of future events. But this minimal kind of faith is the stuff that lubricates everyday living. So once more, if this is what the theistic challenge has in mind, the accusation is true but undamaging.

This being said, it must be admitted there's at least one motive among many naturalists that has a faith-like aroma. It may not be quite accurate to call naturalism a "faith," but supernaturalists who make the charge may be picking up on it.

For all his loyalty to scientific methodology, it would be disingenuous of the naturalist to insist that he's arrived at his position exclusively by way of an objective, clinically detached scrutiny of the facts. Naturalists no less than supernaturalists lean in the direction they do partly out of intellectual conviction, but also partly out of inclination. The naturalist *wants* the universe to be all that there is, just as the supernaturalist *wants* there to be a God. Each has a personal, emotional stake in his respective position that goes beyond intellectual assent. Philosopher Thomas Nagel offers a forthright confession of this role of personal desire in choosing worldviews.

I want atheism to be true and am made uneasy by the fact that some of the most intelligent and well-informed people I know are religious believers. It isn't just that I don't believe in God and, naturally, I hope that I'm right in my belief. It's that I hope there is no God! I don't want there to be a God; I don't want the universe to be like that. (Nagel 2001, p. 130)

Nagel's choice of words is illuminating. In any other context, expressions like "I *hope* there is no X! I *don't want* there to be an X," would suggest wishful thinking. In his psychological account of religious belief (which we'll examine in Chapter 5), Sigmund Freud argued that theists base their belief in the existence of God—their faith, in other words—on wishful thinking. But wishful thinkers, he continued, are almost always in error because they interpret reality as they desire it to be, not as it is. Their picture of reality is a wish-fulfillment rather than a reliable snapshot.

It's a fair question to ask of naturalists how much of their confidence in their worldview is wishful thinking born of deep personal commitment to a particular model of the universe. Theologian Alister McGrath (who's also a trained biochemist) argues that "nature is open to many legitimate interpretations. It can be interpreted in atheist, deist, theist and many other ways—but does not demand to be interpreted in any of these" (McGrath 2007, p. 23). What he means is that a careful scrutiny of natural phenomena entails no single metaphysical interpretation, religious or otherwise. To claim otherwise is going beyond both the facts on the ground as well as the canons of scientific methodology. This may be an honestly mistaken over-reach, or it may be a move that's motivated by personal desire—Freud's wishful thinking.

Physicist Owen Gingerich makes a similar point. The moment that the naturalist says anything more about the universe than what can be verified in a physical or scientific sense, he's gone beyond the limits of the method he claims to follow and sailed off into the waters of metaphysics (Gingerich 2006, p. 101). Speculation about the existence of God or the supernatural is perfectly legitimate. We have a right to decide how we will think about the deep-down nature of the universe. But the choice is a matter of nonscientific opinion or ideology which is hard to separate from personal preferences. The naturalist who claims to know that there's nothing beyond nature is entitled to his opinion. But he has no warrant for believing that his naturalism can support the claim.

Nagel's confession also suggests another factor that, along with wishful thinking, is viewed by philosopher Robert Solomon as a religious characteristic: belonging. Solomon says that the traditional way of thinking about religion is to see it as a matter of belief. Traditionally, the understanding has been that what one believes defines one's membership in a religion. But Solomon thinks that beliefs are "for the most part" secondary when it comes to religion. After all, "many adherents to the major religions of the world do not understand the belief of their particular religion." What *is* primary is the sense of belonging to a group of like-minded individuals who place their trust in something greater than themselves, and investing intellectually and emotionally in the group to such an extent that one's own identity becomes dependent upon it. Belonging bestows a sense of orientation, a place to stand from which to view and cope with the world. Belonging provides a home base (Solomon 2002, p. 12).

The urgency with which Nagel voices his need for the universe to be godless, for nature to be all that there is, suggests that he is invested in belonging to a particular community—the community of naturalists—which provides him with a reference point, a place of safety, and a barricade across which to fire when he's uneasily confronted by "intelligent and well-informed" theists. If other naturalists are similarly invested in a need to belong to a community of like-minded believers, then once again it may not be too off the mark to see naturalism as possessing at least some of the hallmarks of religion. Considerations like these may account for naturalist John Searle's disapproving observation that there is a sense in which naturalism "is the religion of our time . . . . Like more traditional religions, it is accepted without question and it provides the framework within which other questions can be posed, addressed, and answered" (Searle 2004, p. 48).

THE VIRTUE OF HUMILITY

The worldview of ontological naturalism is the foundation on which the atheist ultimately denies the existence of God and the supernatural. Although it's sometimes identified by its proponents with science, I hope enough has been said here to suggest that naturalism, although rightfully associated with a scientific outlook, is also metaphysically speculative, and that commitment to it hinges on temperament and desire as well as a rational appraisal of the way things are. Neither of these factors necessarily falsify it, much less point to the truth of supernaturalism. But they do caution against a too-easy conviction that naturalism, when compared to supernaturalism, is pellucid. They encourage an atheistic naturalism whose defenders argue for it, as Kai Nielsen says, "in a fallibilistic, and sometimes even in a moderately skeptical, manner . . . 'Dogmatic atheism' is not a pleonasm and 'fallibilistic atheism' is not an oxymoron" (Nielsen 2001, p. 30).

NOTES

[1] Readers who know something about the philosophy of science will recognize here an allusion to what's known as the Duhem-Quine thesis, the argument that it's impossible to test any scientific hypothesis in isolation. For a good summary of the thesis, see Gillies (1998).

[2] An excellent summary of the scientific method was written by 72 Nobel laureates (and others) in 1987 as an *amicus curiae* brief in Edwards v. Aguillard, one of the recent test cases on the teaching of creationism in public schools. It includes a statement about the goals of science. The brief may be accessed at www.talkorigins.org/faqs/edwards-v-aguillard/amicus1.html (accessed December 15, 2009).

[3] For data on scientists who are also God-believers, see Beit-Hallahmi (2007).

[4] Sorel (1994) offers an excellent analysis of scientism.

[5] Kurtz's "coduction" is very much like E. O. Wilson's (1998) "consilience." Adapted from William Whewell, consilience (which literally means "jumping across"), occurs when inductions generated from one class of facts coincide with inductions from other facts: thus a "jumping across" conventional disciplinary boundaries.

[6] For more on religious separatism, see Haught (2000, pp. 28–44).

[7] It's worth pointing out that this drive to absorb isn't characteristic only of religion. All worldviews seek to explain reality in a totalizing way.

[8] The distinction, which we'll return to in Chapter 6, is intuitive. Factual statements *describe* ("is"), while value statements *prescribe* ("ought"). More specifically, factual statements reflect discoveries while normative ones reflect consensus. Hume argued that the former are never derivable from the latter. "In every system of morality, which I have hitherto met with, I have always remarked, that the author proceeds for some time in the ordinary ways of reasoning, and establishes the being of a God, or makes observations concerning human affairs; when all of a sudden I am surprised to find, that instead of the usual copulations of propositions, *is*, and *is not*, I meet with no proposition that is not connected with an *ought*, or an *ought not*. This change is imperceptible; but is however, of the last consequence. For as this *ought*, or *ought not*, expresses some new relation or affirmation, 'tis necessary that it should be observed and explain'd; and at the same time that a reason should be given; for what seems altogether inconceivable, how this new relation can be a deduction from others, which are entirely different from it" (Hume 1972, p. 203).

CHAPTER 3

REFUTING THEISTIC "PROOFS"

The fool says in his heart that there is no God, but whoever says in his heart or to men: Wait just a little and I will prove it—what a rare man of wisdom is he! If in the moment of beginning his proof it is not absolutely undetermined whether God exists or not, he does not prove it; and if it is thus undetermined in the beginning he will never come to begin, partly from fear of failure, since God perhaps does not exist, and partly because he has nothing with which to begin.
    Soren Kierkegaard, Philosophical Fragments

When people think about the debate between theists and atheists, what probably comes to mind are "proofs" for the existence of God. This is understandable for two reasons: first, and most obviously, because the wrangle between theists and atheists revolves in large part around whether a deity exists; second, because most of us feel a deep need to distinguish between reality and illusion, and that need intensifies in proportion to the perceived importance of whatever it is whose reality is being debated. (Most likely, a debate about whether leprechauns are real won't generate as much heat as a debate about God's existence.) So it's not surprising that people who feel strongly one way or the other about God would spend a lot of energy coming up with arguments that either prove that God is real or prove that God is an illusion.

Not surprising, perhaps, but a bit strange. As we saw in the last chapter, acceptance or rejection of God is one of those basic beliefs that flow from the embrace of a particular worldview—in this case, supernaturalism on the one hand or naturalism on the other. If one embraces the supernaturalist worldview, God-belief is built into one's core convictions. Similarly, God-disbelief is hardwired into the

53

naturalist worldview. The strange thing about debates over the existence of a God, as Kierkegaard slyly suggests, is that the fix seems to be in before the conversation ever begins. A naturalist operates from an atheist perspective, while a supernaturalist operates from a theistic one. Each has already made up his mind about whether or not there is a God, and the chance of a genuine give-and-take dialogue between them seems slim. This needn't mean that they are dogmatic or have closed their minds, but simply that their visions of the nature of things are so different that they can neither agree on first principles nor honestly suspend their convictions for the sake of discussion. Given their respective worldviews, it's hard to see how things could be otherwise.

So the first strange thing about debates over the existence of God is that it's not clear for whose benefit they're intended. Arguments for the existence of God surely aren't for the instruction of believers, any more than arguments against God's existence are for the instruction of unbelievers. For a naturalist, arguments *for* God's existence are simply irrelevant. Why waste time refuting them? Doing so only bestows on them a faux respectability. For the supernaturalist, arguments *against* God's existence are willfully obtuse. Why bother trying to open the eyes of someone who refuses to see the obvious?

Despite this, philosophers have been coming up with arguments for the existence of God for centuries, and other philosophers have been knocking them down for the same length of time.[1] To a certain extent, both sides may be speaking not so much to one another as to the undecided. But if that's the case, it would make more sense to offer defenses or criticisms of their respective worldviews rather than God's existence, since the latter rides upon the former. That arguments for and against the existence of God have such a long history underscores the fact that the debate has been fueled by apologetic and adversarial motives. Religious disagreements are often heated ones in which adversaries, while perhaps loving truth, too often come across as loving victory more, precisely because deep worldview loyalty is at play. (The latest incarnation of religious dispute, this time between the New Atheists and Christian fundamentalists, is an obvious example of how easy it is for the light of reason to give way to polemical heat.) Christian missionaries are taught standard arguments for the existence of God to help them respond to religion's cultured despisers, but mainly to convert non-Christians. Atheist manuals are written to

REFUTING THEISTIC "PROOFS"

school nonbelievers in talking points and strategies for trouncing believers in take-no-prisoner debates over God's existence.[2]

There's a second reason why debates about God's existence are rather strange, and it has to do with the word "existence." As we'll explore more closely in the next chapter, it's not at all clear what we mean when we affirm (or reject) a proposition like "God exists." When the naturalist uses the word "existence," he means it to refer to natural objects whose reality can be verified in some measurable manner. But when the supernaturalist uses the word in reference to God, she must mean something quite different. How, after all, can one measure or even comprehend the existence of an entity which is supposed to be infinite and eternal? As we saw in Chapter 1, some theists, like Thomas Aquinas, insist that God's mode of existence should be understood analogously rather than univocally—we can infer the general contours of what God's existence is like by reflecting on what it means for a natural object to exist, but we should never presume that material existence is the same as divine existence. But other theists such as Paul Tillich claim that God's mode of being is so utterly different from nature's mode that even to use the word "existence" in reference to God is misleading. It tempts us to think of God as just another thing in the world, existing pretty much like other natural objects—only "supernaturally" rather than "naturally" (Tillich 1973).

What this suggests is that it's entirely possible that theists and atheists are talking at cross purposes when they debate the existence of God. This will become more apparent shortly when we examine a couple of standard criticisms of the cosmological argument for God's existence that assume that God must share, at least in some respects, certain characteristics of the natural order. The theist responds by saying that it makes no sense to make such an assumption because doing so reduces the way God exists to the way that natural objects do. This seems a reasonable objection. But the atheist's reply, that the only model of existence we know is the existence of natural objects, is also reasonable.

It's necessary to make two additional points, both of which are likely to underscore the strangeness of traditional proofs for the existence of God. First, strictly speaking, most aren't proofs at all, if by "proof" one means an argument which aims to establish its conclusion beyond a shadow of a doubt. Instead, most of the arguments aim more modestly to show that belief in God is consistent with reason and everyday experience. Indeed, of all the arguments examined in this chapter, only one—the ontological argument—can properly be called a "proof" in the rigorous sense of the word. This point is important to keep in mind, because arguments for God's existence are frequently criticized by opponents for failing to "prove" their conclusions. But this is an unfair charge. Such arguments should be evaluated in terms of how strong a case they can make rather than held up to an unreasonably rigorous standard of proof.

Second, it should be noted that not all theists will accept the legitimacy of arguments for the existence of God. Some theists, taking a cue from claims about the lack of analogy between natural existence and divine being, argue that human reason is simply too limited to tackle the infinite. Others argue that rational proofs of God's existence would coerce consent and hence violate the free choice to believe in the absence of persuasive evidence that is the necessary condition for faith.

Notwithstanding their oddity, debates over the existence of God aren't likely to go away anytime soon. In this chapter we'll examine atheist rebuttals of three of the most common arguments for God's existence: empirical arguments from design and causation, and the nonempirical ontological argument. In the following chapter, we'll take a look at several positive arguments against the existence of God offered by atheists.

THE ARGUMENT FROM DESIGN

The argument from design, like all empirical (or "*a posteriori*") arguments for the existence of God, is based on an inference from a feature of the world to a divine explanation of that feature. These *a posteriori* arguments are best thought of as hypotheses: they examine a pattern observable in the natural realm and seek to come up with the single best explanation for it. It's just that for the theist, the best hypothesis is God.

In the case of the design argument, the natural feature that the theist wants to account for is orderly complexity. There appears to be a deep-down and intricate order to the way things are. Seasons predictably come and go; objects fall down instead of up (at least on earth); the logical law of identity (something is identical to itself) pertains in any possible world; and the very possibility of both science and everyday survival presupposes physical regularities that we codify as natural laws. It's precisely this orderliness, regularity, and predictability in nature that the theist wishes to account for. The distinctive characteristic of his scrutiny of these phenomena is his conviction that orderliness and complexity can't be accounted for without positing cosmic purposefulness or design, and this in turns leads him to the God hypothesis. This emphasis on the purposefulness of natural order accounts for the fact that the design argument is also frequently called the "teleological" (Greek *telos* = purpose, end) argument.

Arguments from design stretch back at least as far as the Hebrew Bible's Wisdom of Solomon, probably written in the second half of the first century BCE, in which the author claims that both the existence and qualities of the deity can be inferred from an observation of the beauty, power, and energy of creation: "through the grandeur and beauty of the creatures we may, by analogy, contemplate their Author" (13: 5). At around the same time, Cicero asks in his *De natura deorum*: "What could be more clear or obvious when we look up to the sky and contemplate the heavens, than that there is some divinity of superior intelligence?" (Cicero 1972, p. 124). Two important points are suggested by these passages. The first is that the argument from design, perhaps more than any other traditional argument for God's existence, seems prompted by sheer wonderment at the beauty and majesty of nature. The second is the assumption that the natural features which overwhelm us with their grandeur can only be adequately described and appreciated when interpreted as divine handiwork. As we'll see in the final chapter, atheists insist that a rejection of God and cosmic purposefulness in no way diminishes a sense of awe and even gratitude in the face of the natural realm. But this is a minority opinion (which is not, of course, to say that it's false).

There are several varieties of the design argument. The two strongest and most commonly invoked ones are the argument from analogy (gestured at in the Wisdom of Solomon) and the more recent anthropic or fine-tuning argument.

The classic statement of the *analogy argument* is from William Paley's *Natural Theology* (1802), a textbook that was required reading for two generations of British students (including Darwin, who confessed being absolutely won over by it when he read it as a young man; his admiration for Paley's ingenuity endured even after he rejected the book's conclusions). In it, Paley introduces his famous watch analogy. If we examine the mechanics of a timepiece, asserts Paley, we quickly recognize that its obvious orderliness suggests a purpose or design: "we perceive . . . that its several parts are framed and put together for a purpose, for example, that they are so formed and adjusted as to produce motion, and that motion so regulated as to point out the hour of the day" (Paley 1802, p. 2). It would be obtuse, Paley argues, to refuse to see in the watch "proof of contrivance." But "contrivance" presumes a contriver, and the more intricate or complex the contrivance, the more clever the design from which the contriver worked. Simply by observing the inner workings of a watch, then, we can observe that its orderliness and complexity point to a designed purposefulness which in turn points to the existence of an intelligent watchmaker. "Design" logically presumes a "designer."

Now, says Paley, consider nature. "Every indication of contrivance, every manifestation of design, which existed in the watch, exists in the works of nature; with the difference, on the side of nature, of being greater and more, and that in a degree which exceeds all computation" (pp. 17–18). By analogy, then, we can conclude that the "manifestation of design" in nature likewise points to the existence of an intelligent designer. But since no human is capable of designing and creating such a complex ("exceeding all computation") universe, it follows that nature's intelligent designer is God.

Paley didn't invent the analogy argument. That it was in the air is indicated by the fact that David Hume savaged it in his *Dialogues Concerning Natural Religion*, a book published a full quarter of a century before Paley's *Natural Theology* (but only after the cautious Hume's death). Hume's objections to the design argument focus especially on what he sees as the faulty reasoning behind the analogy between human artifacts and the natural order. He denies that there's enough similarity between the two to draw an interesting comparison. When we see a house or a watch, we're habituated by past experience to presume that they had a builder or watchmaker. But the dissimilarity between watches and houses on the one hand and the universe on the other is so great that the most one can "pretend to is a guess, a conjecture, a presumption concerning a similar cause" (Hume 1998, p. 16).

Even if we do allow the analogy, asserts Hume, the conclusions that it generates about the divine Contriver are startling. Working on the argument's assumption that "like effects prove like causes," we're warranted in concluding that God is more like a vegetable or an animal than a cosmic watchmaker, because the world is more organic than mechanical; that God is error-prone and fallible, because events and processes in the world at times seem gratuitous, bizarre, or unnecessarily destructive; and that God may in fact be a committee of deities, each member of which is charged with a specific task, because there are so many different systems at work in nature. In short, the analogy is so sloppy that it allows for "a hundred contradictory views . . ., and invention has here full scope to exert itself" (p. 49).

If none of these objections are compelling, Hume offers two more to sympathizers with the design argument which he thinks clinches things. The first objection is that there's no good reason for privileging mind over matter when it comes to describing the world: "What peculiar privilege has this little agitation of the brain which we call thought, that we must thus make it the model of the whole universe?" Hume can only conclude that human vanity, "our partiality in our own favor," leads us to re-write the physical realm in our own image (p. 23).

Hume's second objection—and it may be his single strongest one—is that there's no compelling reason to suppose that order necessarily points to underlying design. Any universe, if it's to exist at all, must display coherence between its parts and stability in the whole. So from the fact that we observe order in the natural realm—a necessary condition for there being a natural realm to observe in the first place—we can make no inference about design. "It is in vain, therefore, to insist upon the uses of the parts in animals or vegetables, and their curious adjustment to each other. I would fain know how an animal could subsist unless its parts were so adjusted?" (p. 51). Order by itself doesn't point to design. The missing step is showing that order can come about *only* through design. Thus philosopher Antony Flew (1966) famously insists that the argument *from* design more accurately ought to be called the argument *to* design.

Since the 1859 publication of Darwin's *Origin of Species,* criticisms of the design argument's analogy tend to dispute it on scientific rather than purely philosophical or logical grounds. But their refutations of design tend to follow the lines of Hume's insistence that order is possible without design. New Atheists Daniel Dennett and Richard Dawkins contend, for example, that proponents of the design argument in the eighteenth century as well as today build their case on a false disjunction: either the order of the universe is designed or the product of chance. If the former, complexity and orderliness are easily accounted for by the God hypothesis. If the latter, the emergence of complexity and orderliness stretches credulity beyond reasonable boundaries.

Dennett and Dawkins argue that this is a false choice because there is a third explanation of order: natural selection. The mechanism of natural selection allows for the emergence of both complexity and order in the organic realm, and does so without appealing either to design or chance. Natural selection works with genetic changes that appear "by chance," but the selection process itself is anything but chance. We understand the mechanics of natural selection, even though we can't predict the genetic mutations that influence it. In other words, the natural order, understood in evolutionary terms, is able to "subsist" on its own steam without dragging in design on the one hand or having to answer charges of wild improbability on the other. Natural selection, as Dennett concedes, doesn't demonstrate that God doesn't exist. But it *does* show that God isn't necessary to explain order and complexity in the natural world—which was exactly Hume's conclusion (Slack 2007, p. 118).

Dennett also echoes Hume's worry that the design argument shows a privileging of mind that confuses more than clarifies. An evolutionary understanding of the world, writes Dennett, liberates us from the traditional Greco-Christian mind-bias which insists that the universe's orderliness only makes sense if it's the product of a divine intelligence. (Recall his "skyhook" metaphor from the previous chapter.) Such a bias inevitably generates "trickle-down" models like the design argument which presume that "it takes a big fancy smart thing to make a less fancy thing" (Dennett 2007, p. 135). The Darwinian worldview deflates this bias and replaces it with a "bubble-up vision" in which intelligence *emerges* by natural selection rather than being supposed as a preexisting divine quality (p. 136).

A version of the argument from design called the *anthropic* or *fine-tuning* argument has received much attention recently. Proponents favor the argument at least in part because it shifts focus from the world to the cosmos, thereby avoiding the difficulties natural selection presents to design. The anthropic argument contends that the universe is so exquisitely fine-tuned to sustain life that the balancing act can only be reasonably explained by attributing it to a divine intelligence. The working assumption behind this claim is that the greater the number of conditions necessary for life, the less likely that they're satisfied by chance. Since an incredible number of conditions are necessary (such as, for example, the fact that the post-Big Bang expansion of matter had to occur at just the right rate to allow for the gradual unfolding of complexity), and since they apparently are satisfied (life exists), there must be a "life-giving factor [that] lies at the center of the whole machinery and design of the world" (Barrow and Tippler 1988).[3] Somehow, the universe "knew" we were coming.

Debate over the anthropic argument has been lively. Detractors object that the argument fundamentally confuses the direction of the fine-tuning. It's carbon-based life, they contend, that has adapted itself to the universe, not the other way around. Other critics argue that the universe isn't finely-tuned for life at all, since the vast majority of it seems to be empty space inhospitable to life. Still others contend that reality may hold multiverses rather than a single universe, and that there's no reason to suppose that any of them besides our own is "finely-tuned" for life. (It's worth pointing out that physicist Paul Davies rejects the multiverse thesis on the grounds that "like a blunderbuss, it explains everything and nothing" [Davies 1994, p. 49.])

As pointed out earlier, atheist repudiations of the design argument in both its analogy and anthropic versions aren't intended to dispute the awe at the grandeur of the physical cosmos that motivates its defenders. Ultimately, what the atheist objects to is the argument's assumption that the universe was constructed for the sole benefit of humankind. The extraordinary nature of this assumption is perhaps best captured by Douglas Adam's parable of the "sentient puddle."

This is rather as if you imagine a puddle waking up one morning and thinking, "this is an interesting world I find myself in—an interesting hole I find myself in—fits me rather neatly, doesn't it? In fact it fits me staggeringly well, must have been made to have me in it!" This is such a powerful idea that as the sun rises in the sky and the air heats up and as, gradually, the puddle gets smaller and smaller, it's still frantically hanging on to the notion that everything's going to be alright, because this world was meant to have him in it, was built to have him in it; so the moment he disappears catches him rather by surprise. I think this may be something we need to be on the watch out for. (Dawkins 2001)

THE ARGUMENT FROM CAUSATION

Arguments from causation, frequently called "cosmological arguments," are operationally similar to design arguments: they seek to explain a feature of the natural world by positing God as a hypothesis. In their case, however, what they seek to explain is the sheer existence of physical reality. "Why is there something rather than nothing?" is the question proponents of causation arguments wish an answer to. Philosopher J. L. Mackie once referred to the cosmological argument as "par excellence the philosophers' argument for theism," presumably because of the depth of the questions it asks (Mackie 1988, p. 81).

The classic *First Cause* formulation of the argument from causation—and the one that most appeals to common sense—is found in the second of Thomas Aquinas' thirteenth-century *Quinquae viae* or "five ways" of demonstrating God's existence. Experience tells us that everything which exists has been caused by something outside itself. Since the universe exists, consistency suggests that it too must have an external cause. But the only entity powerful enough to cause the universe to exist is God. Therefore, there must be a God.

This argument has an intuitive plausibility, especially if we think of "cause" simply as a prior event serving as the necessary condition for the emergence of a consequent one; think of a line of toppling dominoes. But more than one critic has pointed out that the argument's exemption of God from the universal rule that everything which exists has an external cause is fishy. Whichever way one plays it, either exempting God from the universal causal claim or subsuming God under it, the argument doesn't work. If God is exempt, then the claim ought to be that *most* things which exist have external causes. But if this is the case, why not exempt the universe rather than God from causal dependence? The choice seems arbitrary. If, on the other hand, one concedes for the sake of consistency that God, like everything else which exists, must have an external cause, then the claim that God caused the world to be is uninteresting because then the obviously more important puzzle is "what caused God to be?" And the moment one asks this kind of question, the whole investigation becomes (as Thomas Aquinas himself noted) endlessly regressive: "What caused the cause of God to be?" "And what caused the cause of the cause of God to be?" And so on. As mathematician John Allen Paulos points out, the whole thing soon begins to look like an elaborate Ponzi scheme that "quickly leads to metaphysical bankruptcy" (Paulos 2008, p. 13).

In an effort to end-run this recursive difficulty, several other versions of the causation argument have been offered by theists. The two strongest are the argument from contingency and the *kalam* argument.

The *contingency* argument begins with the observation that every physical object in the world exists in a contingent rather than necessary way. Something which exists necessarily cannot not-exist. It cannot fail to be, nor can it even be imagined to not-be. Obviously, however, no physical object enjoys this kind of existence. Every physical object comes into being, changes over time, and eventually ceases to be. This kind of existence, one which has no necessity, one in which it's entirely possible for something either to not-have-been or to not-be, is called "contingent."

Everything encountered in the universe appears to be contingent. Therefore, so the argument continues, it makes sense to presume that the universe as a whole is likewise contingent. But if this is the case, then an explanation for the universe is called for, because if the universe is contingent then it could just as easily have not-been. Yet it is. Why?

The only possible explanation for the existence of a contingent universe is that its existence depends on the existence of a necessary being. This being's existence has to be necessary rather than contingent. Otherwise, the same question mark that applies to the the existence of the universe applies to it. The reason why there's something rather than nothing is because of the underlying necessary existence of this being, and we can call it "God." God is the necessary foundation which sustains the contingent universe.

One of the strongest atheist responses to the contingency argument was offered by Bertrand Russell in the BBC radio debate, mentioned in Chapter 2, between him and Catholic philosopher Frederick Copleston. Russell's criticism is that the contingency argument commits the fallacy of composition: the (hasty) presumption that the whole must have the quality of its parts. Sometimes this *is* the case: the ocean, for example, is just as wet as the billions of gallons of water that comprise it. But most often, there's no reason to presume that the whole is like its parts. This can be seen pretty clearly if one thinks of the whole as a set or class, and the parts as everything that legitimately falls within the set or class. Obviously it's foolish to claim that the set of red objects is itself red, or that the set of thin books itself shares the quality of thinness. Consequently, even if we grant that every object within the set of "universe" is contingent, it doesn't follow that the universe itself is as well. There's no logical contradiction in presuming that the universe is necessary even though its objects aren't. But if this is the case, then the pivotal assumption in the contingency argument seems unwarranted.

Proponents of the contingency argument embrace the principle of sufficient reason: for everything that is, there must be a sufficient explanation for its existence. If the universe is contingent (leaving aside for the moment the atheist charge of a fallacy of composition), it can't be a sufficient explanation for its own existence because it could just as easily not exist. But critics of this move point out, first, that postulations of God as the sufficient explanation for a contingent universe themselves violate the principle of sufficient reason, because no explanation of the existence of God is offered by theists. More tellingly many atheists agree with Bertrand Russell's conclusion that "the universe is just there, and that's all." In other words, it's a waste of time to search for an explanation of the physical universe that pretends to go beyond the boundaries of the physical universe. The universe is simply a brute inexplicable fact.

Finally, some critics argue that the entire contingency argument rests on a misuse of the terms "contingent" and "necessary." Defenders of the argument intend them as metaphysical descriptions of two types of existence. But critics respond by saying that the terms are properly designations of two types of propositions or statements. In other words, they're linguistic rather than metaphysical categories. A proposition is necessary if it's logically necessary—that is, if its denial is self-contradictory. A proposition is contingent if its denial is not self-contradictory. "Bachelors are unmarried men" is a logically necessary statement. But the sentences "God exists" or "God exists necessarily" aren't, because the denial of them leads to no apparent contradiction (although Anselm of Canterbury, whose ontological argument will be examined shortly, would disagree).[4]

The contingency argument attempts to avoid the classic argument from causation's seemingly arbitrary exemption of God from universal causality by distinguishing between necessary and contingent existence—God is exempt from the need for a cause because God's existence is necessary. The *kalam* argument, which has roots in medieval Islamic thought (hence its Arabic name, which is sometimes translated as "speech" or "philosophical dialogue") but recently has been revived by Christian theists, likewise avoids recursion by focusing on temporality.

Defenders of the *kalam* argument typically take Big Bang as their starting point. Agreeing with cosmologists who claim that the universe had a definite temporal beginning, they conclude that it also must have a cause because everything that has a beginning has a cause for its beginning. The metaphysical claim that everything which has a beginning is caused is the heart of the *kalam* argument. When applied to the beginning of the universe as a whole, it suggests that the only cause powerful enough to bring about such a beginning is God. Therefore, God exists.

Although many defenders of the argument are content to appeal to the scientific Big Bang theory as the basis for their claim that the universe had a temporal beginning, others such as William Lane Craig, the *kalam* argument's strongest champion, also offer a number of mathematical arguments. The strongest of these is an argument based on the impossibility of an actual infinity of past moments (Craig 1995; 2000b). Presume that there is an infinity of past moments, and assign each of them a number such that all numbers (an infinity of them) are assigned to past moments. Now for every present moment that recedes into the past, a new number must be assigned. If the number of past moments was less than infinite, this would be easy. We could simply renumber the past moments in order, such that the moment already assigned the number "1" now becomes "2," "2" becomes "3," and so on, with the renumbering following down the line sequentially. But if we're talking about an infinity of past moments, then all possible numbers have already been assigned. On the one hand, then, how could we possibly recount such that a "new" number is available to assign to the new past moment? But on the other hand, who wants to deny that all actually existing entites, including new ones, can be counted? So claiming that the universe has no beginning embroils us in a paradox—the fact that we both can and cannot assign a "new" number to new past moments—and this, as Craig says, is a metaphysical absurdity. Reason, then, affirms that the universe is not beginningless.

Atheist philosopher Michael Martin criticizes Craig's mathematical rejection of an actual infinity of past moments on the grounds that it makes perfect sense simply to renumber past moments. Although his reasoning is a bit opaque, Martin's point seems to be that successive addition to an infinite set does no damage to the notion of infinity unless one claims a beginning point for the successive addition. If a beginning *is* claimed, infinity—defined as that which has no beginning or end—is of course violated. "But there is an alternative—namely, that an actual infinity can be constructed by successive addition if the successive addition is beginningless" (Martin 1990, p. 105). Craig stipulates that successive addition must begin at some point, but according to Martin offers no argument for the stipulation. Instead, he merely begs the question.

Critics of the *kalam* argument generally respond in two additional ways, one focusing on its causal claim and the other contending that the argument's denial of the possibility of an existing infinity of items (such as past moments) cuts both ways.

The first (and quite strong) objection is that the kalamist's claim that all beginnings have causes is neither self-evident nor empirically verifiable. Every instance of causation that humans experience is a change or transition from one state to another: cold to warm, alive to dead, hunger to satiation. What we *don't* experience are *de novo* creations, genuine beginnings from nothing to something. Our experience teaches us that transitions are caused by intermediate agents—a blanket is the cause of my change from cold to warm, a cancer causes a living creature to die, and so on—but we have no warrant for presuming that a *de novo* beginning likewise has a cause. In short, it's not as obviously bizarre as *kalam* advocates claim that while the universe had a genuine beginning, there was no cause for that beginning. It may be contrary to our experience of transitional change. But transitional change isn't a good analogy for *de novo* beginnings.

The second problem with the *kalam* argument speaks directly to the denial of actually existing infinities. Critics point out that taking this claim seriously seems to entail a denial of God's omniscience. If, by divine omniscience, one means that there is an infinity of knowledge items in God's mind—items that represent not only actual past, present, and future states of affairs but also the entire range of unactualized possibilities—then omniscience must be denied for the same reason that an infinite number of past moments was denied. This latter consequence obviously doesn't bother an atheist, but it ought to give a proponent of *kalam* pause for thought.

This second objection to *kalam* doesn't seem to have the strength of the first, if for no other reason than the items of knowledge in God's mind are presumably simultaneously present rather than *ad seriatim*. Nothing gets "added to" the divine mind in the way that present moments get "added to" the set of past ones.

Before moving on to the ontological argument, it's worth closing this discussion of causation arguments with two general criticisms that have been leveled against all of them.[5]

First, whatever else theists believe about God, they agree that God is atemporal—that is, is eternal and exists outside of time. Even theisms that teach some kind of incarnational, in-time event—the Christian doctrine of Jesus as the second person of the Trinity, for example, or the avatar appearances of Krishna in Hindu tradition—affirm that God essentially exists outside of time.

Leaving aside perplexities about what timeless existence would be, the notion of an eternal God raises a problem for any kind of cosmological argument seeking to establish God as either First Cause or *kalam* Cause of the temporal beginning of the universe. That problem is how a timeless or outside-of-time being can act as a cause in the first place. A cause is a temporal event in which a change from State A at Time t to State B at Time t+1 occurs. But how can an entity which is outside time possibly perform an act which is necessarily temporal? It might seem that the argument from contingency avoids this difficulty because its attention is focused on God as the necessary reason or explanation of contingent existence. But surely the implicit claim of the contingency argument is that contingent existence wouldn't be except for an original act of creation by a necessary being. So the argument from contingency seems to entail an assumption of First Cause or *kalam* Cause, and the same perplexity of explaining how a nontemporal being can perform temporal acts remains.

The second general criticism that can be leveled against cosmological arguments is similar to the one Hume raised against design: even if we acknowledge that they establish a first cause or a temporal beginning, or sustain contingent existence, there's no reason to presume that they also establish a personal deity. Thomas Aquinas himself noted that his arguments from causation fall short of demonstrating the existence of the Christian God. At most, they argue for the existence of a metaphysical principle of order. Faith provides the personal touch.

Moreover, in the case of the First Cause and *kalam* arguments, what reason is there to suppose that the entity which set the universe in motion has endured? Even if we grant that a God (or, to invoke Hume again, a committee of gods) was the originator of the universe, that doesn't mean that this deity or deities are still around. At least when used by theists—believers in a personal God—cosmological arguments seem to fall far short of where their advocates want them to go.

THE ONTOLOGICAL ARGUMENT

The ontological argument, first proposed by Anselm of Canterbury in the eleventh century, is by almost everyone's reckoning the most intriguing argument going for the existence of God. It has had several defenders since Anselm, most notably Rene Descartes in the seventeenth century and Charles Hartshorne, Norman Malcolm, and Alvin Plantinga in the twentieth. But it's also provoked a wide range of critics, beginning with Anselm's contemporary, the monk Gaunilo, and including Thomas Aquinas in the thirteenth century, Kant in the eighteenth, and a wide range of contemporary philosophers. Some of these critics admire its ingenuity even while utterly rejecting both its method and conclusion. As Arthur Schopenhauer famously said of it, "considered by daylight . . . and without prejudice, this famous ontological proof is really a charming joke" (Martin 1990, 95). Others are simply baffled by it, sensing that the argument is illicit but not quite able to put their finger on where it goes wrong. Undoubtedly this is one of the reasons for its perennial interest.

The ontological argument is quite different from design and cosmological ones. First, it doesn't claim to be empirical in even the slightest way. Instead, it is a completely "*a priori*" or "prior to experience" argument, based solely on a rational appraisal of what the word "God" means. If the meaning of the word God entails perfection, then God necessarily exists: this is the fundamental reasoning behind all versions of the ontological argument. Second, unlike all the cosmological arguments and some versions of the design argument, the ontological argument, at least Anselm's version of it, culminates not simply in a metaphysically abstract deity but a good, benevolent, and wise one as well. It isn't precisely the Christian God, but it *is* a personal one.

Anselm actually offers two versions of the ontological argument. The first focuses on the meaning of "God" as "that than nothing greater can be conceived," and the second on the proposition "God exists" as logically necessary. In the first argument, Anselm says that even the "fool"—presumably an atheist—acknowledges that he has a mental notion or concept of God: "that than which nothing greater can be conceived." But once this is understood, it's apparent that the actual or real existence of this "that than which nothing greater can be conceived" must be granted. Otherwise, one winds up in a contradiction:

> Surely that than which a greater cannot be thought cannot exist only in the understanding. For if it exists only in the understanding, it can be thought to exist in reality as well, which is greater. So if that than which a greater cannot be thought exists only in the understanding, then that than which a greater cannot be thought is that than which a greater can be thought. But that is clearly impossible. Therefore, there is no doubt that something than which a greater cannot be thought exists both in the understanding and in reality. (Anselm 2001, p. 7)

Anselm goes on to infer that "greater" in this context also means that God is "just, truthful, happy, and whatever it is better to be than not to be." So "that than which nothing greater can be conceived" turns out to be a personal deity.

The second version of the ontological argument argues that once one understands the meaning of the word "God," it's impossible to think of God as *not* existing. "Everything that exists, except [God] alone, can be thought not to exist. So [God] alone among all things [has] existence most truly . . . so truly that it cannot be thought not to exist" (p. 8). The sentence "God exists," therefore, carries logical necessity. To deny it is to assert a contradiction.

In his *Dialogues Concerning Natural Religion*, Hume responds to the second version by contending that it's an "evident absurdity" to try to prove the existence of God by a priori arguments. His reasoning is that the only way to prove something a priori is by showing that its opposite implies a contradiction, something that goes beyond the powers of reason even to conceive (how to conceive, for example, of a circle which is also a not-circle?). But regardless of how strenuously one claims logical necessity for the proposition "God exists," it's entirely possible to conceive of God not existing (Hume 1998, pp. 56–7).

Several objections to the first version can be raised as well. One is that it's not at all obvious, contrary to Anselm, that either a fool or a wise person is clear on what it means to have an idea of "that than which nothing greater can be conceived." What meaning, for example, should we assign to "greater"? Moreover, is it really the case that an actually existing entity is "greater" than a mentally existing one? Is the concept of a triangle somehow less than one drawn on paper? What if existence actually detracts from greatness rather than enhances it? As Norman Malcolm points out, it's puzzling as to why existence in and of itself adds to greatness.

> It makes sense and is true to say that my future house will be a better one if it is insulated than if it is not insulated; but what could it mean to say that it will be a better house if it exists than if it does not? My future child will be a better man if he is honest than if he is not; who would understand the saying that he will be a better man if he exists than if he does not? (Malcolm 1965, p. 139)

In addition to these charges of vagueness, a number of critics have chipped away at Anselm's argument by showing that its mode of reasoning lends itself to parody, the implication being that any argument so easy to poke fun at is suspect. The first person to do this was Anselm's contemporary, Gaunilo, who used the structure of Anselm's own argument to "prove" that the perfect island (or, by implication, any other "perfect" thing) must exist, since an actually existing perfect island is more perfect than one merely conceived (Anselm 2001, pp. 31–2). A more recent and especially cunning parody of the argument comes from Douglas Gasking. The world, argues Gasking, is the most marvelous achievement imaginable. The merit of achievement is determined in part by the ability of its creator; the greater the disability that must be overcome, the greater the achievement. The most extreme form of disability imaginable is non-existence. If, therefore, we can conceive of an existent God creating the world, we can think of an even greater Being—one who created the world despite the handicap of not being. An existing God, therefore, is not "that than which nothing greater can be imagined," because one can imagine something greater: a non-existing God who overcomes his nonbeing in order to create (Grey 2000). Granted, this is a perfectly silly argument. But that's exactly the point. If Gasking can use the ontological argument's structure to defend such a non-sensical conclusion, mightn't there be something fundamentally wrong with the argument?

The standard objection to the ontological argument (although some have argued that it applies more to Descartes' than Anselm's version [e.g., Brian Davis 1993, p. 66]) is Immanuel Kant's famous claim that the content of a concept is not added to by the claim that it exists. "A hundred real thalers do not contain the least coin more than a hundred possible thalers" (Kant 1965, p. 505). There are many attributes or characteristics that provide genuine information about an object. But Kant denied that existence is one of them. Gottlob Frege made a similar point later when he argued that statements of existence are really just statements of number answering the question "How many?" Existential statements don't express properties. They simply answer the question of how many of a particular object with certain characteristics there are (Frege 1980, p. 65).

If Kant and Frege are correct, the ontological argument's claim that an actually existing X is greater than a merely conceptual X is suspect. Ascribing existence to X adds nothing significant to it. But let's consider for a moment the possibility that existence in fact *is* a property. Does this salvage the ontological argument? Probably not, because all that might be going on then is that the existence being attributed is simply stipulative—that is, it's merely a definitional property of the concept under consideration. But definitional existence is a far cry from actual existence, and critics of the ontological argument have long noted that its proponents fail to appreciate the distinction.

There have been several contemporary attempts to salvage the ontological argument. Alvin Plantinga's version, which appeals to a modal logic analysis, is probably the best known. Plantinga argues that if God exists, God is a necessary being because something is greater if its existence is necessary rather than contingent (this is the obvious connection between Anselm and Plantinga). So if God exists, God cannot not-exist. Now the question is whether God actually exists. Plantinga argues that if it's possible that God exists—and he thinks there's no obvious reason to deny the possibility—then there must be some possible world in which God exists. But since God's mode of existence is necessary, his existence in *any* possible world entails existence in *all* possible worlds. Therefore God exists (Plantinga 1977).

Plantinga himself admits that the argument is inconclusive because the claim that there is a possible world in which God exists can be denied by rational people. But he maintains that the premise isn't contrary to reason, and that his new ontological argument therefore establishes the rational acceptability of God's existence.

But philosopher Patrick Grim isn't so sure, and to show why he parodies Plantinga's argument by offering an ontological argument for the existence of fairies. Suppose, Grim writes, there is a possible world in which there is a special fairy who possesses the property of having magical powers in every possible world. It follows that this fairy would exist in all possible worlds, and thus in our world too. The ascription of necessary magical powers in every possible world is no more contrary to reason, Grim asserts, than Plantinga's claim that if God exists, God exists necessarily. Therefore, the fairy argument is "rationally" acceptable—although surely no rational person would accept it. And neither, concludes Grim, should we accept Plantinga's "rationally" acceptable argument for God's existence (Grim 1979).[6]

A CAUTIONARY REMINDER

Kierkegaard reminded us at the beginning of this chapter that God-belief always precedes the launching of arguments for God's existence. Otherwise, he says, there's no motive for coming up with such arguments. Why would someone who disbelieves in leprechauns waste time and energy seeing if he could devise an argument that demonstrates their existence?

In a similar vein, I suggested that atheists who respond to the design, cosmological, and ontological arguments have already made up their minds about God's existence too. It's certainly possible for a theist to examine and reject another theist's argument for God's reality. As we've seen, for example, Thomas Aquinas had no use for Anselm's. But when an atheist takes on the ontological argument, she goes into the enterprise thinking that it's a bad one. Her only goal is to demonstrate why.

These two considerations—not to mention the fact that if something like the traditional theistic God exists, it's a bit unreasonable to presume that a single argument could establish as much—suggest that the whole enterprise of demonstrating or refuting God's existence needs to be kept in perspective. Taken in and of itself, no single "proof," regardless of how compelling it is, ought to be taken as sufficient grounds for God-belief. Similarly, no single refutation of a "proof," no matter how smashingly effective, ought to be taken as sufficient grounds for disbelief. Formal demonstrations and refutations of God's existence are just part of the puzzle about whether or not God is real. Their appraisal needs to be made against a broad backdrop that includes the worldview possibilities examined in the previous chapter as well as questions of morality, meaning, and spirituality that will be explored in future ones. Decisions to believe or disbelieve in God are—or at least should be—cumulative ones that consider as much evidence as possible. Despite sudden conversion stories from both theists and atheists, there's no grand slam approach to resolving the issue—at least if one wishes to do so rationally.

NOTES

[1] Hick (1964) offers a convenient compendium of the historical debate about God's existence.

[2] See, for example, Johnson (1983).

[3] Other proponents of the anthropic argument include Swinburne (1998), Rees (2001), and Gingerich (2006).

[4] For other treatments of sources of the cosmology argument, see Burrill (1967), Rowe (1998), and Craig (2001).

[5] For a thoroughgoing analysis of the *kalam* argument, see Nowacki (2007).

[6] For more on the ontological argument, see Hartshorne (1965), Plantinga (1965), Dombrowski (2006), Oppy (2007), and Hick and McGill (2009).

CHAPTER 4

WHY GOD CAN'T EXIST

I've been worshipping the sun for a number of reasons. First of all, unlike some other gods I could mention, I can see the sun. It's there for me every day, and the things it brings me are quite apparent all the time: heat, light, food, reflections at the park—the occasional skin cancer, but hey! There's no mystery, no one asks for money, I don't have to dress up, and there's no boring pageantry.

George Carlin, American comic

George Carlin was a funny guy, but his jokes often had a serious edge. His routine on sun-worship gestures at three arguments against the existence of God frequently appealed to by atheists. For the wise skeptic, it's not enough just to show that theistic arguments for the existence of God such as the ones examined in the last chapter are illicit. It's also necessary to come up with *positive* arguments against God's existence. Such atheists, in other words, want to be more than reactive in their denial of deity. They want to be proactive. They want to provide arguments that demonstrate, independently of refuting traditional theistic ones, that God can't be. This is another piece in the cumulative argument against God.

Carlin says that one of the advantages of sun religion is that the worshipper at least "can see the sun" and so there's "no mystery." This tongue-in-cheek observation reflects three of the strongest philosophical objections to God-belief. Some atheists argue against God's existence on the grounds of divine hiddenness: if God really existed, surely God would make his existence more apparent. Others defend related arguments on the grounds of divine impossibility: the qualities that theists typically attribute to God are logically contradictory. Still others reject God on the grounds that the word itself is literally meaningless. God-talk isn't false so much as nonsensical.

In this chapter, we'll explore the claim that God can't exist by focusing on these three arguments against God's existence as well as a fourth one, the position that's frequently called the "problem of evil": if God exists and is good, why is there so much evil in the world? As we'll see, all four arguments are strong. But this last one is probably the most dramatically compelling for atheists, as well as the most troubling to theists. It's surely the rock against which many a person's religious faith has shattered.

DIVINE HIDDENNESS

The 1976 Australian film *The Devil's Playground*, written by Thomas Keneally (of *Schindler's List* fame) focuses on the religious doubts of a handful of students in a pre-Vatican II seminary. One of them, a lad of 13 who's struggling mightily with his adolescent sexual awakening, is especially tormented by his growing attraction to life in the world. At one point in the film he retreats to an abandoned shed on the seminary grounds and pleads in agony for a consoling and counseling word for God. He shouts that he follows all the rules, that he prays day and night for illumination, but that God remains silent—as God does this time, too. Shortly after this latest nonresponse from heaven, the youth leaves the seminary.

The poignant sense of despair in "The Devil's Playground" is generated by the fact that God, rather than being a palpable presence, comes across more as a *deus absconditus* or "hidden deity." Most people have never experienced a revelation of God. Even believers generally fall back only on secondhand revelations as recorded in their holy scriptures. As the gospelist John acknowledges, "No man has seen God at any time" (1: 18).

The hiddenness of God invites the question "why?" If God exists, why doesn't he simply reveal himself so that humans will finally know, once and for all, that he's real? If he wants to establish a loving, intimate relationship with humanity, this is surely the best way to do so. How can we love an abstraction, an entity that has no face, as it were? And if God is truly all-powerful, he should have no difficulty in figuring out a way to reveal himself that humans can comprehend. He could, for example, provide detailed, verifiable information about future events. He could perform miracles. He could show the world that he exists in such a way as to eliminate once and for all the despair and forlornness experienced by millions of people who, like the young seminarian, anxiously await a sign of his existence. He could make himself as non-mysteriously present as Carlin's sun.

But he doesn't, and the explanation for this hiddenness is either that God can't, or God won't, or that God doesn't exist. If the first, God's omnipotence must be called into question. If the second, God's omnibenevolence must be doubted. But take away either of these attributes, and what's left is something quite less than the traditional theistic notion of God. The only reasonable option seems to be the third one: God isn't hiding; God just isn't real.

The theologian Richard Swinburne, well aware of the strength of this objection to God's existence, responds to it by saying that God chooses to be *absconditus,* but that this hiddenness underscores rather than calls into question both his goodness and his wisdom. God chooses to remain hidden because a beyond-doubt revelation on his part would be unduly coercive. It would deprive humans of their moral freedom since they would of course do good or at least abstain from evil out of fear of God's wrathful and certain punishment. Absolute certainty of God's existence would reduce humans to moral slaves (Swinburne 1991, pp. 211–12).

An argument similar to Swinburne's worry about moral coercion is one once (but no longer) defended by Alasdair MacIntyre. MacIntyre is concerned to respond to those believers who worry about the fact that standard arguments for the existence of God rarely convince. In this context, God remains hidden from the critical tool of logic or reason. The atheist argues that this is because God isn't real. But the theist, says MacIntyre, can argue that the hiddenness of God here is deliberate because a theistic proof would constitute coercion that leaves no room for the choice of faith. The upshot is that the hiddenness of God is a divine virtue rather than a cause for regret or skepticism.

> If we could produce logically cogent arguments we should produce the kind of certitude that leaves no room for decision; where proof is in place, decision is not. We do not decide to accept Euclid's conclusions; we merely look to the rigor of his arguments. If the existence of God were demonstrable we should be as bereft of the possibility of making a free decision to love God as we should be if every utterance of doubt or unbelief was answered by thunderbolts from heaven. (MacIntyre 1957, p. 197)

WHY GOD CAN'T EXIST

Both of these theistic justifications for God's hiddenness are weak. In response to Swinburne, it may be asked why certainty of God's existence would be any more coercive than certainty of laws prohibiting evil actions or certainty of swift retribution if those laws are violated. Swinburne's argument also bizarrely implies that, all things being equal, the moral behavior of an atheist is more pure than the behavior of a theist, since the atheist isn't coerced in any way out of fear of God's judgment. Equally bizarre is the implied denial that belief in God *isn't* conducive to moral behavior, since a standard theist claim is that God is the foundation of moral value (more of this in Chapter 6).

MacIntyre's religious coercion argument also fails. As John Hick points out, a "verbal proof of God's existence cannot by itself break down our human freedom." Invoking Cardinal Newman's distinction between "notional" and "real" assent, Hick argues that although the logic of such an argument may coerce a notional or abstract assent to the argument, it in no way coerces a real assent in the sense of "actual living belief and faith in God" (Hick 1971, p. 107). Moreover, MacIntyre's argument, if taken seriously, can lead to a fideism which rejects all efforts at rational investigation into God's existence and nature—a position lampooned by Douglas Adam's delightfully equivocal Babel Fish parable in which God stubbornly refuses to prove that he exists, "for proof denies faith, and without faith I am nothing" (Adams 1979, p. 60).

An obvious theistic objection to the atheist hiddenness argument is that it's overworked. God *does* reveal himself. Millions of people in all religious traditions claim to have had personal experiences of him. The argument at its most basic is simply stated. There are certain experiences which simply have an uncontestable "feel" of truth to them, a kind of basic trustworthiness which no reasonable person would think of doubting. Reasonable people are generally able to distinguish, for example, between waking states and dreaming states. The former have a rough edge of reality to them that for the most part is unmistakable. Similarly, genuine experiences of God such as mystical encounters or miraculous revelations, are likewise difficult to mistake for anything but what they are. The degree of immediate certainty to which they give rise is unassailable, in much the same way that it is inappropriate to doubt an individual's experience of the taste of vanilla or the sensation of yellow.

But for all its popularity, this appeal to experience is problematic. The obvious fly in the ointment is its substitution of experiential authenticity for logical persuasion. Subjective experiences may indeed be trustworthy, but the gauge of their credibility can't be their intensity. We can be intensely certain and yet totally mistaken about the meaning of any number of experiences. Anyone who has ever experienced a "crush" or "puppy love" recognizes how easy it is to misread cues from another person. How much easier it is to misread cues that purportedly have a divine source. Psychologists remind us how commonplace religious neurosis is, and dramas such as Peter Shaffer's *Equus* or John Pielmeier's *Agnes of God* that focus on religion-inspired delusion are so gripping because so utterly plausible.

Critics of the appeal insist that subjective experiences must be weighed against how well they correlate with actually existing states of affairs. Truth value, not intensity, is the proper measure. If someone claims to taste vanilla, it's reasonable to test whether the bit of ice cream they just ate has crushed vanilla beans in it (or more likely, alas, artificial vanilla flavoring). It may or may not. If not, and the person still insists that she tasted vanilla, it's beyond our call to dispute her private experience. But we *can* say that it doesn't correspond to reality.[1]

Similarly, with putative God experiences, we can invoke the rule of thumb that David Hume offered for the investigation of miracles. Where lies the preponderance of evidence (with evidence here meaning actual states of affairs, not intensity of experience): on the side of the God experience or against it? Hume thinks it clear that "no testimony is sufficient to establish a miracle, unless the testimony be of such a kind that its falsehood would be more miraculous than the fact which it endeavors to establish" (Hume 1998, p. 112).

There is, however, one theistic justification for God's hiddenness that deserves to be taken seriously. The standard atheist claim has been that if God exists but is *absconditus,* then divine omnipotence must be questioned: God *can't* reveal himself. But most religious traditions argue that the hiddenness is more likely the result of a weakness on the part of humans rather than God: humans, by virtue of our finitude, simply aren't capable of a full-fledged experience of the infinite God. Such an experience would either destroy us or slide totally past our comprehension. So God deliberately refrains from revealing himself directly out of consideration for us. Instead, he settles for safer, less combustible revelations. This leaves unanswered the question of how an infinite God is capable of "safe" finite revelations, or why the revelations are experienced by some but not all. But it's nonetheless an intriguing argument.[2]

DIVINE IMPOSSIBILITY

Perhaps the first skeptic to object to God's existence on the grounds of divine impossibility was Carneades of Cyrene, whom we met in Chapter 1. He pointed out that the concept of God defended by theists is internally inconsistent or self-contradictory. Since it's impossible for a self-contradiction to exist, God's existence is likewise impossible. Specifically, Carneades argued that God cannot be both omnipotent and good, or virtuous. Omnipotence implies a state of eternal perfection, but moral virtue implies imperfection overcome. Courage, for example, is a virtue that consists in mastering one's fear of a dangerous situation. What sense does it make to say that an all-powerful God, who presumably has nothing whatsoever to fear, has ever been in a place to practice the virtue of courage? Perhaps Carneades was guilty of equivocation in assuming an identity between divine goodness and virtue. Nonetheless, internal inconsistencies such as this, he concluded, so strain rational belief in God that we'd be better off dropping the whole idea of deity (Thrower 2000, p. 41).

Divine impossibility arguments since Carneades generally follow the spirit of his strategy by taking three related approaches: (1) find two attributes or qualities of God which are said to be necessary and show that they're inconsistent; (2) show that in exercising any one of his attributes, God necessarily contradicts the attribute; and (3) show that an attribute standardly predicated of God is impossible.

Consider, for example, the standard theistic claim that God is both omnipotent (all-powerful) and omniscient (all-knowing). If God is omniscient, he can predict everything, including his own future acts. But if God is omnipotent, he can overrule everything, thus making all predictions about the future, including predictions about his own behavior, uncertain. So the attributes of omnipotence and omniscience are inconsistent. God can be one or the other but not both, in the same way that Carneades argues that God can be omnipotent or virtuous but not both.

A simple way of illustrating the second strategy of a divine impossibility argument—showing that in exercising an attribute

God contradicts the attribute—is to recall a question that most first year philosophy students encounter: Can God make a rock too heavy for God to pick up? On the surface, the question seems silly. But it gestures at a more serious puzzle: can God perform an act which entails God's limitation? If God is omnipotent, then the obvious response is "yes." But if so, then God's omnipotence destroys his omnipotence. If, startled by this outcome, we respond "no," then our claim is that God isn't omnipotent after all. And if this is the case, why call him "God"?

Another example of the second strategy comes from Antony Flew, who argued that the attributes of "incorporeality" and "person" are inconsistent. Theists claim that God is personal, and Christian theists even speak of God in terms of a trinity of persons. But they also insist that God, being eternal and infinite, is without body. In ordinary usage, however, the notion of "person" only makes sense in terms of embodiment. The notion of a person without a body, says Flew, is contradictory (Flew 1966).

But this argument isn't as compelling as the previous one. As we saw in the discussion in Chapter 1 of the "personal" theistic God, most theists would argue that they attribute personhood to God in an analogous sense, not in the univocal way Flew does. God exists in a way that is similar but not identical to the way in which humans exist. One of those similarities is the possession of "personal" characteristics such as the ability to love, to know, and so on. This needn't mean that God's personhood entails divine embodiment. Theists who make this distinction are still obliged, of course, to justify the claim that God is analogous in certain ways to humans, and doing so may lead to assertions that are inconsistent or contradictory.

The third way of arguing against God's existence on the grounds of impossibility consists in showing that a particular power attributed to God just can't be the case. Take omniscience, the ability to know everything that is knowable. But surely what is knowable includes experiences such as evil-doing, jealousy, sickness, and sexual desire. Yet God doesn't seem capable of any of these sorts of experiences, precisely because of the sort of entity—perfectly good, immortal, and sexless—he is. So God can't be omniscient; omniscience is an impossibility for God.

An obvious and strong objection to divine impossibility arguments is that they claim more than they accomplish. What they clearly show is that there are problems—perhaps insurmountable ones—with the classical notion of an omni-attributed deity. But this doesn't necessarily lead to the conclusion that God doesn't exist. It may mean simply that if God exists, God can't be the omni-attributed being believed in by many theists. The atheist assumes that showing that God can't be omnipotent or omniscient leaves no alternative but the denial of God's existence. But several schools of contemporary theology argue that God exists and yet isn't omnipotent or omni-scient in the classical senses of the words. In Chapter 1, we saw that process theologians such as Charles Hartshorne argue that God's knowledge is necessarily limited because even God can't know with certainty what hasn't yet happened. At best, God can know the total sum of possibilities (Hartshorne 1983). Other theologians in both the Judaic and Christian traditions similarly dispute divine omnipotence by arguing that God is neither impassable nor impervious to suffer-ing, contrary to what theologians influenced by Greek philosophy have insisted on for centuries. God suffers in response to the afflic-tions of humanity. Otherwise, argue theologians such as Wolfgang Pannenberg, Dietrich Bonhoeffer, and Reinhold Niebuhr, there's no meaningful sense in which God can be said to be "personal." This notion that God is limited in some way goes back at least to Thomas Aquinas, who argued that God is incapable of performing logical impossibilities (for example, making a square circle). But the sense that God is much more limited than that has become standard fare in Christian theology today—as early as 1959, theologian Daniel Day Lewis called it a "structural shift in the Christian mind"—and athe-ists who wish to appeal to divine impossibility arguments need to take the shift seriously (Lewis 1959, p. 138).[3]

THE MEANINGLESSNESS OF RELIGIOUS DISCOURSE

Carlin's quip that he prefers sun worship because he can see the sun every day and can therefore avoid wrestling with mystery gestures at a third type of argument to which atheists appeal to show that God can't be. It's to show that the "mystery" behind God talk is just a euphemism for nonsense. Whatever is said about God is meaningless.

Strictly speaking, this isn't an argument against God's existence so much as one against taking discourse about God seriously. After all, there's a possibility that something we can call "God" actually exists, even if everything we say about God is nonsense. And in fact some ultra-fideistic theologians take this very position, although it's difficult and perhaps impossible to apply consistently (for example, is discourse about the meaninglessness of God-discourse self-contradictory?). But when atheists invoke the argument, it's pretty clear what they have in mind. If nothing can be said about a topic that isn't nonsensical or meaningless, why take it seriously? Their intuition is akin to the one that motivates proponents of divine impossibility arguments when they claim that a contradiction can't exist: if language that purports to describe an entity is nonsense, a good prima facie case presents itself for presuming that the entity is an illusion. As the nineteenth-century atheist Charles Bradlaugh put it, "the atheist does not say 'There is no God,' but he says: 'I know not what you mean by God; I am without the idea of God; the word "God" is to me a sound conveying no clear or distinct affirmation'" (Bradlaugh 1980, p. 10).

David Hume famously prepared the way for the claim that religious discourse is meaningless in his *An Enquiry Concerning Human Understanding* when he expressly singled it out as nonsense: "If we take in our hand any volume; of divinity or school metaphysics, for instance; let us ask, Does it contain any abstract reasoning concerning quantity or number? No. Does it contain any experimental reasoning concerning matter of fact and existence? No. Commit it then to the flames: for it can contain nothing but sophistry and illusion" (Hume 1955, p. 173). For Hume, only those propositions or statements which express either the relations between ideas ("abstract reasoning") or facts ("experimental reasoning") make any sense. The former can be tested for logical consistency, and the latter can be measured against observable states of affairs. No other standard of appraisal is available or necessary. Propositions that fail to meet Hume's two criteria have no truth value, but instead are illusory, or meaningless. And the value of meaningless claims is suggested by Hume's advice to toss them into the fire.

Inspired by Hume, proponents of the twentieth-century philosophical school known as logical positivism proposed a theory of meaning based on verifiability. According to this model, statements may possess formal meaning, factual meaning, and cognitive meaning. A necessary and sufficient condition for formal meaning is that the statement be either analytic or self-contradictory (this corresponds to Hume's first standard). A necessary and sufficient condition for factual meaning is that the statement can be at least in principle empirically verified or falsified (Hume's second standard). Any statement which meets either of these two meaning standards thereby possesses cognitive meaning, is either true or false, and deserves to be taken seriously. Any other statement is neither true nor false but nonsensical and good only for the flames.

Now propositions about God—such as "God exists"—fail to exhibit either formal or factual meaning, and therefore lack cognitive meaning as well. They're neither analytic (Anselm notwithstanding) or tautologous nor self-contradictory. So there's no way to establish their truth or falsity on purely formal grounds. Additionally, there is no way to verify or falsify the proposition by appealing to experience, because users of the word "God" mean by it a transcendent—that is, nonempirical—being. Consequently, God discourse is meaningless. Strictly speaking, one can neither assert nor deny the existence of a God, because all such claims are gibberish. As A.J. Ayer pointed out, "if the assertion that there is a god is nonsensical, then the atheist's assertion that there is no god is equally nonsensical, since it is only a significant proposition that can be significantly contradicted" (Ayer 1952, p. 115). But as we've already seen, showing that God discourse is nonsense is for all practical purposes a dismissal of the whole God issue.[4]

Although the question of whether religious discourse is verifiable greatly exercised philosophers for a good part of the twentieth century, the debate is no longer as lively as it once was. This isn't because theists found a way to compatibalize religious discourse with the verifiability principle, although some tried. Most famously (and bizarrely, in the eyes of many), John Hick argued that religious claims are "eschatologically" verifiable—that is, their truth or falsity are verifiable or falsifiable after death (Hick 1966, pp. 176–99). The main reason for the decline is that many philosophers, including one-time logical positivists, have called the verifiability theory of meaning into question. They argue that it lacks justification (must the theory itself conform to the verifiability principle?) or seems arbitrary (why should truth or falsity be confined only to formal or factual propositions?), or is too porous to prevent metaphysical or transcendent claims from seeping through into factual discourse.

Telling as these criticisms are, they don't warrant relegating the debate to the dustbin of philosophical history. There are at least two reasons for this. The first is that the critics of religious discourse are quite right to point out that religious language is slippery. Its users frequently insist on a much wider leeway than we would allow speakers in other language contexts. On of the best expressions of its slipperiness is Antony Flew's well-known parable of the Gardener:

> Once upon a time two explorers came upon a clearing in the jungle. In the clearing were growing many flowers and many weeds. One explorer says, 'Some gardener must tend this plot.' The other disagrees, 'There is no gardener.' So they pitch their tents and set a watch. No gardener is ever seen. 'But perhaps he is an invisible gardener.' So they set up a barbed-wire fence. They electrify it. They patrol with blood-hounds. (For they remember how H. G. Wells's The Invisible Man could be both smelt and touched though he could not be seen.) But no shrieks ever suggest that some intruder has received a shock. No movements of the wire ever betray an invisible climber. The bloodhounds never give cry. Yet still the believer is not convinced. 'But there is a gardener, invisible, intangible, insensitive to electric shocks, a gardener who has no scent and makes no sound, a gardener who comes secretly to look after the garden which he loves.' At last the Sceptic despairs, 'but what remains of your original assertion? Just how does what you call an invisible, intangible, eternally elusive gardener differ from an imaginary gardener or even from no gardener at all?'[5] (Flew and MacIntyre 1955, p. 96)

Flew's gardener is obviously a stand-in for God, and his point is that users of religious language feel little compunction about stretching their definitions of God to meet any and all challenges. No objection that a skeptic might offer can possibly falsify the God-believer's claim because the response is to amend the original definition with enough qualifications to absorb the objection. Surely, even at a common sense level, there's something so suspicious about this strategy that we would quickly lose patience with it in other contexts. For any assertion to be meaningful, it must exclude *something*. Why, then, ought we to privilege the religious assertion that excludes *nothing*?

The second reason for taking the meaninglessness of religious language thesis seriously is the analysis offered by Canadian philosopher Kai Nielsen, perhaps the best-known contemporary defender of a revised verifiability theory of meaning. For Nielsen, the verifiability standard simply offers a criterion for distinguishing between factually meaningful and factually meaningless statements by stipulating that the former depends on the possibility of at least one observational statement that would count for or against it (Nielsen 1971[6]).

Unlike defenders (like Ayer) of earlier verifiability standards, Nielsen argues that his version doesn't reduce all religious propositions to nonsense. Statements frequently associated with folk religion, particularly crude anthropomorphic descriptions about God, are clearly falsifiable. If we hear the claim that God is a powerful spatial-temporal being who lives in the sky, we both understand what the claim signifies and we can reasonably infer, given everything that we know about reality, that it's quite false. In addition, Nielsen allows that more sophisticated religious claims possess enough meaning, syntactically as well as semantically, to allow us to draw inferences from them. If someone tells us that "God is immaterial and yet acts in the world," we clearly understand the sentence well enough to infer, for example, that God's way of acting in the world must be different from our embodied human way.

So it's too simple to say that religious claims are sheer nonsense. Some religious propositions ("God is a big man with a white beard") are meaningful and factually falsifiable. Others ("God is nonmaterial but acts in the world") are meaningful in the sense that inferences may be drawn from them. But the sticking point for Nielsen is that this doesn't make the second set of statements *factually* meaningful. Factual meaning depends upon knowing what would count for or against a proposition, and discourse about a transcendent God with transcendent qualities such as infinity, eternity, omniscience, and so on (think of Flew's invisible gardener), just doesn't meet this test.

The virtue of Nielsen's position is that it allows the skeptic to distinguish carefully between different kinds of religious propositions instead of treating them all equally in a willy-nilly sort of way. Moreover, Nielsen believes that his position also speaks to the experiences of theists, who themselves distinguish between different levels of religious discourse. But whereas a theist would accept sophisticated God-talk as both meaningful and somehow metaphorically or allegorically true, Nielsen would insist that its meaning doesn't stretch far enough to allow conclusions about its truth or falsity.

THE PROBLEM OF EVIL

The more Charles Darwin discovered about the organic world, the more convinced he became that suffering and death were the two great constants in it. Animals prey on animals; most offspring perish before they can reproduce; and hunger, disease, and predation can bring down entire species. Although the phrase is Tennyson's rather than his, Darwin had no difficulty in sizing up nature as "red in tooth and claw."

The ichneumon wasp, a beautiful and delicate creature, came to symbolize for Darwin the inherent cruelty of nature. The female of the species lays her eggs inside living caterpillars which she's paralyzed with a sting. The larvae hatch inside the live caterpillar and devour it from the inside out. After describing this horribly carnivorous mode of birthing in a letter to Harvard biologist Asa Gray, Darwin concluded: "I cannot see, as plainly as others do, evidence of design & beneficence on all sides of us. There seems to me to be too much misery in the world." In a later letter to Gray, Darwin returned to the theme: "An innocent & good man stands under [a] tree and is killed by [a] flash of lightning. Do you believe (& I really shd like to hear) that God designedly killed this man? Many or most persons do believe this; I can't & don't" (Darwin 1993, pp. 224, 275).

Darwin's reflections on the palpable presence of "too much misery in the world" gesture at an argument against God which many people, atheists and theists alike, consider to be stronger than any other. It's frequently called the "problem of evil" or the "argument from evil," although a more accurate title for it would perhaps be the "problem of innocent suffering" or the "argument from innocent suffering." In its simplest terms, it calls God's existence into question based on the widespread and indiscriminate suffering that afflicts both humans and animals. The argument is so powerful because it focuses on a phenomenon—suffering—that's personally close to all humans. Whenever a natural disaster occurs that slays hundreds of people, whenever a child dies of leukemia, whenever a spouse or parent sinks into dementia, the obvious response is to ask oneself how such tragedies square with the existence of a wise, good, and powerful God. It's been said that the great Lisbon earthquake of 1755, which struck on All Saints Day, destroyed the city, and killed upwards of 100,000 people, did more to shatter the modern era's religious faith than the writings of Enlightenment freethinkers such as Voltaire, Diderot, and Hume.

In order to appreciate the argument, it's important to be clear on what its proponents mean by "evil" or "innocent suffering." What they don't intend is transitory pain that either doesn't permanently harm (the skinning of a knee) or actually leads to some greater good (the jab of an inoculation needle). Nor need they mean either short-term pain or long-term suffering which I willfully bring upon myself through my action or inaction (the lung cancer, for example, caused by my deliberate decision to smoke cigarettes). Instead, what they have in mind is an affliction that inflicts great physical and mental damage or death, which serves no salutary purpose, and which is unde-served. The affliction can be short and intense (being murdered or killed by an earthquake) or drawn out and progressively debilitating (enduring Lou Gehrig's Disease or being devoured by ichneumon wasp larvae). It can be caused by a force of nature such as an earth-quake, flood, tidal wave, nonhuman animal or virus, or it can be inflicted by another human. The former is generally referred to as an act of "natural evil," and the latter "moral evil."

One of the earliest formulations of the argument from evil comes to us from the Stoic philosopher Epicurus (341–270 BCE). When thinking about the relationship between God and innocent suffering, he suggested a tetralemma, or a set of four possibilities: either, (1) God wants to eliminate evil but can't; or (2) God can eliminate evil but won't; or (3) God neither can nor wants to; or (4) God wants to and can. (Hume 1998, p. 63) If (1), we must jettison divine omnip-otence, one of the classical omni-attributes; if (2) we must abandon divine benevolence; if (3) we must conclude that God is evil; and if (4) we're obliged to explain why there's so much innocent suffering in the world. Epicurus' point is that any horn of the tetralemma we grasp is undesirable. We're saddled either with a crippled God, an evil God, or a God who has no obvious connection with the real world. In either case, what post-Epicurean theists are left with is a God that falls far short of the traditional understanding. At that point, they must ask themselves which is a more likely model for making sense of innocent suffering: that God is either less than perfect or even downright malevolent, or that God doesn't exist and innocent suffer-ing is simply an irreducible fact of life. The atheist obviously thinks the second option the more reasonable one.

So, surely, do many theists, who nonetheless can't quite bring themselves to make the break with belief which atheists recommend. Like the biblical Job, they alternate between angry rebellion against what appears to be the indifference of their deity to suffering, and submitting in silence to the "mystery" of how an all-powerful, all-knowing, and all-good God can co-exist with innocent suffering.

The religious skeptic may be impatient or even disdainful of their clinging to God-belief in the face of such counterfactual evidence. But he can hardly refrain from sympathizing with the existential burden they take on in the process. The uneasiness and even despair a theist can experience from the dissonance between noisy evil and a silent God has been grippingly captured by Dostoyevsky in his character Ivan Karamazov. Although Dostoyevsky himself was an intensely religious man, Ivan the atheist surely speaks for him when he cries out in anger and misery: "I want to see with my own eyes the lion lie down with the lamb and the murdered man rise up and embrace his murderer. I want to be there when everyone suddenly finds out what [suffering] has all been for" (Dostoyevsky 1980, p. 225).

But Job and Ivan offer us existential cries from the heart rather than philosophical arguments that justify or acquit God in the presence of evil in the world. (Such arguments are known as "theodicies": *theos* = God; *dike* = justice.) But before turning to some of them, it's good to dismiss one response to the problem of evil that crops up more in New Age literature, certain strains of Hindu thought, and the occasional Christian mystic than in mainstream theism. This is the claim that evil is illusory or unreal. The general argument for the claim is that everything that happens is but a step in the acting-out of a cosmic divine plan that will culminate in a state of perfect completion and fulfillment. From a limited human perspective, some or even most of these steps appear evil. But if we could but acquire a God's-eye view and experience the totality of things, we would see individual components of the totality quite differently. We would recognize their fittingness and purposefulness in the grand plan, and that even though they may occasion suffering, they can't be evil.

The obvious objection to this denial of the reality of evil is that it flies in the face of ordinary experience. Surely no reasonable person would deny that the sexual murder of a child or the systematic slaughter of Tutsis by Hutus is evil. To do so is not only to refuse to open one's eyes to the world in which one lives, but also to risk falling into a moral passivism. Moreover, it's also reasonable to dismiss as sophistry the claim that suffering is real but evil isn't. Most people consider suffering to *be* evil.

Rather than denying the reality of evil, the theist typically will acknowledge its existence and then account for it in such a way as to avoid Epicurus' tetradilemma. This typically entails distancing God from evil, thereby absolving him of direct responsibility for it. The hope is that this distancing allows the believer to retain the traditional omni-attributed God while at the same time acknowledging that bad things happen to good people.

Perhaps the single most popular way of doing this is by invoking human free will. Free will, so the argument goes, is a good. It is better to be a creature capable of making free decisions than to be an automaton programmed to act in a certain way, even if that way appears to be good. God in his omniscience knew this when he endowed humans with free will, but he also knew that the gift of free will could be maliciously misused to do evil and cause suffering in the world. Still, the actual goodness of free will outweighs the potential evil to which it can give rise—so much so, in fact, that it would be a greater evil for God either to have not granted free will originally, or to violate free will by intervening to prevent an evil human act. The genius of this theodicy is twofold: although the reality of evil seems to suggest that God is neither all-wise, all-good, nor all-powerful, the argument from free will manipulates the very existence of evil to underscore God's omniattributes (he knows that it's better not to interfere with human actions even though he could); and God is taken off the moral hook with the claim that evil arises from the malicious abuse of free will by humans.

Reservations to one side about whether it makes sense to posit free will in humans in the first place (we'll examine this topic more closely in Chapter 7), there are several objections to this argument. One is that not all evil comes from human immorality, or the malicious use of free will. It frequently springs from human error: I miscalculate how fast I can make the next bend in the road, lose control, and collide with another car, killing all its occupants. If this is the case, then it isn't true that all human-made evil is the result of wickedness, and this in turn calls into question the rather simple interpretation of evil as the result of human malice accepted by defenders of the free will argument.

A more pointed response is to deny the argument's claim that divine interference with human free will is a greater evil than not interfering. This denial takes on weight if we move from thinking about God to thinking about humans. It's absurd to claim that a parent's intervention to prevent her child from playing with a firecracker is a greater evil than allowing the firecracker to blow off a finger or two. If the theist replies by saying that the example is disanalogous because the child hasn't reached the age of reason and isn't capable of the sound judgment that a parent exercises, the atheist can respond by saying the same thing about adult humans. In comparison to God, our judgments are immature and potentially dangerous. If it's morally appropriate for a parent to step in to protect a child, why isn't it even more appropriate for our Godparent to step in to forestall our own destructiveness? When one thinks of the bloodied and battered course of recent history in which the Hitlers, Stalins, and Pol Pots of the world have wreaked so much havoc, the question takes on a certain urgency.

Two additional points need to be considered. One is that there's a distinction between free will and free act. When a parent prevents a child from playing with a firecracker, all that's obviously been interfered with is the child's freedom of action. Her capacity for free will is undamaged. Similarly, God's intervention to prevent or forestall evil acts need not damage the human capacity of free will. Hitler's ability to freely will evil endures even if God limits his ability to act on that will. The second point is that not all constraints of free will are coercive and hence unjustifiable. Whenever we engage in reasoned discussion with others in the hope of persuading them to abandon their opinions and adopt ours, we're surely endeavoring to influence the exercise of their will. Why can't God similarly nudge—but not coerce—the Hitlers of the world toward more enlightened opinions?

At this juncture the theist may adopt a different theodicy tactic by claiming that a certain amount of suffering/evil is necessary for the spiritual and moral quickening of human beings. Suffering, as theologian John Hick (following the third-century Irenaeus) says, is soul-making. It serves as a spiritual catalyst by jolting us out of complacency and obtuseness. It encourages self-examination, deep reflection, and compassion for other suffering beings. Without the presence of suffering, humans would possess less depth and goodness than they do. So suffering is, if you will, a *felix culpa* that hurts us but at the same time tempers us (Hick 2007).

But there are at least three objections to this argument. The first appeals to ordinary experience: suffering doesn't always or even usually improve us morally or spiritually. On the contrary, it more typically tears down our physical health and psychological well-being to the point where life becomes unbearable. St. Paul tells the Corinthians (1 Cor. 10: 13) that God doesn't mete out more than humans can bear. But the slightest knowledge of the world shows that this is clearly false. The second objection, related to the first, is that the extent and intensity of the suffering that befalls humans seems disproportionate to the goal of soul-making and contrary to the goodness of God. Surely humans don't need to writhe to the extent that they do in order to achieve self-reflection and compassion. Even if suffering is necessary, why is *so much* of it necessary? The third objection takes us back to Darwin: suffering in the nonhuman animal world is mind-bogglingly horrible. To what end is *it?* Surely not to stimulate soul-growth in animals. It seems pointless and hence cruel on the part of a Creator to allow it.

So far the discussion has focused on moral evil—the sort of evil that the theist claims comes from the malicious misuse of free will. But the Darwinian reminder that nonhuman animals also suffer recalls the second kind of evil in the world: the "natural" evil caused by disasters, illnesses, and ultimately death. How does the theist acquit God from responsibility for this?

The strongest theodicy argument offered (and it *is* a strong argument) is that while God out of his omnipotence, omniscience, and omnibenevolence has created the best world possible, the best world possible necessarily includes the risk of natural disasters and the inevitability of illness, decay, and death. Creating a physical world which contains embodied, sentient creatures and is governed by uniform natural laws is a gigantic balancing act on the part of God. The world has to operate in accordance with certain constant natural laws which generally nurture life but occasionally allow for local conditions that result in tsunamis, earthquakes, and volcanic eruptions. Moreover, the same sentient embodiment that brings pleasure necessarily carries certain opportunity costs such as the ability to experience excruciating pain, the risk of being slain by a microscopic bacterium, and the necessity for life to feed upon life. All of this is simply the price that must be paid for being human. Most people would agree that the returns are worth it (Reichenbach 1982; Lewis 2001).

It seems unquestionable, regardless of whether one is a theist or an atheist, that natural pain, decay, and death are inevitable in organic creatures. The question that may be posed to the theist is whether there needs to be as much pain and decay as there is. Would any violation of natural law unbalance the cosmos if God, for example, made regions of the earth that are particularly prone to natural disaster so inhospitable to humans and animals that they were virtually uninhabited? Is it necessary that there be quite so many horrible viruses out there waiting to assail us? Is it really the case that an all-powerful God couldn't have created a friendlier physical world? Or if not, would an all-good God have gone ahead anyway? After all, adult humans sometimes refuse to procreate on the grounds that the world is too dismal a place to bring new life into.

The argument from evil is a devastating assault on theism. It compels us to flesh out abstract arguments for and against the existence of God with the harsh stuff of real life. Many people who at one time considered themselves religious turned to atheism not because they were persuaded by logical argument but because the horror of the world's evil shattered their faith. Elie Wiesel poignantly speaks for them in recalling his experiences in a Nazi death camp: "Never shall I forget those flames which consumed my Faith forever. Never shall I forget that nocturnal silence which deprived me, for all eternity, of the desire to live. Never shall I forget those moments which murdered my God and my soul and turned my dreams to dust. Never shall I forget these things, even if I am condemned to live as long as God Himself. Never" (Wiesel 1982, p. 32).

The argument from evil haunts theists. Qualify his understanding of God as much as he will in order to distance the deity from responsibility for evil, the theist no less than the atheist is painfully aware of how short all arguments fall. The problem of evil is an overwhelming burden for the theist. It is his great tragedy.

A DAUNTING PROSPECT BY WAY OF CONCLUSION

Atheist positive arguments against God's existence seek to take the initiative from theists by arguing that there's no evidence of divine reality (hiddenness argument), that the qualities typically ascribed to God contradict one another (impossibility argument), that for the most part we don't have the slightest idea what we intend when we use the word "God" (meaninglessness argument), and that the presence of evil suffering in the world is incompatible with the existence of an all-knowing, all-loving, and all-powerful God (the problem of evil argument). All in all, people who find these arguments persuasive would agree with George Carlin that a much less problematic form of devotion would be sun worship. Be that as it may, it should be kept in mind that the arguments are more limited in scope than their defenders sometimes admit. As atheist arguments they specifically take on the God of theism: the omni-attributed and personal deity worshipped by Jews, Christians, and Muslims. In this regard, they're curiously unlike the standard theistic "proofs" for God's existence examined in the previous chapter, because all of the latter, with the exception of the ontological argument, conclude with only an impersonal First Cause or Necessary Being or Great Designer.

Just as standard theistic arguments in no way establish the existence of the theistic deity, so the positive atheist arguments examined in this chapter in no way disprove the existence of an impersonal one. God could exist, say, as the First Cause, devoid of any personal characteristics. In that case, God's hiddenness would be perfectly understandable, and the other objections, all of which revolve around inconsistencies between divine personal characteristics, or between them and factual experience, would be irrelevant. Or God might've existed at one time, but no longer does (one of the possibilities raised by David Hume, by the way), once again making the positive arguments discussed in this chapter beside the point. Of course, if God once existed but no longer does, it is technically correct to say that atheism is true. But such a predicament would surely call for a rewriting of the naturalism upon which atheism stands. And that's a daunting prospect.

NOTES

1 One problem with trying to determine the truth value of subjective experiences, especially ones claiming to be revelations of God, is the difficulty in figuring out how to test them. Thomas Hobbes recognized this. "If a man pretend to me, that God hath spoken to him supernaturally and immediately, and I make doubt of it, I cannot easily perceive what argument he can produce, to oblige me to believe it. If the man says that the divine voice came to him in a dream, that's only to say that he dreamt. If, on the other hand, he claims that the voice came to him while he was awake, how is this distinguishable from day-dreaming?" (Hobbes 1904, p. 270).

2 Two very good resources that look at defenses and objections to the hiddenness argument against God are Howard-Snyder and Moser (2001) and Schellenberg (2006).

3 Additional discussion of the impossibility argument may be found in the essays in Martin and Monnier (2003, especially pp. 323–438).

4 The *locus classicus* of the philosophical discussion of religious language's meaning (or lack thereof) is Flew and MacIntyre (1955). Martin (1990, pp. 40–78) offers an informative overview. An excellent theological exploration of religious language may be found in Macquarrie (1967).

[5] Flew's recent conversion to deism, discussed in Chapter 2, interestingly reverses the question the Sceptics in his parable implicitly asks: "What would it take for a believer to not believe in the gardener/God?" Flew now thinks the Sceptics would be asked: "What would it take for you to take seriously the possibility of God?"

[6] For a good discussion of Nielson on verifiability of religious language, see Martin (1990, pp. 45–55).

CHAPTER 5

THE NATURAL HISTORY OF RELIGION

Religion is based, I think, primarily and mainly upon fear. It is partly the terror of the unknown.
      Bertrand Russell, *"Why I Am Not a Christian"*

Perhaps religion doesn't have a direct survival value of its own, but is a by-product of something else that does.
      Richard Dawkins, The God Delusion

As the atheist sees it, there's no good reason to believe in God. The core conviction of naturalism is that nature is all there is, and that everything science reveals about the universe confirms this belief. Traditional arguments for the existence of God don't work, and there are compelling positive arguments against God-belief. Religious fervor tends to diminish in societies whose educational and economic levels improve. And those who cling to religion tend to be surprisingly tepid in their beliefs or frighteningly fanatical—neither particularly inspiring role models.[1]

All this leaves the atheist with a puzzle. If religious conviction—whose broad but essential definition is belief in the supernatural[2]—is so irrational, why is it still so prevalent? After all, as we saw in Chapter 1, it's still the majority opinion in the world today. How to account for this curious fact? Why do so many people persist in believing what, to the atheist, is nonsense at best and dangerous nonsense at worst?

Regardless of how any given atheist goes about answering that question, one thing is a given: his starting assumption will be that religion, like everything else, is a natural phenomenon which can and should be examined without contriving supernatural explanations.

The God-believer, especially of the theist variety, holds that his religious tradition ultimately originates from a divine revelation, usually recorded in a set of texts that he considers sacred, and that God has subsequently added to the original revelation through miracles, mystical experiences, and ecclesial tradition. He defends, in other words, what might be called a "divine history" of religion. But the atheist searches instead for a "natural history" of religion that accounts for its origins and development without appealing to revelation or the supernatural. For him, religion is just another fact in the world, albeit one of the more influential ones, that reveals a great deal about human beings and society but nothing whatsoever about God. As Kai Nielsen asserts, "the naturalist [must assume] that it is false to say that there is nothing real underlying religious symbols. There is something there very real indeed . . ., only the reality is not what the believer takes it to be" (Nielsen 1997, p. 408).

One naturalistic way of explaining the persistence of religion is by concluding that people are by and large irrational. An atheist acquaintance of mine once put it this way: "Lots of people are stupid and this means that they cling to beliefs for which there's absolutely no evidence—such as the existence of God." If comments on scores of atheist blogs are reliable standards, this sort of dismissal is extremely popular. But despite data which suggest that intellectuals *do* tend to be nonbelievers[3] (Beit-Hallahmi 2007, pp. 306–13), the claim that people are religious because they're irrational isn't much of an explanation. For one thing, it's not at all clear what one means by "irrational" (much less my acquaintance's category of "stupid"). Does it mean uneducated? Slow-witted? Too emotional? Superstitious? Prone to form opinions without evidence? Inability to think logically? But surely believers have no monopoly on these qualities. Second, chalking up the persistence of religious belief to irrationality only begs the question of *why* irrational people are religious. What's missing is an explanation that connects the two.

Perhaps most strongly, it's not at all clear that religious belief *is* irrational in any simple sense of the word. Max Muller (1823–1900), E. B. Tylor (1832–1917), and James Frazer (1854–1941), pioneers in the anthropological investigation of religion, all held that religion in its most primitive historical stage was a genuinely intellectual attempt to understand the world by making connections between different experiences and drawing conclusions. Muller argued that belief in gods sprang from an urge to explain great objects (seas, mountains, the sun, the sky) and events (thunderstorms, droughts, seasonal flooding) in nature (Muller 2002, pp. 109–23). Tylor contended that belief in spiritual beings was a way of making sense of the seeming vitality of inanimate objects (the annual budding of trees, for example) as well as the fact that the dead reappeared in dreams as if they were still alive (Tylor 1903). Frazer claimed that early magic and, later, religion were strategies for both understanding and manipulating natural forces (Frazer 1998). In each of these models, primitive believers adopted a kind of proto-inductive methodology. Ideas were associated with experiences and inferences made, and this ability, says Tylor, "lies at the very foundation of human reason" (Tylor 1903, Volume 1, p. 116). Primitive believers may have held false beliefs. But they weren't necessarily irrational in the way they arrived at them. They simply operated from faulty assumptions.

A similar claim about the rationality of religious belief has been made by sociologist Rodney Stark. He understands religion in terms of rational choice theory. Religion is a system of compensation based on supernatural assumptions. Humans, says Stark, are basically goal-driven and adept at exploring ways to achieve their goals at the lowest possible cost to themselves in proportion to the value of what it is they desire. Denying oneself worldly and transitory pleasures for the sake of an eternity of rewards (the compensation) may be a bargain that has no basis in reality, but it's no more irrational than an economic belt-tightening in the present in order to acquire a future dividend. Seen in this way, religious belief is a species of cost-benefit calculation, even though believers are unlikely to describe it in such terms (Stark and Bainbridge 1996).

So the irrationality thesis won't do. But Stark's model gestures at a more fruitful way to account for the continuation of religious belief, and that's by exploring its function. What does it provide the individual as well as the group? For Stark, religion functions as a cost-benefit calculus for the individual worshipper. For other thinkers such as Auguste Comte (1798–1857), Emile Durkheim (1958–1917), Bronislaw Malinowski (1884–1942), and A. R. Radcliffe-Brown (1881–1955), religion's chief function is social rather than individual. It serves to create and perpetuate group identity— community, if you will—through tradition-specific story, myth, ritual, and values. Along with Stark, they agree that religion may be false but nonetheless has a useful function.[4]

For the most part, atheists have adopted a functionalist approach to charting the natural history of religion and explaining its persistence. In the late eighteenth and nineteenth centuries, the favored explanation was that religion endures because it performs the consolatory function of mitigating death-fear, pain and suffering, and a sense of vulnerability. After Darwin, another focus emerged: religion as an evolutionary phenomenon whose persistence can be understood in terms of natural selection. The two sets of explanation are not incompatible, since it's clear that if religion is a product of evolution, it must serve some kind of selective or useful function (such as consolation). Where they *do* differ is in stress. The consolatory model emphasizes the human fear and desperation that breeds religion. Although sympathizing with individuals who need religion to deal with life, atheists think religion an only partially successful (if that) coping strategy because it's just as likely to feed as to assuage fear. The evolutionary model doesn't deny the consolatory function of religious belief, but its emphasis is on disclosing religion's biological roots rather than analyzing it in strictly psycho-social terms. Some evolutionists allow that religion still performs a useful function, while others argue that it's an evolutionary holdover whose day has passed and whose persistence is due to inertia. But regardless of which approach is taken, the goal, as Nielsen describes it, is to provide an account that

> explains religion's origins, explains its claim to truth, explains how that very claim is in error, the depth of that error, its persistence, in spite of that, in various institutional contexts and in the personal lives of human beings, its various cultural and historical form, how and why it changes and develops as it does, and its continuing persistence and appeal in one or another form. (Nielsen 1997, p. 408)

In the rest of this chapter, we'll examine representative voices from both the consolatory (David Hume, Karl Marx, and Sigmund Freud) and the evolutionary (Richard Dawkins, Daniel Dennett, and E. O. Wilson) camps. Then we'll conclude with a general appraisal of the project to understand religious belief as a natural phenomenon.

HUME: RELIGION AND MELANCHOLY PASSIONS

In Chapter 3, we examined Hume's devastation of the design argument for God's existence in his posthumous *Dialogues Concerning Natural*

Religion. An equally important treatment of religion as natural phenomenon is the subject of his 1757 *The Natural History of Religion.* In it, Hume laid the groundwork for the claim that the primary function of religion is to console us in our travail.

Just as he would do in the *Dialogues* nearly 20 years later, Hume punctuates his *Natural History* with assertions that "the whole frame of nature bespeaks an intelligent author" (Hume 1956, p. 21) and that nature's "regularity and uniformity is the strongest proof of design and of a supreme intelligence" (p. 42). And just as in the later work, it's unclear how seriously to take such statements. One interpretation is that Hume was hedging his bets to escape a charge of infidelity. Another is that he genuinely wished to distinguish between an abstract "intelligent author" arrived at by philosophical reflection and the personal deity of popular religion, affirming the first as a reasonable inference while rejecting the latter as superstition. But however one reads Hume, the assurances of belief with which he punctuates his text seem at odds with the overall thrust of the *Natural History.*

One indication that Hume's talk about an "intelligent author" is disingenuous is his unmistakable conviction that there's a wide gulf between any claim that God-belief is rationally defensible and the actual historical origins of religion. An examination of the latter reveals that religious sensibility is based on something quite contrary to rational reflection. Nor is God-belief a "natural instinct"—an innate idea, or perhaps Alvin Plantinga's notion of a basic belief that we looked at in Chapter 1. Instead, it's an historical artifact that arises from human responses to nature.

That response is fundamentally negative. Hume explicitly denies that a sense of grateful wonderment at the orderliness of nature and the gifts it bestows is the original impetus for religion. The more accustomed we are to nature's regularity, he argues, the more we take it for granted as a scarcely noticed backdrop: "Prosperity is easily received as our due." What we *do* attend to are those perceived ruptures in nature's uniformity—a breakdown in health, a drought or flood that ruins the harvest, the death of a loved one—that evoke anxiety, fear, and panic in us. It's these negative emotions, not positive ones of "cheerfulness and activity and alacrity and a lively enjoyment of every social and sensual pleasure" that inspire religious belief.

[I]f we examine our hearts, or observe what passes around us, we shall find, that men are much oftener thrown on their knees by the melancholy than by the agreeable passions . . . [E]very disastrous accident alarms us, and sets us on enquiries concerning the principles whence it arose: Apprehensions spring up with regard to futurity: And the mind, sunk into diffidence, terror, and melancholy, has recourse to every method of appeasing those secret intelligent powers, on whom our fortune is supposed entirely to depend. (Hume 1956, p. 31)

Hume's analysis here is reminiscent of the old chestnut that there are no atheists in foxholes. It's only when things are going badly that we feel particularly religious, and even then only to beseech the divine powers-that-be to get us out of a fix. Religious sentiment, then, is founded on a most unsalutary motive: the panicked, desperate urge to curry favor with a Protector powerful enough to keep us from harm's way.

One criticism of Hume's argument to this point might be that his description fits "primitive" religious traditions but not more "sophisticated" modern ones. Polytheistic cultures regularly sacrificed to the gods in hope of winning their favor or staying their wrath. But with the rise of more reflective monotheistic traditions on the one hand and scientific progress in understanding the forces of nature on the other, ancient terrors and superstitions that prompted the bribery of fickle gods have vanished. So even if Hume's claim that religion was born from "melancholy passions" is historically correct, there's no reason to think that the same passions motivate religious belief today.

For his part, Hume is wary of drawing this kind of hard distinction between "primitive" polytheism and "sophisticated" monotheism. He sees monotheism as nothing more than believers pledging their loyalty to the one god who strikes them as more powerful than all the rest. So monotheism isn't a move away from the ancient terror so much as a last ditch effort to seek protection from it.

It should come as no surprise, continues Hume, that monotheism is saturated with remnants of polytheistic rituals and ways of thinking. This makes it inherently ambiguous and even unstable in at least two senses. In the first place, there is the tendency to anthropomorphize God in order to make him personal, compassionate and, most of all, petitionable. This is a hangover from polytheism. But there's also the later monotheistic-generated philosophical tendency to reify God, making him abstractly impersonal and incomprehensible. Similarly, our fear of present and future dangers, the original motivation for religion, sometimes prompts in us an ancient desperation that decries God as cruel and uncaring. At other times, however, the monotheistic "spirit of praise and eulogy" persuades us that God is benevolent and loving. These two instabilities in monotheism create a perpetual "flux and reflux in the human mind" that juggles the emotions of believers, causing them "to rise from idolatry to theism, and to sink again from theism into idolatry" (pp. 46–7).

So monotheism is by no means immune from the "melancholy passions" that prompted polytheism. If anything, they're enhanced by monotheism's fundamentally ambiguous understanding of the deity: on the one hand personal and caring, on the other hand abstract and cruel. Believers today "fluctuate between these opposite sentiments" (p. 48)—which brings us back to Hume's fundamental claim that there's no rational basis for religious belief. Were it founded on reason, it wouldn't give rise to inconsistencies such as these, nor the sectarian intolerance they inevitably breed. In an utterly ironic turn of events, religion too often exacerbates the very negative emotions from which its believers seek succor. Hume finds this a state of affairs as commonplace as it is deplorable.

> Survey most nations and most ages. Examine the religious principles, which have, in fact, prevailed in the world. You will scarcely be persuaded, that they are any thing but sick men's dreams: Or perhaps will regard them more as the playsome whimsies of monkeys in human shape, than the serious, positive, dogmatical asservations of a being, who dignifies himself with the name of rational. (p. 75)

The upshot for Hume is that the consolatory strategy of religion is too irrational to work well. At the same time, however, the same fears, suffering, and dread that originally motivated it, endure, and so does the superstitious longing, especially in our darkest moments, to find gods to bribe.

MARX: RELIGION AS PROP OF PRIVILEGE

Hume had the sort of coolly rational temperament that's associated (not wholly accurately) with Enlightenment thinkers. His written dissections of religion were never vitriolic or even heated. There was, if you will, nothing "personal" in his disagreement with God-believers. He merely thought them mistaken.

Karl Marx (1818–1883) is of a different, much more choleric temperament, and his denunciations of religion are frequently so brutal that one suspects he felt personally affronted by it. As early as his 1841 doctoral thesis, he took as his own a line from Aeschylus' *Prometheus Bound*: "In sooth I hate all gods!" (Niebuhr 1969, p. 15) But there's also a less personal reason for the intensity of his dislike. Marx was convinced that it was philosophy's role both to understand the world and to change it. Success in the former task revealed that the economic world order was "inverted," just the opposite of the way things should be. It followed, for Marx, that all the ideologies springing from that cracked world order are likewise inverted and, worse, in the business of providing intellectual and emotional defenses of the status quo. One of the most powerful of them is religion. So the vivisection of it is one way in which philosophy can take action to change things for the better. And Marx was passionately committed to change.

To gain an appreciation of what Marx meant when he said that the world order and the religion to which it gives rise are inverted, it's useful to turn to an elder contemporary of his, Ludwig Feuerbach (1804–1872). Feuerbach famously argued that God is nothing more than a fiction, the outward projection of noble human qualities such as wisdom, love, hope, and compassion.[5] Humans, of course, are unaware that they create God in their own (best) image. The same fears that Hume wrote about prod them to feel the need of a divine protector who will save or at least reassure them in times of peril. And what better protector than a God who, while personal and endowed with all the qualities admired by humans, is without the taint of human weakness? (Feuerbach 2004).

But, argued Feuerbach, there's a large price tag for this kind of projection. It robs humans of a sense of pride in and control over their own best attributes by stripping them away and assigning them to an external, divine source. This assignation is really an insidious draining of vitality: humans decrease so that God may increase. Predictably, the drainage leaves a self-consciousness or sense of personal identity that is "inverted," disassociating the subject from his true nature by making his very essence seem foreign to him. Feuerbach hoped that once humans are able to discern the projective mechanism behind their religious beliefs, they can re-appropriate "divine" qualities as their own, close the tap on the drainage, right the inversion, and overcome the disassociation. When the gods die, humans become fully human.

Marx was influenced by Feuerbach's analysis, and especially struck by the claim that religious belief and the inversion it gives rise to damages human self-consciousness. But he worried that Feuerbach had failed to explain *why* the inversion occurred in the first place. What motivates people to think less of themselves in order to think more of a God-projection? To answer that question, Marx believed, is to understand the origin of religion and open the way for breaking its hold.

As an unapologetic materialist, Marx argued that the ideological systems which characterize a society—religions, philosophies, jurisprudences, the arts, popular culture, and so on—are direct reflections of that society's material, economic base. Ideas aren't the motors of history. Economic conditions are, and the economic conditions that happen to be prevalent at any given historical period inevitably spawn ideological justifications (what Marx usually calls the "superstructure") of the established order.

The economic base with which Marx was particularly concerned was, of course, capitalism. Although acknowledging its efficiency, Marx insisted that capitalism was a broken system that fundamentally deformed the creative value of human labor by commodifying it: "buying" it from the worker and thereby quantifying it as an objective product to be sold, bought and owned by purchasers. In doing so, the capitalist system alienated (or disassociated) the worker from the object of his labor, because he felt himself to be nothing but an expendable cog in the industrial machine; from his fellow workers, because he was always competing with them in trying to sell his labor; and from himself, because his work allowed him no outlet for individual expression and creativity—not to mention that he typically lived in a state of near penury because the capitalist bosses refused to pay a fair price for the labor they purchased from him. Capitalism promised to bring prosperity and progress, but in fact led to a social situation in which those who did all the work to bring about prosperity shared in few of its benefits, while those who had no direct hand in creating prosperity enjoyed its benefits. In other words, thought Marx, capitalism gives rise to an inverted world order.

This is the point at which Marx's analysis of religious belief provides the causal explanation he thought Feuerbach had missed. Religion, like all other superstructural ideologies, reflects the material base on which it rests. As Marx wrote in *Das Kapital,* "the religious world is but the reflex of the real world" (Niebuhr 1969, p. 135). As we saw earlier, if the real world of capitalism is inverted, then the ideologies to which it gives rise must likewise be. So the alienation wrought by the economic system is mirrored in religion. In the former, human labor is disassociated from the individual worker's creativity. In the latter, as Feuerbach noted, virtues and potentialities are dissociated from humans and handed over to a God-projection. In this "inverted world order," the human being can attain "no true reality" (Marx 1982, p. 131). "Religion is only the illusory sun about which man revolves so long as he does not revolve about himself" (p. 132). Re-setting the human orbit demands a total overhaul of capitalism's inversion.

> Since the existence of religion is the existence of a defect, the source of this defect can only be sought in the nature of the state itself . . . . We do not change secular questions into theological ones. We change theological questions into secular ones. History has for long enough been resolved into superstition: we now resolve superstition into history. (McClellan 1976, p. 26)

Like all ideologies, religion is conveniently in the service of the economic status quo. Its social principles "justified the slavery of Antiquity, glorified the serfdom of the Middle Ages, and equally know, when necessary, how to defend the oppression of the proletariat, although they make a pitiful face over it" (Niebuhr 1969, pp. 83–4). Religion achieves its goal by "preach[ing] the necessity of a ruling and an oppressed class," urging the former toward a no-risk charity and the latter toward a meek acceptance of the way things are. It discourages dissent by condemning it as sinful rebellion against God's order. And it corrupts believers by encouraging a moral code that effectively breeds "cowardice, self-contempt, abasement, submission, dejection, in a word all the qualities of the canaille" (pp. 83–4).

But—and this is the unique cunning of religion—it also seeks to console believers in their misery even as it defends the political and social structure that abuses them. In a passage that contains one of the most famous lines he ever wrote, Marx asserted that "the wretchedness of religion is at once an expression of and a protest against real wretchedness. Religion is the sigh of the oppressed creature, the heart of a heartless world and the soul of soulless conditions. It is the opium of the people" (Marx 1982, p. 131).

Marx's observation that religion is both symptom and protest when it comes to wretchedness is astute, and demonstrates that for all his animosity toward religion he wasn't incapable of sympathy for the aching need of people (at least those from the rank and file) for religious consolation. Religion as a superstructural prop of economic and political privilege is an accomplice in the economic order that condemns the underprivileged to wretchedness. But ironically, personal religious yearning—for a heavenly homeland in which justice rolls down like water and suffering is no more—is a protest, albeit one lacking clarity or self-understanding, against impoverishing and alienating material conditions. Institutional religion's counsel of humble forbearance in this world and promise of a better life in the next may indeed be an opiate that beclouds the insight and defuses the anger needed to right the inverted world order. It may be a totally false and ultimately pernicious compensation for the ills that believers endure at the hands of church and state. But it also, even if unwittingly, offers a genuine if near-sighted consolation, and as such has more staying power than mere superstition or self-deception.

FREUD: RELIGION AS WISHFUL THINKING

Hume's argument that religious belief is ultimately traceable to fear and propitiation exerted a remarkable influence on subsequent skeptics. Yet it's unlikely that his *The Natural History of Religion* was widely known, much less read, by the public at large. Today, most people instantly recognize Marx's one-liner about religion being the "opium" of the people. But few have any notion of the assertion's context and full significance. Things are different, however, with Sigmund Freud's naturalistic explanation of religious belief. His account has seemed so plausible to so many that it's almost become received wisdom. It is unquestionably the most influential of all efforts to describe religious belief as a natural phenomenon.

Freud, who according to his daughter Anna liked to think of himself as a "wicked pagan" and raised his children in a "totally nonreligious" manner, was nonetheless fascinated by religion (Freud 1963, p.17). He wrote three books devoted to exploring the psycho-history of religious belief: *Totem and Taboo* (1913), *The Future of an Illusion* (1927), and *Moses and Monotheism* (1939).

The first and third of Freud's studies of religion are provocative but bizarre. In *Totem and Taboo*, he argued that God-belief is an attempt to deal with the ancient traumatic memory of sexual rivalry between sons and father which culminates in patricide. After the patricide, the sons are burdened with guilt and the need for expiation. So they endow a totem, or animistic spirit, with the qualities of the slain father (who, after all, is the only person capable of bestowing on them the forgiveness they crave). Sexual conflict and unresolved guilt, then, are the bases of religion. In *Moses and Monotheism*, Freud argued that Moses was actually an Egyptian, and that the monotheism he brought the Hebrew people was an offshoot of the teachings of the heretical pharaoh Akhenaton. Ultimately, Freud surmises, the Jews murdered Moses, and the same dynamic (minus the overt sexual rivalry) of patricidal guilt and expiation introduced in *Totem and Taboo* is repeated.

Freud's argument in *The Future of an Illusion* is less speculative and, consequently, more convincing. Civilization, he claims, is made possible by the sublimation of destructive fears and instinctive urges that, left unchecked, would create a hostile climate of each against all. By hook or crook, however, humans have stumbled upon a number of strategies by which to channel passions into less violent outlets. Freud mentions artistic expression as one of the paths along which instincts are redirected. Jurisprudential systems, presumably because they transform raw lust for vengeance into rational systems of justice, are another. But neither of them is anywhere as effective in controlling fears and instincts as religion.

Religion is particularly suited to supervise the passions that threaten civilization because it specifically addresses three primal human fears: fear of nature, fear of other humans, and fear of death. Freud's assumption here, although he doesn't explicitly state it, is that fear is a strong catalyst for other more explicitly violent passions. Social mechanisms that tame fear, therefore, stabilize communities and enhance the possibility of civilization.

Religion promises believers that nature, despite the fact that it seems coldly indifferent to human welfare, in reality is the creation of a benevolent personal deity and therefore bears the stamp of its all-good Maker. Religion addresses death-fear by assuring believers that death is not personal extinction, but rather the beginning of a new, better life. And because God is good, justice will be dispensed in the afterlife. (We'll see the philosopher Immanuel Kant make a similar claim in the next chapter.) People who harm others in this life will be punished in the next, and their victims will be given crowns of glory. So there's no real reason to fear others, because things will be made right in the end.

In short, religion for Freud, as for Hume and Marx, is functionally consolatory. It helps humans deal with fears which otherwise would be too burdensome to endure, and in doing so historically promotes stability at both the individual and social levels. What makes Freud's account of religion unique is his insistence that God-belief isn't merely erroneous (as Hume suggested) or oppressive (as Marx said), but a form of psychopathology. To be more precise, Freud diagnoses religious belief as an infantile obsessive neurosis.

Religion is infantile because the deity to whom believers pay homage is actually a father substitute. When we're children, we look to our fathers for protection, counsel, and consolation. But as we grow into adulthood, our biological fathers either die or the childish trust we once placed in them lessens. Yet, by then, the habit of needing a powerful father figure is so engrained that we can't do without one. So a projection reminiscent of the one Feuerbach wrote about (as well as the one explored by Freud in his *Totem and Taboo*) takes place: the earthly father is replaced by a heavenly one purified of all the former's weaknesses and foibles. God-belief is the product of a "father-complex" that was "never wholly overcome" in the maturation process (Freud, 1961, p. 30). It's a symptom of arrested development or infantilism.

Moreover, this fixation on a divine father figure is obsessive, a constant preoccupation with a fixed idea that the believer simply can't imagine foregoing and which she "verifies" regularly by consulting sacred scriptures, attending worship services, and praying. The obsession is so powerful because the three primal fears that beset humans, which God-belief functions to allay, are so threatening.

But Freud's charge that religious belief is infantile and obsessive is clinched by his third accusation: religion is also neurotic. The hallmark of neurosis in this context is the insistence on believing that something is the case even when there's not the slightest rational evidence for doing so—and when, in fact, there's a great deal of counter-evidence ready to hand. Instead of accepting what his senses and reason tell him, the neurotic insists on clinging to what he *wishes* to be so. Religious belief is nothing more than neurotic wishful thinking. It is a "fairy tale" the faithful superimpose upon experience in order to bend reality to their will (p. 29).

This is the secret of religion's persistence: it affirms for us in the strongest, most authoritative terms what we want to believe. Religious beliefs are "fulfillments of the oldest, strongest and most urgent wishes of mankind; the secret of their strength is the strength of those wishes" (p. 30). But precisely because they *are* reflections of our most fervent wishes, they are suspect. Freud posits the general rule that any belief which is even slightly infected by wishful thinking is thereby dubious. We ought always to be wary of interpretations of the world which too comfortably suit what we want to believe. "It would be very nice if there were a moral order in the universe and an after-life; but it is a very striking fact that all this is exactly as we are bound to wish it to be" (p. 33).

But a critic might ask Freud, or for that matter any other defender of a consolatory model of religion, if there's really any harm in believing that the world is as one wishes it to be. Surely the individual is entitled to believe whatever gets her through the day so long as her belief doesn't harm others. As Thomas Jefferson wrote, "it does me no injury for my neighbor to say there are twenty gods, or no god. It neither picks my pocket nor breaks my leg" (Jefferson 2002, p. 59). Philosopher William James agreed. In his classic essay "The Will to Believe," he argued that in the absence of evidence one way or another, an individual is perfectly entitled to believe in God if the belief improves his quality of life (James 1911).

Freud has two responses to this objection. One of them is practical, and the other rather touchingly idealistic for a hard-nosed realist. The practical observation is that the more strongly a false belief is held, the more severe the backlash is likely to be when believers discover they've been deceived. "Civilization runs a greater risk if we maintain our present attitude to religion than if we give it up . . . Is there not a danger here that the hostility of . . . [the] masses to civilization will throw itself against the weak spot that they have found in their task-mistress?" (Freud 1961, pp. 35, 39). Moreover, Freud is convinced that there's a practical alternative to religion. The sciences are now ready to assume the role that religion historically has played. Science can tame the wilder aspects of nature, influence human behavior to ameliorate crime and warfare, and prolong life and health, even if it isn't able to defeat death. So the illusion of religion, however useful it once was in establishing and sustaining civilization, is no longer necessary to defuse the three primal fears. And Freud is confident that just as healthy individual adults eventually cut the apron strings and strike out on their own, so the human race will gradually mature to the point where it no longer clings to a divine parent.

The idealistic objection is Freud's rock solid conviction that "ignorance is ignorance" and should never be tolerated, regardless of the temporary benefits it might bestow (p. 32). Freud was a great believer in the claim that the truth makes us free. It was, after all, the guiding star of his psychoanalytic method: patients are freed from the bondage of repressed traumas by facing up them. For him, self-deceit was an intolerable offense against the truth, and religious superstition, regardless of how consoling it is, even more so. "In the long run nothing can withstand reason and experience, and the contradiction which religion offers to both is all too palpable" (p. 54). There is a moral obligation both to oneself and one's fellows to believe only that which has been verified.[6] It's not entirely clear on what grounds Freud posits this obligation. But his passionate commitment to it is undeniable, as is his opposition to religion.

DAWKINS, DENNETT, AND WILSON: RELIGION AS EVOLUTIONARY PRODUCT

Post-Darwinian atheists don't dismiss earlier consolatory explanations for the persistence of religion, but they do argue that they need to be complemented by evolutionary analysis. Richard Dawkins and Daniel Dennett are the best known contemporary defenders of this position. Although acknowledging the insights of the consolatory model, they worry that it doesn't dig deeply enough. It doesn't ask *why* religious belief is the coping mechanism humans typically invoke when confronted with fears and anxieties. But if this question isn't asked, says Dennett, inquirers into the origins of religious belief will succumb to "premature curiosity satisfaction" (Dennett 2006, p. 103). Dawkins agrees. Consolatory models, he says, settle for "proximate" psychological explanations. But his and Dennett's concern is with "ultimate" ones that explain religion in terms of natural selection (Dawkins 2006, p. 168).

When searching for an evolutionary account of religion, the temptation is to presume that there's something about belief in the supernatural, specifically, that has survival value. As Dawkins says, the question around which most evolutionists mold their inquiry is "Why did those of our ancestors who had a genetic tendency to grow a god centre survive to have more grandchildren than rivals who didn't?" (Dawkins 2006, p. 169). Biologist E. O. Wilson, for one, accepts the "genetic tendency to grow a god centre" assumption. "The predisposition to religious belief," he writes, "is the most complex and powerful force in the human mind and in all probability an ineradicable part of human nature" (Wilson, 1978, p. 169). The genetic accident that gave rise to it is undiscoverable. But the reason for its survival is no mystery.

At a social level, the convictions shared by co-religionists create a bond that serves them well in conflicts with other communities.[7] This bond nurtures qualities such as love, devotion, and hope that are necessary for a sense of group identity and loyalty. Moreover, the believer's conviction that there is a hierarchical order to the universe, topped off by the gods, then followed by shamans and tribal leaders, is another source of group stability. In the absence of some system of leadership, internecine squabbles can quickly weaken a community. Religion provides leaders and thereby serves the fundamental human need for society. Biologically, psychologically, and developmentally, humans (and most other primates) require the company of others.

At an individual level, the hardwired religious predisposition is just as important. There it provides humans with a feeling of transcendence which, according to Wilson, is essential to a fulfilled life. "For many the urge to believe in transcendental existence and immortality is overpowering. Transcendentalism, especially when reinforced by religious faith, is psychically full and rich; it feels somehow right" (Wilson 1998, p. 261). Of course Wilson, as a naturalist, believes that the supernatural claims made by religious faith are utterly false. But, he concludes, "the human mind evolved to believe in the gods; it did not evolve to believe in biology" (p. 262).

For Wilson, the religious predisposition is a happy biological/cultural accident that favored the survival of humans. "Acceptance of the supernatural conveyed a great advantage throughout prehistory, when the brain was evolving" (p. 262). But if this predisposition is now an "ineradicable part of human nature," it's reasonable to presume that it, like every other essential aspect of what it means to be human, rides on a gene or gene-cluster. Specific forms and practices of religion may be culturally transmitted, but the initial impetus—what Wilson sees as the hunger for transcendence—must be hardwired. Geneticist Gene Hamer agrees, and believes he's located a "God gene." This gene, whose scientific label is VMAT2, correlates with the personality trait of self-transcendence, a term which denotes self-forgetfulness, a strong sense of unity with reality, a tendency towards mysticism (but also psychosis), and a highly developed moral sense. Self-transcendent people don't necessarily believe in God or subscribe to a particular religious tradition, but they're certainly more likely to than individuals who aren't hardwired with VMAT2 (Hamer 2004). There's an obvious correspondence between the character traits associated with VMAT2 and the behavioral qualities Wilson thinks are necessary for early primitive humans to develop a sense of group loyalty.

Hamer's thesis is contentious, and even he admits that assigning religious belief to a single gene is dangerously reductionistic—not because he accepts the possibility of the supernatural, but because it's likely that more than one gene is responsible for the self-transcendence trait.[8] This difficulty of isolating or even making sense of a gene or gene-cluster that accounts for Wilson's religious predisposition and Hamer's self-transcendence is one of the reasons Dawkins and Dennett suggest that perhaps evolutionists are asking the wrong question. Instead of thinking about religion as a specific trait which has endured because it possesses survival value on its own steam, what would happen if we instead thought of it as "a by-product of something else that does"? (Dawkins 2006, p. 172).

The merits of this approach, Dawkins thinks, make it a serious contender. Religion as a by-product liberates us from having to posit a God gene, much less a biologically programmed hunger for the transcendent. Both claims are simply too problematic— unverifiable on the one hand, conceptually confusing on the other—to generate fruitful explanations. Moreover, the by-product hypothesis accounts for the persistence of religious belief despite its utter irrationality and destructiveness: it tags along with some other quality that possesses genuine survival value. To use another metaphor, it is a parasite that feeds off and travels with a host, unable to survive on its own. It is, as Dawkins frequently refers to it, a "virus of the mind."

So what is the biologically-based trait favored by natural selection which accidentally encourages religious belief? Dawkins suspects that it's childish credulity.

> More than any other species, we survive by the accumulated experience of previous generations, and that experience needs to be passed on to children for their protection and well-being. Theoretically, children might learn from personal experience not to go too near a cliff edge, not to eat untried red berries, not to swim in crocodile-infested waters. But, to say the least, there will be a selective advantage to child brains that possess the rule of thumb: believe, without question, whatever your grown-ups tell you. (Dawkins 2006, p. 174)

Dawkins' claim that credulity has strong survival value is compelling, particularly given the relatively drawn-out maturation period required by humans. But, as he says, the trait "can go wrong." The same biological tendency to believe experienced elders with unquestioning trust can be directed not only to practical advice about which berries to eat and which to stay away from, but also to religious counsel from shamans and priests. As Wilson argued, obeying such counsel may be conducive to survival to the extent that it strengthens the cohesiveness of the group. But if so, what natural selection favors isn't a religious so much as an underlying credulity predisposition that, in this case, just happens to misfire religiously. So there may not be a God *gene*, concludes Dawkins, but there's definitely a God *meme*—that is, a culturally transmitted unit of meaning—which arose as the by-product of a credulity gene that enhances survival. The God meme, as well as the entire religious "memeplex" of which it's a part, gets transmitted from one generation to the next in proportion to how well it addresses psychological needs such as security, anxiety-inhibitors, and love—which brings us back, of course, to earlier consolatory explanations for the persistence of religion.

The religion as evolutionary by-product thesis, impressive as it is, might be accused of a curious blind spot. Recall that Dawkins and Dennett insisted that a natural history of religion needs to shoot for ultimate (in the Darwinian sense) rather than proximate (in the consolatory sense) explanations of religion. Otherwise, the temptation to settle for "premature curiosity satisfaction" is too great. But a reasonable criticism of their position is that they've mistaken what's actually a proximate explanation for an ultimate one. If we presume that religion arose from a biologically selected predisposition to obey authority, this begs the question of how the religious authority being obeyed arose in the first place.

Daniel Dennett recognizes this difficulty and has a response to it. He argues that natural selection favors a tendency on the part of humans (and other animals as well) to overshoot in attributing agency. The basic survival principle here is that in a predatory world it's better to be over- than under-cautious. This tendency, says Dennett, is the origin of belief in the supernatural.

> At the root of human belief in gods lies an instinct on a hair trigger: the disposition to attribute agency—beliefs and desires and other mental states—to anything complicated that moves. The false alarms generated by our overactive disposition to look for agents wherever the action is are the irritants around which the pearls of religion grow. (Dennett 2006, p. 114)

The point of Dennett's postulation of an instinctual "disposition to attribute agency"—which actually seems little more than an evolutionary restatement of E. B. Tylor's anthropological thesis—is to argue that raw material for the religious misfiring of the credulity gene *can* be accounted for. Operating separately but in tandem, the biologically selective predispositions toward agency attribution and credulity enjoy a symbiotic relationship with one another. The former endows the external world with agency in the form of spirits or gods, and the latter perpetuates belief in spirits and gods through the authority of elders, shamans, priests, sacred scriptures, and religious institutions.

CONFLATIONS, LEPRECHAUNS, AND JOY

Atheists who wish to account for the persistence of religious belief in ways that go beyond simplistic assertions that the faithful are "stupid" are quite right to search for naturalistic explanations. Both the pre-Darwinian model of religion as consolation that reconciles humans to the hard facts of life and the post-Darwinian one that sees religion as a product of biological evolution are informative and, as we've seen, complementary models. Taken together, they not only offer a cohesive (although certainly incomplete) account of the origin and remarkable staying power of religion. They also resist the temptation of reducing religion to a one-dimensional phenomenon. Even strong critics such as Marx, Freud, and Dawkins recognize that in some historical periods and in some contexts religion is capable of affecting people's lives for the better.

Intriguing and insightful as they are, natural histories of religion such as the ones examined here are not without their faults. One of the most common objections to them is their frequent failure to draw clear distinctions between individual God-belief and religious institutions. Granted, there's disagreement as to whether individual God-belief is ever separable from its social expression. Comte, Durkheim, and Radcliffe-Brown, for example, hold this position. But others (William James is the most famous example[9]) think that there's a crucial difference between what the individual does in solitude with her God and what she does when publicly interacting with the religious institution or faith tradition to which she belongs. If this distinction has any merit, then it's possible that natural histories of religion commit an equivocation when they collapse the two into a single category. Put simply, religion as a *social institution* may be a natural phenomenon perfectly explicable in terms of group psychology and natural selection. But if religion isn't identical to God-belief, naturalistic explanations of the former don't necessarily apply to the latter.

Closely related to the conflation of God-belief and religion is a tendency to collapse all notions of God and religion into one. Typically, atheists who want to explain religion as a natural phenomenon use some variety of theism as their model. Thus Marx's critique of religion as a superstructural defender of capitalism clearly has Christianity (and particularly nineteenth-century European and Russian Christianity) in mind. (It also ignores the insights of later thinkers such as Italian communist Antonio Gramsci and Latin American liberation theologians that Christianity can be a force of opposition to the economic and political status quo.) Likewise, when Freud claims that God is nothing more than a projected father figure, he's thinking of the three great monotheisms and totally ignoring other religions (such as Buddhism or Jainism) in which a God-father is absent.

Another possible objection is that natural histories of religion tend to fall victim to the genetic fallacy: the assumption that the historical origin of a phenomenon exhausts its meaning or establishes its truth-value. But this obviously need not be the case. Even if the atheists we've surveyed in this chapter are correct about the origins and appeal of religion, it doesn't necessarily follow that religious belief is false. Believers may be correct in their convictions—there may really be a God—even though they hold their convictions for all the wrong reasons. The cause of their belief in God may be that they need a divine parent to look after them, or that their biologically adaptive credulity predisposition has misfired. But this only offers a causal explanation of how they arrived at the belief, not a refutation of it. If I ask you how many coins I have in my pocket, you may just luck out and give me the right answer, even though you think you've come to know it because an invisible leprechaun whispered it to you. I can certainly call your leprechaun theory into question. But your answer will still be correct.

Finally, the atheist who wishes to provide a naturalistic account of religion needs to be aware that his disbelief in and perhaps dislike of religion can color his account. One of the more obvious examples of this is the frequent claim that religious belief is born from the "melancholy passions," as Hume calls them. Most pre- and post-Darwinian atheists presume that religion, as Bertrand Russell says in this chapter's epigraph, is based on a fearful response to the world. But if the testimony of thousands of believers may be taken seriously, religious belief is just as likely to spring from sheer celebratory joy at the world's beauty, or awed wonder at its sublimity. Religion can emerge out of passions that are anything but melancholy. If this is so, then the consolatory model, as well as the post-Darwinian ones that accept it as a proximate explanation, needs revisiting.

NOTES

[1] I suspect this latter claim overreaches. But it's a frequently stated conviction of the New Atheists in particular, who argue that the tolerant tepidity of liberal believers bestows an implicit stamp of approval on the excesses of fundamentalists.

[2] Defining religion is a notoriously difficult enterprise, and I've opted here for the definition that seems most inclusive. Thinking of religion solely in terms of God-belief is contentious because doing so excludes (for example) Buddhists who worship no deity. Some scholars of religion prefer *substantive* definitions which define religion in terms of the conceptual content that religious people commit to. Others opt for a *functional* definition that focuses more closely on how religion operates than on the beliefs that comprise it. This is the approach typically taken by atheists interested

in exploring the natural history of religion. For an enlightening discussion of the difficulties in defining religion, see Pals (1996, pp. 3–15, 268–84).

3 In fact, it's become a convention among the New Atheists to refer to unbelievers as "brights," with the accompanying implication that believers are dim (-witted). Christopher Hitchens is the only New Atheist of note who finds the label offensive, admitting that he's annoyed at "Professor Dawkins and Daniel Dennett for their cringe-making proposal that atheists should conceitedly nominate themselves to be called 'brights.'" (Hitchens 2007, p. 5). A website devoted to brights is available at http://the-brights.net/ (accessed December 15, 2009).

4 See Radcliffe-Brown (1976), Malinowski (1992), Durkheim (2008), and Comte (2009).

5 Feuerbach's argument, of course, has a long pedigree. Recall the mention of Xenophanes in Chapter 1, who claimed that if animals could, they would fashion gods like themselves. This is a less sophisticated forerunner of Feuerbach's projection thesis.

6 Freud's claim that we have a duty to pursue the truth, regardless of how consoling a falsehood may be, is reminiscent of philosopher W. K. Clifford's famous argument in *The Ethics of Belief* that we are morally, not just intellectually, obliged to believe only what we definitely know. See Clifford (1999, pp. 70–96). William James took Clifford's thesis on in "The Will to Believe."

7 In saying this, Wilson suggests that natural selection favors groups as well as individuals. Other evolutionists, including Daniel Dennett, disagree.

8 For more on efforts to locate a God gene, see Noelle (2003).

9 According to James' well-known definition, religion is "the feelings, acts, and experiences of individual men in their solitude, so far as they apprehend themselves to stand in relation to whatever they may consider the divine" (James 1994, p. 36).

CHAPTER 6

A GODLESS MORALITY

It is putting a very high price on one's conjectures to have a man roasted alive because of them.

Montaigne, *"On the Lame"*

Although credited with the line, Dostoyevsky never actually wrote "If God doesn't exist, everything is permitted." But it's a sentiment he would've wholeheartedly endorsed. It's also the worry behind one of the most common challenges to atheism, namely that the denial of God breeds moral nihilism. The reasoning behind the worry is that God is a necessary foundation for genuine morality, because only God can ground objective and universal moral duties. Eliminate the foundation and you eliminate the basis of moral accountability. Eliminate moral accountability, and people will allow their ugliest passions to run hog wild.

It's important to be clear that most defenders of this position aren't saying that atheism is a slippery slope to moral nihilism because atheists are wicked persons. That may be the opinion of a minority of religious fundamentalists, but it's not shared by more thoughtful believers. Instead, the point is that without a metaphysical guarantee that values are objective, there's no compelling reason for anyone to do the right thing. In such a situation, in fact, there is no "right thing."

There are two atheist responses to this, one negative and the other positive. The negative response is that it's actually religion rather than skepticism that encourages immorality because the religionist, as Montaigne noted, is willing to kill or at least persecute for his faith. The positive response is that an ethic that's autonomous from religious belief—a Godless morality—is not only possible but more desirable than religion-based ones. In this chapter, we'll explore both responses.

"SO GREAT THE EVILS TO WHICH RELIGION CAN PROMPT!"

One of the earliest and most eloquent critics of religious morality was the Roman philosopher Lucretius (94–55 BCE), who in his *On the Nature of the Universe* railed against religious "superstition" not only because it encouraged false beliefs about reality but because it also "has given birth to sinful and unholy deeds" such as human sacrifice. Lucretius illustrates his claim by recounting the hair-raising account of Agamemnon's sacrifice of his daughter Iphigenia on the eve of the Trojan War, and concludes the sad tale with the observation: "So great the evils to which religion can prompt!" (Lucretius 1940, pp. 70–1). It's not surprising that the early Church took a dim view of Lucretius.

Ethics-based criticisms of religion—particularly of Christianity—hit their stride during the eighteenth-century Enlightenment. The British deists, although accepting a minimalist and impersonal First Cause deity, were nearly unanimous in their denunciation of institutionalized religion's immorality. On the Continent, Voltaire's battle cry against the Church, "*Ecrasez l'infame!*", became famous. Baron d'Holbach acidly reminded his readers that it wasn't skeptics such as Epicurus, Lucretius, and Hobbes who killed for their beliefs: "Hobbes did not cause bloodshed in England where in his lifetime religious fanaticism put a king to death on the scaffold" (Thrower 2000, p. 108). And Denis Diderot, the driving force behind the Enlightenment's greatest achievement, the *Encyclopedie,* expressed his repugnance for the immorality of religion by writing a parable in which a misanthrope, hidden away in a cave and pondering on how best to harm the human race, is suddenly seized with inspiration. Racing from his cave, he begins shouting "God! God"! at the top of his lungs. "His voice resounded from pole to pole," writes Diderot, "and behold, men fell to quarrelling, hating, and cutting one anothers' throats. And they have been doing the same thing ever since that abominable name was pronounced and they will go on doing it till the process of the ages is accomplished" (Thrower 2000, p. 106).

Denunciations of religion on moral grounds continued throughout the succeeding two centuries. But the rise of Christian fundamentalism in the United States, the violent repression practiced by the Taliban in Afghanistan, the religious-inspired terrorism of al Qaeda, and the horrific attacks on Manhattan's Trade Center towers on September 11, 2001, have infused a unique urgency—some would say vehemency—into the moral critique of religion. New Atheists Sam Harris, Richard Dawkins, Christopher Hitchens, and Daniel Dennett have been especially vocal in their insistence that religious belief breeds intolerance, repression, and violence.

Harris contends that the root cause of religion's immorality is the irrationality of its central tenets. Religious people may not be generally insane, he writes, but "their core beliefs absolutely are" (Harris 2004, p. 72). Those beliefs include the claim that God demands absolute obedience, that his commands trump ordinary ethical duties, and that the particular faith tradition to which one belongs is the only correct one. These "mad beliefs" inspire violence in two ways: the faithful kill "infidels" because they believe God wants them to, and they identify the moral community with their religious affiliation, and thereby at least implicitly deny that they have ethical obligations to anyone but fellow believers (Harris 2006, pp. 80–1). Belief in God, then, is "intrinsically dangerous" (Harris 2004, p. 44).

Harris is quite harsh in his moral condemnation of religion, particularly Islam. Even so, he's less splenetic than Richard Dawkins or Christopher Hitchens. Dawkins famously argues that religious norms in general and Christian and Muslim ones in particular are so oppressive that exposing youngsters to religious education is a form of child abuse that brainwashes them in the exclusivity and intolerance that breeds violence. (Dawkins 2006, Chapter 9).[1] Moreover, he refuses to draw moral distinctions between moderate and fundamentalist believers. "The teachings of 'moderate' religion, though not extremist in themselves, are an open invitation to extremism" (p. 306). Hitchens agrees, tersely asserting that "religion kills," and alliteratively citing as evidence his personal experiences of faith-inspired violence in Belfast, Beirut, Bombay, Belgrade, Bethlehem, and Baghdad (Hitchens 2007, Chapter 2).

Dennett, a New Atheist whose tone is usually less incendiary than his colleagues', agrees with them about the moral dangers of religious belief. He argues that religion is like a swimming pool in that both are "what is known in the law as an attractive nuisance." Each lures people who don't know any better—youngsters in the case of the pool, theists in the case of religion—and grievous injury is often the consequence. Just as pool owners are properly held responsible for harm that befalls innocent people, so religions ought to be held liable too. "Those who maintain religions, and take steps to make them more attractive, must be held similarly responsible for the harms produced by some of those whom they attract and provide with a cloak of responsibility" (Dennett 2006, p. 299).

Although not a member of the New Atheist clique, atheist philosopher Michel Onfray agrees that religion is morally condemnable. His challenge to those who adopt a live and let live attitude toward faith is one that Harris, Dawkins, and Hitchens would endorse:

All discourse does not carry the same weight: the discourse of neurosis, hysteria, and mysticism proceeds from another world than that of the positivist. [Onfrey means a "naturalist."] We can no more tolerate neutrality and benevolence toward every conceivable form of discourse, including that of magical thinking [faith], than we can lump together executioner and victim, good and evil. Must we remain neutral? Can we still afford to? I do not think so. (Onfrey 2008, p. 219)

There's a shrillness of tone and a tendency to hasty generalization in the New Atheists' and Onfrey's moral denunciation of religion that quickly wear on the reflective reader. They ignore the fact that in the twentieth century, much more violence has been perpetrated by secular totalitarian regimes than by religious repression. They conflate fringe and violence-prone religious groups with mainstream ones, possibly because they see 9/11 as a symbol of what religious belief inevitably brings. And they overlook the complex intermingling of culture, politics, and faith that may lead to violence expeditiously justified by religious rhetoric but actually inspired by quite secular factors.[2] The six cities of "religious" violence that Hitchens discusses are a case in point.

Still, it can't be denied that the New Atheists' moral critique of religious belief, even if too polemical, has some merit. Faith has often been used as a bludgeon against nonbelievers. One only need recall the persecution of heretics, the Inquisition, the European religious wars, or the Church's collaboration in the mistreatment of American Indians and African slaves. Even Pascal, certainly no atheist, noted that "men never do evil so completely and cheerfully as when they do it from religious conviction" (Pascal 1958, p. 254).

This observation echoes Montaigne's observation that religious beliefs, claiming as they do to be based on the absolute and unquestionable revelation of God, not only allow but urge believers toward either a quiet or noisy intolerance of people from other traditions or no traditions. This is because the disagreement isn't simply intellectual or abstract. It's based instead on a deep investment in a sectarian identity that entails emotional as well as cognitive commitment. The possibility of being mistaken in their religious convictions is unimaginable for many believers because it would expose their entire lives as an error—or, worse, as self-deception. Consequently, hostility to what they perceive as heterodox challenges is highly fueled. Even if the hostility isn't physically violent, it can inflict grave emotional damage through sectarian censure or excommunication. One thinks here of the chilling scene in Luis Bunuel's film *The Milky Way* in which sweet-faced Catholic school girls are trotted out at a school exhibition to pronounce solemn anathema on various heresies. Or one is reminded of the poignant passage in Charles Darwin's *Autobiography* where he expresses indignant grief at Christianity's insistence on separating orthodox sheep from heterodox goats:

> I can indeed hardly see how anyone ought to wish Christianity true; for if so the plain language of the [scriptural] text seems to show that the men who do not believe, and this would include my Father, Brother and almost all my best friends, will be everlastingly punished. And this is a damnable doctrine. (Darwin 1958, p. 87)

GOD AND MORALITY

A theist might reasonably reply to the moral despisers of religion that even if their criticisms have merit, they don't speak one way or another either to the existence of God or the connection between morality and God. Individual humans are prone to passion-driven error, prejudice, and irrationality. Institutions, even religious ones—perhaps *especially* religious ones, given their appeals to divine authority—are liable to become monolithic, resistant to internal reform and hostile to external challenges.

So it's not surprising that, historically speaking, religious bigotry and violence are common. But despite the wicked actions and policies perpetrated in the name of religion, the very possibility of morality still depends on the existence of a God who gives universal, objective, and absolute moral laws that establish our ethical responsibilities. The very fact that atheists are capable of criticizing religion on ethical grounds indicates that they have some notion of objective right and wrong. But normative objectivity is possible only because of the existence of a divine lawgiver whose very being grounds value. Philosopher Hastings Rashdall summed up the theistic position this way:

> On a non-theistic view of the Universe . . . the moral law cannot well be thought of as having any actual existence. The objective validity of the moral law can indeed be and no doubt is asserted, believed in, and acted upon without reference to any theological creed; but it cannot be defended or fully justified without the presupposition of theism. (Rashdall 1963, p. 92)

Many theists are so convinced of the dependence of morality on God that they defend arguments for God's existence based on morality. Although not cosmological, these arguments often operate similarly by focusing on a phenomenon in the world—in this case, the ability to make value judgments and recognize moral duties—and looking for an ultimate explanation of it. Moral arguments for the existence of God are generally reckoned to be thin, but they're frequently appealed to in order to firm up the alleged connection between morality and God. They also try to address the problem of evil.

Perhaps the most famous moral argument for God's existence was defended by no less a philosopher than Immanuel Kant. He argued that morality makes no sense unless it requires us to set our normative sights on a supreme end, the complete or highest good. All moral law necessarily "commands us to make the highest possible good in a world the final object of all our conduct" (Kant 1909, p. 34). But the complete or highest good doesn't simply mean a world in which everyone obeys the moral law. It also means one in which everyone who obeys the moral law is rewarded with happiness. After all, the highest good surely includes normative proportionality: people receive what they deserve. This is the demand of justice, which itself is a virtue and hence inseparable from the highest good.

It takes little experience of the world to realize, however, that reward is often disproportionate to behavior. Wicked people flourish and good people suffer. So if morality is to be salvaged—if the highest good is to be taken seriously as our normative standard—the existence of a beneficent and just God who ultimately guarantees that the righteous will be rewarded with happiness is a necessary postulation. "It is," Kant concludes, "morally necessary to assume the existence of God" (p. 130).

Whatever else Kant's argument does, it clearly gives voice to the conviction that a divine grounding is necessary for morality. Without God guaranteeing the reality of justice in the face of an unjust world, and thereby likewise guaranteeing the actuality of the highest good, our moral striving would be farcical. Note also that his argument appears to offer a way around the problem of evil: good people who are ill-rewarded for their rectitude in this life—that is, those who endure unmerited suffering—will be given justice in the next.

Our concern here isn't with Kant's argument as a demonstration of God's existence—in all fairness to Kant, he himself denied that one could "prove" God's existence, and offered his argument only as a "practical" or "prudential" one—so much as with his underlying claim that justice and happiness are possible only if God guarantees them. This contention can be challenged on several grounds, not the least of which is the simple denial that ethical aspirations are somehow inauthentic or empty in the absence of a divinely grounded proportionality between rectitude and happiness. But the more pertinent challenge in the context of this chapter is that Kant posits but leaves unexplained the relationship between the good and God. What exactly is it? This is a puzzle that Plato famously explored in his dialogue "Euthyphro," and his analysis of it seriously undermines the theist's claim that morality depends on God.

In the dialogue, the eponymous Euthyphro, an earnest, somewhat priggish youth, runs into Socrates as the young man's on his way to the authorities to accuse his father of murder. This shocking act of filial disrespect, Euthyphro tells Socrates, is motivated by piety, and this launches a conversation between the two about how to define piety: is an act beloved by the gods because it's pious, or is the act pious because it's loved by the gods? In the context of our examination of the relationship between ethics and religion, we may rephrase the question: does God command a morally good act because it's good independent of God's commanding it, or is an act morally good precisely because God commands it? Are loyalty, charity, and justice intrinsically virtuous or virtuous because God decides they are? Is a Kantian proportionality between rectitude and happiness good in itself, or good because God says so?

What emerges is a dilemma whose two horns most theists find equally unacceptable. If God commands a particular act because it's intrinsically good, that presumes that there is something independent and antecedent to God: the good. But this appears both to call his sovereignty into question as well as his primordiality. In point of fact, this horn of the Euthyphro dilemma effectively sunders any substantive connection between God and the morally good. At best, God's role is reduced to exhorting humans to do the good. His authority is that of an endorser. In other words, God doesn't seem necessary for morality.

But the other horn of the dilemma—an act is good because God commands it—is even more problematic. This position, frequently called "divine command theory," has it that the only reason an act is moral is because it's been commanded by God—period. This position salvages divine authority, but at the steep price of grounding morality on what appears to be caprice, or at least arbitrariness. If an act is moral simply because God designates it as such, there's no reason why God can't change his mind one day and designate everything now forbidden by him to be moral. So it's conceivable on the divine command model that acts such as torture, rape, and serial murder have the possibility of being not only morally acceptable but obligatory. The atheist contends that this is a nightmarish foundation for ethics.

The theist may respond at this point that even though God has the power and prerogative to reverse what he now designates as good, he won't. God isn't about to call wicked acts moral because God is omnibenevolent. God's essential goodness is a safeguard against whimsy or arbitrariness in divine commands.

But this isn't much of a response, because it begs the question. As philosopher Kai Nielsen points out, "without a prior conception of God as good or his commands as right, God would have no more claim on our obedience than Hitler or Stalin except that He would have more power" (Nielsen 1990, 54). Nielsen's point is that one is confident that God won't abuse his authority by reversing the moral order only if one already believes that God is irreproachably good. But typically no argument is offered for the claim. It's simply presumed by believers to be "part of the definition" of what the word "God" means (a distinctively Anselmian move, by the way). There's a reason for this: if the can of worms of asking why God is good is opened, one risks having to conclude that the same independent-of-God goodness that grounds moral acts also grounds God. God's very goodness, then, would be a quality that depends for its being on something outside of God. It's a variety of the Euthyphro dilemma's first horn.

There's another difficulty with the divine command model, and it's one suggested by the famous story in the Hebrew bible (Genesis 22: 1–24) of Abraham's near-sacrifice of his son Isaac. Grant for the sake of the argument that an act is moral solely because God commands it. That means that human reason is totally unnecessary when it comes to acting morally. All one needs is to hear the command of God, as Abraham did, and obey it. But the problem is this: even if we assume that we can trust God to make good judgment calls in issuing moral commands, how can we be sure that we're hearing those commands accurately? If we receive what appears to be a bizarre divine command—take your son to the mountaintop and sacrifice him to God—how can we possibly call it into question? A command is a command, not a rational request. But this in turn opens a pandora's box in which there seems no reliable way to distinguish between genuine divine commands and psychotic delusion.

The Euthyphro dilemma is a strong objection to the theist claim that morality ultimately is somehow dependent on God. There's a final objection to the morality-religion connection that deserves mention. It isn't a particularly strong one, but it's frequently invoked.

Many atheists reject religious ethics on the grounds that any moral system which encourages agents to be good solely for the sake of reward (heaven) or to refrain from doing evil solely to escape punishment (hell) is unworthy of the name. As Daniel Dennett puts it, religion's "most important role in supporting morality" is to give believers an "unbeatable reason to do good: the promise of an infinite reward in heaven, and . . . the threat of an infinite punishment in hell" (Dennett 1996, p. 279). But philosopher Colin McGinn claims that "to do good only for the sake of reward is corrupting" (McGinn 2005), and humanist Jim Herrick dismisses religious ethics on the ground that it tends to offer "a carrot and stick approach to morality" (Herrick 2005, p. 22). Many would agree.

There are at least two responses to this criticism. The first is that it's a crudely economic misreading of what ethically motivates religious believers. It would be surprising if there were no theists who walked the straight and narrow primarily because they saw it as a bus ticket to heaven. But if religious scriptures as well as centuries of personal testimony are taken at their word, more common than self-interest in religious ethics is the motive of love. Love of God and neighbor are stronger incentives to moral behavior among religious people than the hope of heaven or the fear of hell. The second response is that a carrot and stick approach isn't unique to religious ethics. Any secular normative model that encourages morally acceptable behavior with a reward system and discourages morally unacceptable behavior with a punishment system is waving the carrot and stick. There's no prima facie reason for presuming that doing so tempts moral agents to hypocrisy or reveals the normative model under which they're operating to be corrupt. Consequently, there's no reason to see it as a strong criticism of religion-based ethics either.

Still, it can hardly be denied that the religious stick of divine displeasure and damnation can complicate the theist's motives for doing good by lacing the purer motive of love with self-interest. This possibility led philosopher Louise Antony to formulate a clever argument that underscores the "doublethink," as she puts it, of presuming that morality is dependent on God.

Antony notes that in her Roman Catholic youth she desired to make a perfect act of contrition: that is, she wanted to be sorry for committing wrong *because it was wrong,* not out of a fear of damnation. But she came to realize that the only possible way she could be contrite in this pure way was to disbelieve in God.

> I was struck by a perverse insight: that the perfect contrition that had eluded me hitherto might finally be achieved *if I became an atheist.* If I didn't *believe* in God, then fear of eternal damnation could hardly be a reason for me to repent anything. If I, as a non-believer, felt contrite for having done something wrong, it could *only* be because it *was wrong.* If I ceased to fear God's judgment, then the only possible reason I could ever have for doing good would be *goodness* itself. (Antony 2009, p. 69)

The argument that this insight generated is both deliciously paradoxical and revealing. If perfect contrition, even without belief, is more pleasing to God than imperfect contrition, even with belief, and if the only way humans can achieve perfect contrition is by not believing in God, and if humans ought to do what's most pleasing to

God, than humans ought to cease believing in God in order to better honor God. The lesson to be taken from this charming argument is not unlike the lesson given us by Plato in the "Euthyphro": basing one's morality on religion is an enterprise that, when examined closely, only confuses.

ETHICS WITHOUT RELIGION

Given that a great deal of wickedness is fueled by religious belief, as well as the fact that efforts to establish a necessary connection between God and the good are problematic, most atheists believe that we'd be better off with a self-consciously secular morality. Contrary to the fear of many theists (and, as we'll see at the end of this chapter, a few atheists), the collapse of belief in God doesn't necessarily lead to moral nihilism. As Richard Dawkins writes, "It seems to me to require quite a low self-regard to think that, should belief in God suddenly vanish from the world, we would all became callous and selfish hedonists, with no kindness, no charity, no generosity, nothing that would deserve the name of goodness" (Dawkins 2006, p. 227).

Dawkins and other atheists believe that a post-God regress into callous and selfish hedonism is unlikely because humans have the necessary equipment—a hardwired propensity to moral behavior and the rational ability to think through moral conflicts—to behave ethically without appealing to religious carrots or sticks. Transcendental lawgivers and metaphysical guarantees aren't necessary. In fact, they're nothing more than myths that add psychological weight to the moral intuitions that humans already possess. In keeping with the naturalistic worldview endorsed by atheists, all that's needed to establish an objective morality is an analysis of the sorts of creatures we are, the kinds of needs we have, and the best ways to meet those needs. It will certainly be the case that a secular morality will lack the unchanging transcendental foundation claimed by religious morality. But from the atheist's perspective, this is a virtue rather than a disadvantage, because what makes a given act morally good or evil is in part determined by context. Once divorced from religion, values can still be objective. But they cease to be absolute, and thereby one of the incentives to religious violence—the dogmatic rejection of moral flexibility as somehow displeasing to God—disappears.

Richard Dawkins has been one of the most vocal defenders of the increasingly fashionable atheist position that evolution has hardwired human beings to behave ethically. On the face of things, he admits, "natural selection seems ill-suited to explain such goodness as we possess, or our feelings of morality, decency, empathy and pity" (Dawkins 2006, pp. 214–15). But in fact our "selfish genes" do precisely this in their quest to ensure their survival relative to other genes. According to Dawkins, this is accomplished in four different ways.

First and most obviously, "a gene that programs individual organisms to favor their genetic kin is statistically likely to benefit copies of itself" (p. 214). If successful, the reproduction of the gene in successive generations reaches the point where kin altruism becomes normative. Insects such as bees, wasps, ants, and termites, and some vertebrates such as mole rats and meerkats, care for younger siblings. Numerous species display altruistic patterns of parental care for offspring.

Second, Dawkins argues that selfish genes which favor reciprocal altruism improve their chances of survival and reproduction. Reciprocal altruism is the symbiotic cooperation between members of different species in which deals are "brokered" that result in mutual benefit. A typical example is the relationship between bees and flowers: the bee needs nectar and the flower needs pollinating. This genetic predisposition to enter into "relationships of asymmetric need and opportunity," when displayed in a human context, encourages behavioral repayment of favors as well as anticipation of proportionate payback (p. 217). Our genes "know" that it's in their interest to keep promises so that the behavior will elicit reciprocity.

Kinship and reciprocation, says Dawkins, are the "twin pillars" of natural altruism, but they give rise to a couple of secondary behavioral qualities that serve to further ground human moral actions. One is reputation, the habitual display of behavior which earns an animal the "reputation" of being a good reciprocator. The other is advertisement, in which animals behave altruistically as a signal to others of their dominance or superiority. Birds known as Arabian babblers, for example, "altruistically" donate food to one another to show off. Such displays of superiority are responded to favorably by sexual partners, thereby increasing the likelihood of such altruistic advertising being passed on to offspring.

All four of the phenomena Dawkins observes in nonhuman animals are explicable in totally naturalistic, Darwinian terms. There's nothing mysterious about their origin—genes—or their function—survival enhancement. When transposed to the human species, Dawkins concludes, it's easy to see how genetic tendencies towards altruism would have favored the survival of our prehistoric ancestors. Kinship, reciprocation, reputation, and advertisement established behavioral patterns among members of the in-group kin as well as out-group reciprocators that in turn prepared the way for explicit moral virtues such as loyalty, truth-telling, trustworthiness, generosity, and cooperation.

But the question immediately arises as to how the in-group behaviors that Dawkins describes made the leap to moral virtues that have wider application. How did our ancestors move from favoring their own kin to universalizing behaviors such as loyalty and generosity?

In a move similar to his analysis of religion as an evolutionary by-product, Dawkins' answer is that our "Good Samaritan urges" are biological "misfirings." Sometimes genetic "rules of thumb" that promote behavior conducive to survival get misapplied. The rule of thumb that tells a bird to feed its offspring, while usually good for the perpetuation of the bird's genes, misfires if the youngsters it feeds aren't its offspring—if, for example, a cuckoo has laid its eggs in the bird's nest. The rule of thumb gets misapplied and the feeding of the interloper is the result.

In the case of humans, our ancestor's privileging of kin has misfired into a moral regard for all humans, or at least for a wider range of humans. Just as the sexual urge, which in Darwinian terms has procreation as its only purpose, endures even when sexual partners have no intention of producing offspring, so behavioral patterns that originated with kinship altruism endure when there's no need to limit them specifically to an in-group. They're now a part of who we are, even though the environmental conditions which favored their emergence has changed. So, as Dawkins says, "We can no more help ourselves feeling pity when we see a weeping unfortunate (who is unrelated and unable to reciprocate) than we can help ourselves feeling lust for a member of the opposite sex (who may be infertile or otherwise unable to reproduce). Both are misfirings, Darwinian mistakes: blessed, precious mistakes" (Dawkins 2006, p. 220).

Is this a hopeless reduction of ethics to biology, an unwarranted squeezing of an "ought" from an "is," as David Hume might say? Allowing that our ancestors, as well as other species, displayed survival-enhancing behaviors such as kin altruism and out-group reciprocation, and granting Dawkins his claim that a misfiring of the genetic rules of thumb that selected for these behaviors allowed for a wider, beyond-kin targeting of them: is it legitimate to springboard from the *fact* that these behaviors enhance survival to the norm that we *ought* to practice them? This is a question that not only challenges Dawkins' evolutionary account of morality but any ethics that claims to be naturalistic rather than supernaturalistic. How can description generate prescription?

Daniel Dennett responds by arguing that the is/ought challenge, while it makes perfect sense to a theist, seems awkward to one who has embraced a naturalistic worldview. If one works under the assumption that there are no explanations of the world that are non-naturalistic, whence could one possibly derive values except from facts? It seems strangely misguided to worry overmuch about the distinction. "If 'ought' cannot be derived from 'is,' just what *can* 'ought' be derived from? Is ethics an *entirely* 'autonomous' field of inquiry? Does it float, untethered to facts from any other discipline or inquiry?" (Dennett 1995, p. 467). There's a distinction, Dennett says, between claiming that facts such as Dawkins' evolutionarily selective behavior are necessary to ground moral values and that they're sufficient to ground moral values. No naturalist except the "greedy reductionist" type who seeks to collapse all of reality into a few physicalist categories, wants to defend the latter claim. Instead, the former, more modest one is embraced as the ground but not a full explanation of morality:

> Ethics must be somehow based on an appreciation of human nature—on a sense of what a human being is or might be, and on what a human being might want to have or want to be . . . No one could seriously deny that ethics is responsive to such facts about human nature. We may just disagree about where to look for the most telling facts about human nature—in novels, in religious texts, in psychological experiments, in biological or anthropological investigations. (p. 468)

What Dennett endorses is a temperate or nongreedy reductionism that uses rationality to reflect on the natural facts and potentialities of human nature and then, calling upon a wide range of disciplines, generates from them normative rules of behavior. This will require a balancing act that avoids two errors: on the one hand, thinking that "more rationality, more rules, more justifications" is the magic wand, on the other hand thinking that piling up more and more brute facts will do the trick (p. 506). We'll never arrive at a normative algorithm that automatically prescribes the morally right response to every situation. (Neither do religious ethics, for that matter, even though they sometimes pretend to.) But that's no cause for despair, concludes Dennett, because "we have the mind-tools we need to design and redesign ourselves, ever searching for better solutions to the problems we create for ourselves and others" (p. 510).

ATHEIST ETHICS: TWO EXAMPLES

Regardless of the specific direction a Godless morality takes, atheists agree that it will have a few general characteristics. It will be *naturalistic,* firmly grounded in an understanding of what it means to be a human being. This entails drawing not only on the social and physical sciences for information but also, as Dennett suggests, upon the arts and even religious texts for insight. An atheist morality will be *humanistic,* firmly human- rather than God-centered. Its goals will be earthly rather than heavenly. A morality independent of God will endorse *objective values* in the sense that they're *rationally grounded* and nonsubjective. But these values will also be flexible enough to take into consideration extenuating circumstances arising from context, agent, and situation. In short, atheistic values will be *relative* rather than absolute.

Two philosophers who have thought deeply about the contours of atheist ethics are Kai Nielsen and Paul Kurtz. A brief examination of their respective normative models provides some idea of how the general principles of naturalism, humanism, objectivity, rationality, and relativism can be translated into a viable morality.

Nielsen begins negatively: religion isn't needed, he says, to make sense of morality. In fact, the person who says otherwise, especially a person who falls into existential despair at the thought that God is dead and concludes that nothing matters "is a spoilt child who has never looked at his fellowman with compassion" (Nielsen 1990, p. 118). God's death should neither hurtle us into nihilism nor absolve us of any responsibility to others. On the contrary: precisely because God doesn't exist, the stakes are much higher and the burden much heavier.

What exactly is at stake? For Nielsen, it's happiness. Humans, whether religious or not, desire happiness and hope to avoid suffering: our activities in the world are ultimately motivated by our wish to be happy. This suggests that happiness is a "very fundamental good." (Nielsen doesn't deny that there may be other fundamental goods as well. But acknowledging this, he says, "only complicates the secular picture of morality" rather than providing reason for appealing to theistic concepts" [p. 119]). Reason is necessary to sort out sometimes difficult questions of whether a particular action is conducive to genuine happiness or what constitutes untoward suffering, but what isn't in dispute is the fact that happiness is a good. Nielsen admits that he can't "prove" that this is so, but neither does he feel the need to do so. For him, the belief that happiness is both desirable and good is a basic belief that's affirmed time and again in our behavior and discourse. (It's worth pointing out that if atheist criticisms of divine command theory are cogent, the theist is unable to "prove" her basic values too.)

Given the importance of happiness, the goal of a secular, humanistic ethic is its promotion and maximization. The good life is a happy life and humans are warranted in conducting themselves in such a way as to attain it. But this of course immediately raises the question of how to handle conflicts of interests. If the pursuit of my happiness interferes with yours, should I be bothered by your situation? Do I, in fact, owe moral consideration to others who also desire happiness?

Nielsen answers in the affirmative, and invokes the principle of fairness or justice. Morality requires us to honor the common good, to make sure that happiness is distributed as evenly as possible, and to do so sometimes even at the sacrifice of our own immediate interests. Reason tells me that if I consider happiness a good for myself, I should consider it a good for others as well. Ultimately, vital human interests are what generate the calculus of rights and duties (p. 203). Self-interest tells me that surrendering some of my interests or privileges for the sake of more equitably distributing the resources necessary for happiness is ultimately conducive to my own well-being. And when conflicts arise, as they inevitably will, they are adjudicated rationally rather than by appealing to some supernatural judge.

Still, what if someone simply refuses to act rationally, either out of misguided ignorance or spitefulness?[3] What's to stop someone in a Godless world bereft of absolute moral standards—much less the fear of divine retribution—from thumbing her nose at any values whatsoever? This is a real possibility, admits Nielsen. No absolutely compelling secular justification for choosing to honor the desire of others for happiness can be given. People are always free to choose howsoever they wish. But this isn't unique to atheist ethics. All of us, religious or not, ultimately must decide what kind of person we wish to be and act accordingly. The acceptance of any (or no) moral code involves a choice, regardless of whether that moral code is believed to have been decreed by God or is seen as arising from a naturalistic recognition of human needs and interests. There are, in short, no moral guarantees for either the atheist or the theist (pp. 122–3). The crucial difference between them is that the theist won't or can't live with this.

Paul Kurtz agrees with Nielsen's claim that a naturalistic ethic is unable (and unwilling) to make categorical claims. "Critical ethical inquirers," by which Kurtz means secular, nontheistic inquirers, accept no "unalterable regulation." They recognize a certain contingency or conditionality to all moral pronouncements. This is because they believe that the discourse of rights and obligations are based upon the facts of human nature and are relative to social, cultural, and historical referents. Their factual basis means that they're not subjective. But their relativity means that they're not absolute either (Kurtz 1988, p. 64). As Kurtz writes, "Although there are some *prima facie* general guidelines, what we do depends in the last analysis upon the context in which we decide" (Kurtz 2007, p. 43).

Like Dawkins, Kurtz believes that much behavior which we call "moral" is biologically rooted "in the nature of the human animal and the processes of evolution by which the species adapts and survives" (Kurtz 1988, p. 66). Adaptation is crucial. The exigencies involved in being social animals, the common tasks of living, and the wide range of environmental conditions, require that the moral codes generated by the facts of human biology "have an adaptive function." Ethical principles may be thought of as hypotheses, even though their defenders frequently don't see them as such. As hypotheses, one of the tests of a putative ethical principle is the kind of consequences its acceptance or rejection entails. Kin altruism and reciprocation develop into moral maxims such as "be kind and considerate to people" and "be honest and truthful." Immediate, lived evaluations of these normative hypotheses are based on the results for both individuals and communities they create. Philosophical justifications come later, and generally only if the hypotheses have produced the kind of beneficial consequences that allow them to survive as moral principles.

From this experimental positing, testing, and affirming or rejecting of moral hypotheses, all of which constitute a process of "reflective inquiry" which is indispensible to a humanistic ethic, several virtues which Kurtz calls "common moral decencies" emerge which in turn serve as the foundations for the establishment of rights. The three cardinal decencies are courage, cognition, and caring. The moral atheist must be courageous enough to live in a world without absolute moral guarantees. She must be reflective, deliberative, and informed enough to examine critically moral conflicts and dilemmas when they arise. And she must be sensitive enough to the needs of others to recognize the need to balance self-interest with the common good— even at times, as Nielsen suggested, to the point of sacrifice. Moreover, says Kurtz, given the current context of global ecological crisis, the common decency of caring extends further than traditionally thought. "We also have some obligation to other forms of sentient life and to other species on the planet Earth" (Kurtz 2007, p. 43).

HOMO HOMINI LUPUS EST?

Four years before his death, Benjamin Franklin—hardly a friend to theism—wrote to a correspondent whose name hasn't come down to us (it might've been Thomas Paine), but who apparently was defending an atheist ethics.

> You yourself may find it easy to live a virtuous Life without the Assistance afforded by Religion; you having a clear Perception of the Advantages of Virtue and the Disadvantages of Vice, and possessing a Strength of Resolution sufficient to enable you to resist common Temptations. But think how great a Proportion of Mankind consists of weak and ignorant Men and Women, and of inexperienc'd and inconsiderate Youth of both Sexes, who have need of the Motives of Religion to restrain them from Vice [and] support their Virtue.

In short, concluded Franklin, "if Men are so wicked as we now see them *with Religion* what would they be *if without it?*" (Franklin 1963, pp. 294, 295).

Franklin's fear is a sober warning to those defenders of a natural-istic ethic who presume that reason and restraint come easily to humankind. As noted earlier, it's misleading to presume that reli-gious ethics relies exclusively on a carrot and stick approach. But it can't be denied that religious belief, for all the wickedness which it can and has bred, historically has also served as something of a check on individual excesses. In another letter, Franklin refers to humans as wolves, rapacious for power, possessions, and prestige (Franklin 1995, p. 455). Does an ethic totally autonomous from God-belief have the persuasive force, at least occasionally supplied by religion, to curb our lupine appetites?

A quick affirmative response might be as naïve as Freud's conviction, explored in Chapter 5, that humans can outgrow the "infantile neurosis" of religion by rationally accepting the fact that science is a much better way of explaining reality. Jettisoning an entire world-view is never that easy. We don't pick and choose our deepest, most motivating beliefs solely (or even primarily) on the basis of rational analysis. Similarly, very few of us behave the way we do because we've thoroughly considered the range of possibilities and rationally concluded that one course of action is more conducive to personal and social happiness than another. Human passions are powerful motivators, and reason alone—or even reason coupled with social incentives and disincentives (laws, for example)—seems more often than not unable to curb them. But religious belief in a God who rewards or punishes according to one's deserts just might.

This was the opinion of the fifth century BCE philosopher Critias, a contemporary of Socrates and character in two of Plato's dialogues. In his drama "Sisyphus," he argues that the gods were invented to be ever-present witnesses to human acts done in private.

So that everything which mortals say is heard
And everything done is visible.
Even if you plan in silence some evil deed
It will not be hidden from the gods: for discernment
Lies in them. (Critias 2001)

Plato's story in Book 2 of the "Republic" of the shepherd Gyges who uses a ring of invisibility he stumbles upon to steal and murder underscores Critias' fear that in the absence of overseeing gods—or, in Plato's terms, in the absence of moral visibility to them—human wolfishness will run unchecked. It's interesting to note that Daniel Dennett, one of the more reflective of the New Atheists, seems to agree. Religion, he says, can be "moral viagra." Some people need help being good, and the ever-present eye of God may be the extra push they need. So the eradication of religion as an atheist goal needs to be approached warily (Dennett 2005).

The case can be made even stronger. Although the belief in an all-seeing and punitive God may be the extra jolt that many people need to walk the straight and narrow, surely just as many other theists, as already noted, behave morally out of love rather than fear of punishment or expectation of reward. They've internalized norms such as kindness, compassion, charity, and self-sacrifice out of a love of their God and a desire to live in a way that's pleasing to him, much as a child wishes to be good in order to give joy to a parent. This internalization in turn motivates them to serve others. Even Christopher Hitchens, for whom religion "poisons everything," concedes (albeit reluctantly) that "some of the most dedicated relief workers are also believers" (Hitchens 2007, p. 192).

These considerations bring us back to the question posed at the beginning of this chapter: does a godless universe lead to moral nihilism? Theistic insistences that it does as well as atheist worries about moral collapse if religious illusions are taken away seem, at the end of the day, to have more to do with a sense of meaning than with morality. The assumption is that a universe in which God disappears is one in which any sense of deep meaning or purposefulness also vanishes. Stripped of this ground, which serves to orient and sustain individuals as well as cultures, moral inhibitions fall away because there seems no more point to them than to anything else. If God isn't in his heaven, then all isn't right with the world, there's no rhyme or reason to existence, and no meaning to life. So why should I bother to act rationally or behave morally? What's the use?

The deep and despairing spiritual alienation and moral cynicism that can come from loss of belief in God are much more serious threats to morality than the possibility that humans will take the death of God as an opportunity to run amok. The latter scenario is fixable with time and appropriate societal policing. The former can only be addressed by the discovery of alternative nonreligious sources of deep meaning. It's to an exploration of those alternatives that the final two chapters turn.

NOTES

[1] Hitchens (2007, Chapter 16) enthusiastically agrees with this assessment, Dennett (1996, pp. 321–28) more reservedly (and rationally) so.

[2] For an interesting discussion of the complex similarities and differences between religious and secular violence, see Fine (2008).

[3] Such an unhappy person has been brilliantly portrayed in Dostoyevsky (2009).

CHAPTER 7

SISYPHUS' QUESTION

"Forty-two."

Richard Adams, The Hitchhikers Guide to the Galaxy

Sisyphus, king of Corinth, crafty manipulator of men and women and rebel against gods and death, was finally brought low by an angry and vengeful Zeus. Thanks largely to Albert Camus, Sisyphus' fate is well known to the contemporary world: condemnation for all eternity to the utterly futile task of pushing a huge boulder up the side of a steep mountain, only to have it roll back down time after time after time.

Camus saw Sisyphus' fate as exemplifying the human condition, and used it as an occasion to ask whether life was worth living. If there is no ultimate point to human existence, if life is just one damn thing after another, each ending in failure, then "there is but one truly serious philosophical problem, and that is suicide" (Camus 1955, p. 3). The problem, in other words, is whether it's better to be rid of an existence apparently devoid of inherent purpose and meaning, or to live it as best one can.

But there's a question that logically precedes the one Camus asked. One can easily imagine Sisyphus pondering it as he trudges perpetually up and down his mountain. That question is whether in fact life *does* have a meaning, regardless of how absurd and pointless it appears at times. Theists believe they can answer this second question affirmatively because they presume that the existence of a God infuses meaning and purpose into the physical cosmos as well as human existence, both now and in a hereafter. Atheists, however, don't have the luxury of God to fall back on. As naturalists, they more soberly believe the human condition devoid of any overarching, intrinsic meaning. The issue for them is whether other kinds of meaning more compatible with a naturalistic worldview can compensate for the absence of the divinely-ordained theistic one.

It's no small issue. Most theists will say that the absence of God spells utter loss of purposefulness in their personal lives—"If I didn't believe in God, I'd have no reason for getting out of bed in the morning" is a commonly heard refrain—and a sense of profound alienation in the face of an indifferent, purposeless universe. Atheists, too, wrestle with the same worries. Having rejected the traditional religious model, they must find energy and motive for getting through the day and strength to bear the silence of the heavens and the post-mortem annihilation they believe awaits them. Militant atheists may claim that they're unbothered by such concerns. But even if we take them at their word, we may be assured that their failure or refusal to acknowledge the tragic dimension of a godless life isn't shared by most thinking nonbelievers. If the problem of evil is the theist's burden, the apparent pointlessness of life is the atheist's.

MAKING SENSE OF THE QUESTION

One of the funniest and most memorable scenes in Douglas Adams' *Hitchhikers Guide to the Galaxy* tells the story of a couple of galactic philosophers who set a mega-computer, Deep Thought, the task of answering the question "What is the answer to life, the universe, and everything?" It takes Deep Thought seven and a half million years to run the appropriate programs, but at last the computer declares that it's ready to announce the answer. The descendants of the two philosophers are ecstatic at the prospect. "Never again," they exult, "never again will we wake up in the morning and think *Who am I? What is my purpose in life? Does it really, cosmically speaking, matter if I don't get up and go to work?* For today we will finally learn once and for all the plain and simple answer to all these nagging little problems of Life, the Universe, and Everything!"

And then the great moment comes. As everyone waits with hushed breath for the answer, Deep Thought "with infinite majesty and calm" says: "Forty-two." "Forty-two!" shouts the bewildered audience. "Is that all you've got to show for seven and a half million years' work?" Deep Thought replies that it has worked on the problem very thoroughly, and that forty-two is indeed the answer. But then the computer adds: "I think the problem, to be quite honest with you, is that you've never actually known what the question is . . . [O]nce you do know what the question actually is, you'll know what the answer means" (Adams 1979, pp. 176–7, 181).

Besides being funny, Adams' parable gives pause for thought. It suggests two possible ways of thinking about the meaning of life.

One way is to dismiss questions about life's meaning as themselves meaningless. It would follow, then, that Deep Thought's answer "Forty-two" to the question "What's the meaning of life?" is perfectly appropriate. If the question is nonsense, it's fitting, in a Lewis Carrollesque way, that the answer should be too. The reason commonly given for this dismissal is that meaning is a function of statements, not existence. It makes sense to ask what the meaning is of the statement "Life has meaning," but to ask if life itself is meaningful is a category mistake akin to asking if apples golf on Tuesdays or Saturdays. As philosopher of language J. L. Austin once said, "You've got to have something on your plate before you can start messing it around" (Austin 1962, p. 142). Inquiries about the meaning of life place nothing on one's plate. Sigmund Freud characteristically put a dismissive psychological spin on the asking of such questions. "The moment a man questions the meaning and value of life, he is sick." Such inquiries, Freud says, are indicators of "a store of unsatisfied libido," a psychic "fermentation leading to sadness and depression" (Cottingham 2006, p. 10).

But if this is what Deep Thought's answer is gesturing at, it's hardly satisfying to anyone except a handful of linguistic philosophers or orthodox Freudians. When people wonder about the meaning and purpose of life, what they have in mind is something along the lines of the questions Gauguin famously scrawled on one of his paintings: *Where do we come from? What are we? Where are we going?* What they mean by "meaning" is akin to "significance," "reason," or "importance," and by "purpose" they intend a sense of direction, a definite *telos* or destiny rather than an aimless wandering. Responding to these deeply-felt puzzlements about significance and destiny by insisting that they're based on a technical misunderstanding of "meaning" isn't likely to evaporate the uneasiness that gives rise to the questions. Nor, in all honesty, should it.

The other possibility raised by Adams' parable is more fruitful. It is that the question "What's the meaning of life (and everything else)?" is the wrong one to ask if looking for some clue about the significance of existence. This isn't because the question is nonsensical, but because it's too ambitious, just as the traditional answer to it, "God," is too ambitious (we'll see why shortly). A much more reasonable approach is to reframe the question into manageable pieces, such as "What are the relationships, activities, goals, experiences, and so on that make life meaningful?" In other words, Deep Thought may be suggesting that the question "What is the meaning *of* life" be replaced by "What are the meanings *in* life?" That, at any rate, is the substitution which atheists who concern themselves with such things have tended to make.

Before exploring possible responses to the more modest question about meanings in life, though, it would be helpful to address the theist's insistence that a universe without God is one totally devoid of even the possibility of meaning. One theologian who takes this approach is William Lane Craig, whom we met in Chapter 3 as a defender of the *kalam* argument for God's existence.

Craig claims that there is neither "ultimate significance" nor "ultimate purpose" to the universe if God doesn't exist. Even if humans survived death, their escape from annihilation wouldn't infuse meaning into life in the absence of God. It's not entirely clear what Craig's argument is here, but he seems to be appealing to a species of the design argument. Without God, he writes, "man and the universe would . . . be simple accidents of chance, thrust into existence for no reason" (Craig 2000a, p. 45). In the absence of God, there is no overall plan to the universe; if no plan, no direction; if no direction, no significance to anything humans know or do. Everything is equally pointless. Moreover, continues Craig, it won't do to claim that we can get by on smaller chosen meanings as substitutes for the missing cosmic one. "It is inconsistent to say life is objectively absurd and then to say one may create meaning for his life . . . Without God, there can be no objective meaning in life." To suppose otherwise is "an exercise in self-delusion" (p. 47). (Craig goes on to characterize the move as "pretending" that the universe has meaning, which seems to be different from his earlier claim of self-delusion. But his point is taken: in a Godless universe, objective meaning is impossible.)

Varieties of this argument have a long tradition in both philosophical and popular literature. But Craig's version of it, at least, is questionable on several counts. In the first place, he shifts from talking about "ultimate" significance or purpose of life to "objective meaning" of life as if the two expressions are synonymous or at least necessarily related to one another. On the face of it, however, there's no evident reason for the claim that absence of "ultimate significance" spells an absence of "objective meaning." Perhaps what Craig has in mind when he uses the word "objective" is "intrinsic," in which case his claim makes more sense: unless there's a God, the universe has no intrinsic, built-in, overarching meaning. This is a claim the atheist can agree with. But the atheist (as well as others) doesn't equate "intrinsic" and "objective." As we saw in the previous chapter, atheist ethicists argue that moral values which are based on a rational appraisal of human nature and social criteria for justice and happiness are indeed objective in the sense that any reasonable person can agree with them. Objectivity is a function of reason, not intrinsic meaning.

Second, even if the existence of a deity bestows significance or purpose upon existence as Craig claims, it's neither clear nor necessary that the significance would be *intelligible* to humans. If God is ultimately incomprehensible, as most theists concede, how could he serve as the ultimate explanation of why we're here or the ultimate justification of our existence? How does the mere existence of God bestow meaning when God himself is beyond our ken? If the answer is that anything created by a deity must have a point, a purpose, a meaning, then it's reasonable to respond by asking what the point of God is. After all, as philosopher Thomas Nagel notes, "Can there really be something which gives point to everything else by encompassing it, but which couldn't have, or need, any point itself?" (Nagel 2000, p. 7). It won't help if the theist responds by saying that the meaning God bestows on creation is *in principle* intelligible, but just not by human beings. Assurance of an intelligibility that's beyond human recognition or appreciation is no consolation for a person hungry for cosmic meaning by which to orient his life.

Third, it's not clear that that the mere existence of an intelligible God-bestowed point to the universe would automatically bestow meaning on our lives. What if the meaning of the universe is felt by us to be coercive or distasteful? In that case, we would know that God is in his heaven and that there's an ultimate rhyme and reason to existence, but the knowledge would stunt rather than enrich our existence.

Finally, Craig's claim that "it is inconsistent to say life is objectively [that is, intrinsically] absurd and then to say one may create meaning for his life" seems at the very least to have a vital premise missing. Apparently, Craig's assumption is that one cannot create pockets of meaning from a random or patternless situation. But ordinary experience gives the lie to this assumption. Writers create meaningful novels and poetry by manipulating random letters and words, and musicians create meaningful music by manipulating random notes and chords. Craig may respond by asserting that the very existence of words and chords presupposes meaning in the world, but only at the cost of question-begging.

These difficulties with claiming that God's existence necessarily bestows meaning upon existence recalls a suggestion made earlier: just as the question "What's the meaning of life?" is too ambitious, so also is the theistic response "God." The overly-ambitious question is so encompassing that only an equally encompassing answer will suit it. But this allows for and indeed guarantees a vagueness in both the question and the answer that can only raise perplexities. The economist E. F. Schumacher once observed that when it comes to public policy, it's not always the case that big problems demand big solutions. Often, big solutions only exacerbate the very problem they're intended to fix. For Schumacher, the big problems need to be rethought on a different scale so that small, little-by-little strategies can be envisioned and applied (Schumacher 1999). So far as the atheist is concerned, that rule of thumb applies equally well to the problem of life's meaning. Whatever the solution to the problem is, it won't be the encompassing and vague one offered by the theist.

In addition to the conceptual difficulties with thinking that the existence of God is a necessary condition for objective meaning, there is, in the estimate of many atheists, an undesirable practical effect that can, ironically, impoverish life. Theists who insist that meaning is dependent upon God risk blinding themselves to the actual opportunities for meaning that life offers. As Paul Kurtz writes,

> In the last analysis it is the theist who can find no ultimate meaning in this life and who denigrates it. For him life has no meaning per se. This life here and now is hopeless, barren, and forlorn; it is full of tragedy and despair. The theist can only find meaning by leaving this life for a transcendental world beyond the grave. (Kurtz 1988, p. 235)

Kurtz probably overstates the case. Surely many theists believe that the universe has an ultimate God-given meaning that transcends but also saturates the natural realm, and therefore celebrate rather than denigrate life. But it seems reasonable to suppose that it's quite possible for the theist to undervalue the present for the sake of a supposedly transcendental meaning that is never quite graspable, always just out of reach. Philosopher Andre Comte-Sponville contends that this move exiles us "from happiness by the very hope that impels us to pursue it; cut off from the present (which is all) by the future (which is nothing)." In such a situation, we "condemn ourselves to powerlessness and resentment" (Comte-Sponville 2007, pp. 52, 53).

Finally, at the other end of the scale from Kurtz and Comte-Sponville's worry that a theistic insistence on ultimate meaning directs attention away from this life, are those atheists who argue that the colossal amount of pain and suffering in the world either demonstrates that there is no overarching meaning to everything or, if there is, that it can only be the work of a malevolent God. "The world in which we live," observed Bertrand Russell, "can be understood as a result of muddle and accident; but if it is the outcome of deliberate purpose, the purpose must have been that of a fiend. For my part, I find accident a less painful and more plausible hypothesis" (Russell 1957, p. 93).

SOURCES OF MEANING

If God is no guarantee of meaning, whence can we derive some sense of significance and direction in our lives that rescues us from Sisyphus' seemingly absurd existence and allows us to take Gauguin's three questions seriously?

As naturalists, atheists agree with Steven Weinberg's conclusion that "The more the universe seems comprehensible, the more it also seems pointless" (Weinberg 1977, p. 154). There is no overarching meaning to things. So if there is any meaning at all, they argue, its sources must be found by focusing on what appear to be humankind's basic needs for living a significant life, and then working to meet them. There's a strong loyalty to common sense in this approach, much as we observed when examining atheist morality: stick to the hard facts and then infer possibilities from them. So in exploring meaning from an atheist perspective, the first task is to discover what people actually say makes their lives richer, more significant, and more purposeful than they otherwise would be.

One of the first conditions for a meaningful life most people cite is the ability to set goals for themselves and to pursue them. According to the atheist existentialist Jean-Paul Sartre, the existence of a designer

God would enslave people to a preordained essence. Just as a human artifact such as a paper knife has a set (and confining) definition because designed for a very particular purpose, humans, as the artifacts of God, would likewise be limited to a narrow, pre-set template. Such constraint may be abstractly significant as part of God's overall plan, but it lends either no or a limited sense of meaning and purpose to individual humans. Fortunately, however, the absence of God means that humans aren't artifacts in any sense of the word. In Sartre's well-known phrase, the essence (or design or plan) of an artifact precedes its existence. But when it comes to humans, existence precedes essence. Humans first *are*, and subsequently define themselves through their free choices and behavior in the world. As Sartre puts it,

[M]an first of all exists, encounters himself, surges up in the world—and defines himself afterwards. If man as the existentialist sees him is not definable, it is because to begin with he is nothing. He will not be anything until later, and then he will be what he makes of himself. Thus, there is no human nature, because there is no God to have a conception of it. Man simply is. Not that he is simply what he conceives himself to be, but he is what he wills, and as he conceives himself after already existing—as he wills to be after that leap towards existence. Man is nothing else but that which he makes of himself. (Sartre 1977, p. 10)

Existentialist Hazel Barnes expresses the open-endedness of human existence with what she calls the "homely" example of a gigantic Chinese checkerboard. Religion and traditional philosophy, she says, assume that there's one and only one pattern in which players can arrange their marbles on the board. But in the absence of a designer God, the checkerboard on which humans find themselves has no "correct" pattern. Humans are free to arrange their marbles howsoever they desire. "While this lack deprives man of guide and certain goal, it leaves him free to create his own pattern" (Barnes 1967, p. 107). Note that Barnes' checkerboard analogy doesn't suggest that the lack of a pre-set essence or pattern makes for an absolutely open-ended range of possibilities. Human choice is always circumscribed by the marbles of facticity—individual temperaments and talents, social and historical contexts, and so on. But given the marbles one is given, there's no divinely ordained constraint on how one chooses to play them.

The strongest objection to the freedom touted by Sartre and Barnes comes not from the theistic camp but from the naturalist one. If nature is all there is, and if the objects and events in nature conform to deterministic laws, there's a strong presumption that humans, no less than wasps, meteors, and kidneys, are bound by those laws. As such, it *does* make sense to speak of a preordained human essence. It's just that the ordainer in this case is nature rather than God.

In fact, Sartre to one side, a standard objection to naturalism in general and atheism in particular is that the universe defended by naturalists is deterministic: objects conform to physical laws and are the products of antecedent events. Since naturalism denies the existence of both God and soul, there's no reason to believe that humans somehow enjoy an exemption from this conformity. Therefore there's no good argument to be made for free will, and the source of meaning defended by Sartre and de Beauvoir is just wishful thinking. We may *feel* free. But if we live in a naturalistic universe, the feeling is illusory. We are indeed constrained, as is everything else that exists, by a deterministic web of causal relations. This is a major challenge to the possibility of meaning and purposefulness, not to mention morality. If humans are determined to behave as we do, how can we be held ethically responsible—that is, praiseworthy or culpable—for our actions?

This isn't the place to plunge into an examination of the free will versus determinism debate. But it's worth pointing out both that this is a real problem for naturalists, and that not all of them will concede that their position rules out free will. Daniel Dennett for one resists what he thinks is an overly-reductionistic denial of the ability of humans to make choices. He argues that humans are capable of making decisions even if the physical conditions that allow for decision-making are hardwired and biologically determined. An accurate billiard shot depends in part on good English, which can be understood exclusively in terms of physics. But it also depends on the player's conscious resolution to follow the shot through by, for example, keeping her head low and her wrist straight. Analogously, the fact that humans feel autonomous (that is, able to deliberate and choose) and act on that feeling, even though it's the case that their feeling of autonomy is dependent upon certain brain states, infuses an undeniable element of control, and consequently meaning, to life[1] (Dennett 1984).

Dennett's defense of autonomy may be less than convincing. But one may ask if it really makes any difference, so far as a sense of meaning goes, whether we're free or determined. We feel autonomous; we believe ourselves capable of distinguishing situations in which we're constrained from those in which we're not; we prefer the latter to the former; and we accept personal responsibilities and assign social ones as if we were free. So the experience of autonomy still remains a source of individual and group meaning for us, even if it should turn out that the experience has no factual basis. William Lane Craig would doubtlessly say that this is a form of self-deception or pretending. But the philosopher Richard Rorty might argue instead that it's better understood as an example of "ironic commitment," a commitment to an ideal (in this case, human autonomy) which we recognize can only be provisional or "ironic," but which nonetheless enhances our lives (in this case, by encouraging a sense of meaning) (Rorty 1989).

The sense of autonomy, of being in control of one's destiny, undergirds additional sources of meaning suggested by atheists. Kai Nielsen, for example, thinks that meaning is tied up with well-being, and that the latter depends on certain material and relational conditions such as freedom from pain and want, security, emotional equilibrium, love and companionship, and creativity. These are basic requirements for the good life and for the cultivation of an enduring sense of significance and purposefulness (Nielsen 1990, pp. 116–17). Grounded as they are in an appraisal of foundational human needs, there's nothing mysterious about them. There's also no guarantee. Not all humans will experience well-being because of their life situations, and consequently their sense of meaning will be proportionately diminished. But this unhappy fact is an incentive to ameliorate social conditions that inhibit well-being, not an excuse for either presuming a supernatural significance that will be revealed to us when we die or throwing up our hands in resignation at the death of God. "A man who says 'If God is dead, nothing matters,'" chides Nielsen, "is a spoilt child who has never looked at his fellowman with compassion" (p. 118).

Philosopher Richard Norman likewise presumes autonomy as one of the basic requirements for a meaningful life. Meaning isn't discovered in a grand revelation but in moments in which the disparate elements of life come together in such a way as to help us understand our personal and collective stories (Norman 2005, p. 146). These moments are best encouraged by creative endeavors, the enjoyment of beauty, and the excitement of discovery. Consequently, the possibility of their appearance depends in large part on the choices we make in life—do we cultivate a taste for beauty and the life of the mind, notwithstanding that doing so may also breed a certain level of anxiety or restlessness, or do we allow ourselves to sink into the comfortable quotidian of everyday existence? (pp. 138, 139). Art, especially narrative art, is important in infusing meaning rather than comfort into our lives because the "paradigmatic particularity" of narratives help us to reflect on and make sense of our personal stories while seeing that, for all their particularity, they are also paradigmatic of the human condition (p. 153). This analysis of meaning is reminiscent of John Stuart Mill's famous claim that it's better to be a dissatisfied Socrates than a satisfied pig. Under Norman's account, one of the advantages of being a dissatisfied Socrates is that the possibility of meaning is enhanced.

Julian Baggini agrees with Norman's claim that meaning isn't dependent on extraordinary revelations. There are, he says, no deep secrets of existence to be discovered or anything very special to find out about ourselves or our place in the universe (Baggini 2004, p. 185). So hoping to find meaning by peeling back the veil to disclose a transcendent big picture is futile. Thankfully, it's also unnecessary, because the trick to a meaningful life is to find significance in the present moment, looking neither in longing to the past nor anticipation to the future (a position similar to Comte-Sponville's). Baggini's candidates for the requirements of a meaningful life will, by this point, have a familiar ring to them: service to humanity, happiness, success, freeing the mind, enjoying each day (p. 57). And once again, each of these possibilities presumes autonomy.

What's noteworthy about all of these models is that the conditions for meaning they defend are, to use a distinction invoked by John Cottingham, endogenous rather than exogenous. Instead of resting on the will of an external divine source of ultimate significance, they are efforts to "find meaning 'within,' as it were, constructing it from the inside as a function of [human] choices and commitments" (Cottingham 2006, p. 12). The conviction that underlies them is that life can be meaningful—have a point or significance, such that it's well worth living—even if the universe isn't. What counts is focusing on the short term, not the big picture.

There is a danger, however, of the atheist simply equating meaning with happiness. Kai Nielsen comes close to it when he argues for the connection between well-being and meaning. But if we take seriously the suggestions that creativity, love and service to humanity can be sources of meaning, it's quite clear that a life can be unhappy—sometimes wretchedly so—but still meaningful. There's also the risk of endogenous meaning sliding into a laissez-faire subjectivism in which a choice or lifestyle such as drug addiction or sadism may be defended as meaningful just because its practitioner designates it so. The atheist might respond that the grounding of meaning in basic human needs precludes the possibility of this sort of subjectivism, but his protest isn't completely convincing. As Hazel Barnes notes (and apparently endorses) in defending her Chinese checkerboard metaphor,

> There is no external model according to which one may pronounce the new pattern good or bad, better or worse. There are only the individual judgments by him who makes it and by those who behold it, and these need not agree. If the maker finds value in his creation, if the process of making is satisfying, if the end result compares sufficiently favorably with the intention, then the pattern has value and the individual life has been worthwhile. (Barnes 1967, p. 107)

This is a troubling conclusion.[2]

Finally, the spectre that haunts any effort to claim meaningfulness in the absence of God is the ephemeral nature of life. It's one thing to strive for well-being (Nielsen), search for the moments in which the disparate threads of life come together (Norman), and focus on the present rather than dwelling in memories of things past or anticipations of things future (Baggini). But it's quite another to deal with the fact that it all comes to an end with death. What matters all the beautiful moments, glorious achievements, and loving relationships if they culminate in annihilation? The sense of purposelessness that comes from an awareness of inevitable death can mock even a happy and fruitful existence. As a bumper sticker popular a few years ago put it, "Life sucks—and then you die."

Theists may console themselves with the conviction of a continuation of their personal identity. But for the atheist, this isn't a possibility. If they wish to defend their claim that life can be meaningful even though God doesn't exist, they must come to terms with mortality. Otherwise, critics may point to the fate of Sisyphus as a warning about the futility of a life whose accomplishments inevitably dissolve in death.[3]

THE NIGHT AT ARZAMAS

In early September 1869, Leo Tolstoy wrote a letter to his wife Sonya which began: "Something extraordinary happened to me at Arzamas. It was two o'clock in the morning . . . Suddenly I was seized by a despair, a fear, a terror such as I have never known before. I shall tell you the details later" (Troyat 1965, p. 392).

At the time he experienced his terrible night at Arzamas, Tolstoy was in his early 40s, in excellent physical condition, and a happy husband and father. He was wealthy and acclaimed throughout Europe as one of the greatest writers of his day. Moreover, he'd just put the finishing touches on his masterpiece *War and Peace*. He was at the top of his game.

Tolstoy decided to give himself a holiday by travelling several hundred miles to an estate he was interested in purchasing. On his way, out in the middle of the great Russian steppe, he stopped for the night at a rough hostel in the isolated village of Arzamas. He had a meal and retired for the night to his room, perfectly at ease with himself and the world. But in the dark hours before dawn, Tolstoy awoke with the panicky certainty that there was an uncanny presence in the room with him. Trying to calm himself, he muttered: "This is ridiculous . . . What am I afraid of?" Then he heard a response. "Of me," answered Death. "I am here."

A cold shudder ran over my skin. Yes, Death. It will come, it is already here, even though it has nothing to do with me now . . . My whole being ached with the need to live, the right to live, and, at the same moment, I felt death at work. And it was awful, being torn apart inside. I tried to shake off my terror. I found the stump of a candle in a brass candlestick and lighted it. The reddish flame, the candle, shorter than the candlestick, all told me the same story: there is nothing in life, nothing exists but death, and death should not be! (p. 391)

Tolstoy began his journey homeward an utterly changed man. This horrible night of death-panic in the late summer of 1869 marked him for the rest of his life.[4]

Most of us have experienced our own dark Arzamas night in which we're hit in the gut by the realization that death one day will utterly annihilate us, that the world will continue and we will not. In such disorienting moments, it's no good appealing to Epicurus' ancient argument that where death is I am not, and where I am death is not: so why fear death? (Epicurus 1940, p. 31). A contemporary version of the Epicurean position is defended by Kai Nielsen. We know we must die, he writes, and we regret doing so because no one (at least while happy and healthy) wants to leave life. But what's the use of agonizing over our mortality? "Why must we suffer angst, engage in theatrics and create myths for ourselves? Why not simply face it and get on with the living of our lives?" (Nielsen 2000, p. 155). But reasonable as Epicurus' and Nielsen's arguments are, they're likely to come across as coldly abstract and out of touch with the death-despair that can make life seem utterly pointless. So the challenge for the atheist is to find a way of coping with death which, while avoiding both stormy panic and icy logic, allows him to discover meaning even in a life that's doomed to extinction.

One way to go about it is to realize that surviving death is no solution to the meaning of life. Recall E. D. Klemke's argument that the meaning of life isn't guaranteed by the existence of God, because the meaning that we want is one that clarifies rather than further obfuscates our lives, and God is incomprehensible. Consequently, concludes Klemke, there's no reason to suppose that God is necessary (much less sufficient) for a meaningful life. In a similar vein, Julian Baggini argues that an analysis of what life after death might be reveals that there's no reason to suppose a meaningful life depends on a never-ending life. If we survive death, either our existence will be a mere continuation of the life we now live, or it will be totally different. (The second alternative makes more sense because our entire way of relating to existence is embodied, and it's impossible to conceive how we could remain "us" as disembodied spirits. This perplexity may be one of the reasons why the Christian faith has always insisted in its various creedal statements on the "resurrection of the body.") But neither possible mode of survival does anything to establish meaning in this life. As Baggini notes, "Either the after-life is recognizably like this life, in which case an eternal one does not look very meaningful; or it is not like this life at all, in which case it doesn't look like the kind of life we could actually live" (Baggini 2003, p. 70).

Another way to think about mortality and a meaningful life is offered by the American man of letters Carl van Doren, who argues that only someone who has assumed that life is meaningful in the first place can see death as a challenge to meaning. If life has no intrinsic meaning or purpose, then the cessation of life is a challenge to nothing except survival. Rid oneself of the (fallacious) conviction that life is meaningful, and death becomes less of a threatening absurdity. One quickly realizes that death breaks no promises nor violates any rights (van Doren 2007, p. 140). What van Doren didn't say but could've is that the mere cessation of anything surely isn't enough to qualify as a destroyer of its meaning. Is Dickens' unfinished novel *The Mystery of Edwin Drood* meaningless simply because it's incomplete? Similarly, the slow or abrupt ending of a human life, while a cause of grief to the survivors, surely doesn't rob the deceased's life of meaning. One's life may not have a great deal of meaning because of the conditions into which one is born or the life choices that one makes. But the mere fact that life ends has no bearing.

An objection to this is that the meaning that's longed for is *my* meaning, not the meaning that my life has for outsiders who view it retrospectively. When others "read" the "story" of my life, it may not seem meaningless to them simply because it ends before all the loose threads get tied together. But from my vantage point, the situation is otherwise. Part of what constitutes meaning for me, as we've already seen, is the sense that I am free to set goals for myself and to take advantage of opportunities as they arise. But the prospect of death creates a feeling of entrapment or coercion that radically limits my options. Regardless of how hard I strive, some of my goals will be unachieved and thousands—millions—of opportunities for experiencing beauty, love, creativity, and so on will be taken from me when I die. This sense of coerced lost opportunity is voiced in Bertrand Russell's melancholy observation, muttered shortly before his death at the age of 98, that "I do so hate to leave the world." After nearly a century of life, Russell mourns the world he knows he'll shortly lose—even a world he thinks muddled and accidental.

Much as one appreciates the longing not to miss any of life's opportunities, a bit of reflection suggests there's something strange about the fear that doing so diminishes meaning. I know, for example, that as I write these words, I'm missing tens of thousands of unrepeatable opportunities. But I don't mourn their loss. Although I might feel an occasional twinge of regret at missing an actual picnic or beautiful sunset, or any number of other imagined opportunities, I don't feel especially impoverished. Moreover, whenever I sleep I miss thousands more without mourning them, either. Finally, I know that countless opportunities were missed before I was born. Yet my life doesn't feel less meaningful because of their loss. Why, then, should I feel as if my life is robbed of meaning because of lost opportunities after my death? And if the response is that death not only robs me of immediate opportunities (as does sleep), but also of the possibility of opportunities in general, it seems reasonable to invoke Epicurus' observation that I won't be around after death to know that my opportunities are gone, any more than I'm conscious while in a deep sleep of what I'm missing. When in deep sleep, I worry neither about missed opportunities nor failing to wake up. *I* am annihilated.

Concern about lost opportunities ultimately points to a fear of the transience of both individual experiences and life itself. Since everything is so fleeting, so ephemeral, there's the anxious worry that one must scramble not to miss anything. But of course one will miss lots of things—more than one *doesn't* miss, in fact—and the impossibility of the project can give rise to a number of responses. One can slip into despair and live an existence tormented by thoughts of inevitable annihilation. One can deny the fleetingness of things and anesthetize one's anxieties with a desperate busyness and ravenous consumption. But there is, writes literary critic Eric Wilson, a third option: "we can sit with our anxiety and let it pervade our hearts and thus honestly encounter our own finitude" (Wilson 2008, p. 120).

Wilson's thinking here is not unlike that of German philosopher Martin Heidegger's claim that an authentic human existence entails an "impassioned freedom towards death" (Heidegger 1962, p. 311). According to Heidegger, a meaningful life depends in part on an honest and courageous acknowledgment of one's finitude, in contrast to the usual denial of personal mortality that most of us indulge in. Such an acknowledgment is always anxiety-provoking, but it's a necessary condition for coming to terms with what it means to be a human. As Wilson says in agreement with Heidegger, "my deepest anxieties over passing things makes me who I really am: this unique and unrepeatable possibility, this quivering node of individuality" (Wilson 2008, p. 123).

But acknowledgment of the inexorable passing of things does more than give me a better idea of who and what I am. It also makes me more receptive to the very moments whose passing I regret. "We understand that we have only a very short time remaining to us and that we'd better make the best of it. In this way, just when we experience our extreme limitation, we also become aware of our grand possibilities" (p. 121). Moreover, recognition of mortality also encourages fellow-feeling with other equally mortal humans. Finally, an acceptance of the transience of things and experiences actually enhances our appreciation of beauty. Beauty, as opposed to pretti-ness, is "unpredictably mottled, scabrous, and fractured"—in short, organic, dangerous, and unpredictable (recall Richard Norman's warning that artistic sources of meaning aren't always comfortable). As such, says Wilson, "you can experience beauty only when you have a melancholy foreboding that all things in this world die" (p. 115). What Wilson says about the experience of beauty also applies to the experience of love. An awareness of its fragility adds a poignancy to it that enhances its meaning for us.

If Heidegger and Wilson are correct, the awareness that our life projects end in personal annihilation stimulates rather than destroys meaning. Our sense of the fleetingness of things and the multitude of opportunities that life offers but which we won't have time to embrace ratchets up our appreciation for what we have while it lasts. The narratives of our lives are short. But there's no reason why they can't be rich with novelty, beauty, and love once we accept their brevity as the price for their splendor.

Neither Wilson's nor Heidegger's position, however, rules out a sense of resentment at the recognition that all things die. One can acknowledge that transience stimulates appreciation while also deploring the necessity of leaving the world. In short, one can rebel, shaking a fist at fate and refusing to go gently into that dark night. Ingmar Bergman's unforgettable 1956 cinematic exploration of death, *The Seventh Seal*, offers the character of the Squire, a worldly and realistic man who enjoys the good things of life—wine, food, song, companionship—but who also is honest enough to acknowledge that one day death will bring them to an end. Unlike his tormented mas-ter the Knight, a man terrified of death and desperately longing for one of those big, revelatory answers lampooned by Douglas Adams and denied by Julian Baggini, the Squire is defiant in the face of death. He acknowledges its undesirability but refuses to cringe or bow before it. His rebellious attitude toward mortality is perfectly captured toward the end of the film when, shortly before death comes for him, he tersely says: "I protest!"

LOOKING THE WORLD FRANKLY IN THE FACE

Ultimately, Sisyphus is a rebel too—but, at least in Camus' interpre-tation, a fulfilled one. Sisyphus knows that the task to which he's tied is futile when looked at from the standpoint of the cosmos. But he refuses to bow before the futility. He rebels against it by accepting his lot, by making it his own—"his fate belongs to him," writes Camus. "His rock is his thing"—and thereby infuses it with transformative meaning (Camus 1955, p. 90). His ownership of the rock and the task lends a coherence to his personal narrative. His freely chosen response to what must be bestows significance and purpose on his ceaseless toil up the mountainside. And although Sisyphus surely has moments of anger and despair, his "struggle toward the heights is enough to fill a man's heart. One must imagine Sisyphus happy" (p. 90).

At the end of the day, the atheist's search for meaning and purpose is inspired by Sisyphus' courageous acknowledgment of the way the world is: celebrating its joys and beauty while accepting, as best one can, its tragedies. Meaning will always be provisional. Purpose will always be contingent. Narratives will never be completed. But for all that, life is worth living. Few people have better expressed both the somberness and the promise of such an understanding of life's meaning than Bertrand Russell, who so hated to leave life.

We ought to stand up and look the world frankly in the face. We ought to make the best we can of the world, and if it is not so good as we wish, after all it will still be better than what these others [theists] have made of it in all these ages. A good world needs knowledge, kindliness, and courage; it does not need a regretful hankering after the past or a fettering of the free intelligence by the words uttered long ago by ignorant men. It needs a fearless outlook and a free intelligence. It needs hope for the future, not looking back all the time toward a past that is dead, which we trust will be far surpassed by the future that our intelligence can create. (Russell 1957, p. 23)

NOTES

[1] If chaos theorists are correct, determinism doesn't necessarily entail predictability. So another possibility is that human actions might be autonomous in the sense that they're open-ended.

[2] Sartre, characteristically, puts the point more dramatically. So far as the sheer exercise of autonomy goes, he says that it makes little difference whether one chooses to be a leader of nations or drink alone in bars See Sartre (1969, p. 627).

3   It bears mentioning that one of the reasons Sisyphus was punished was his protest against mortality. On two separate occasions, we're told, Sisyphus defied and defeated death. Such a rupture of the established order of things couldn't be tolerated by the gods—hence another reason for his punishment.

4   Tolstoy's short story "The Death of Ivan Ilych," one of the most gripping and authentic fictional portrayals of the dying process, was born of this experience. See Tolstoy (2003).

CHAPTER 8

AN ATHEIST SPIRITUALITY?

It is not how things are in the world that is mystical, but that the world exists.

Ludwig Wittgenstein, Tractatus Logico-Philosophicus

The true mystery of the world is the visible, not the invisible.

Oscar Wilde, The Picture of Dorian Gray

There are certain peak experiences in life that, although difficult to put into words, are nonetheless so heavy with significance that they stand out in memory and fundamentally influence the way one sees the world and self. In his story "The Adulterous Woman," Albert Camus beautifully captures the essence of these experiences.

Janine and Marcel are a middle-aged French couple living in northern Africa. They're childless and their marriage has become little more than a convenient shelter from loneliness and death-fear. Marcel seems content enough in a bovine sort of way with their life together, but Janine feels suffocated in a "knot tightened by the years, habit, and boredom" (Camus 1958, p. 24).

The knot is severed when Marcel drags Janine on a business trip to a remote desert village. The eerily desolate beauty of sand, rock, and endless sky stirs in her a great longing for liberation from the humdrum existence into which she's fallen. Restless one night, she leaves a sleeping Marcel in their hotel room, makes her way to the parapet of an ancient fortress in the village, and stands gazing at the sky. "In the vast reaches of the dry, cold night, thousands of stars were constantly appearing, and their sparkling icicles, loosened at once, began to slip gradually toward the horizon." Captivated by its vast beauty, Janine opens up to the night, forgetting "the dead weight of others, the craziness or stuffiness of life, the long anguish of living and dying" (p. 32). She feels regenerated, filled with a new vigor.

The last stars of the constellations dropped their clusters a little lower on the desert horizon and became still. Then, with unbearable gentleness, the water of night began to fill Janine, drowned the cold, rose gradually from the hidden core of her being and overflowed in wave after wave, rising up even to her mouth full of moans. The next moment, the whole sky stretched out over her, fallen on her back on the cold earth. (p. 33)

Few readers will fail to resonate to Janine's desert epiphany. Most of us have experienced similar moments in our own life when a starry sky, a thunderstorm coming in from the ocean, a sunset, a poem, or a piece of music swept us out of the present and out of ourselves. Such peak experiences bring a sense of interconnectedness with the universe as well as awed wonderment at the sheer mystery of existence, the unfathomable but marvelous fact that things *are*. Appreciation, gratitude, and a feeling of having learnt something important and liberating typically accompany the experiences.

Religious traditions have a language for these sorts of moments. They refer to them as "theophanies" or "mystical experiences" and claim that they're moments in which the soul, temporarily liberated from most (but not all) of the constraints of embodiment, catches a glimpse of God's absolute being. Religious traditions from around the world testify to the prevalence of these experiences. Although usually couched in the vernacular of the specific religious traditions from which they arise, accounts of these experiences reveal a remarkable uniformity.

What's a naturalist in general and an atheist in particular to make of them? One option is to reject them out of hand as delusions born of superstition. Anthropologist Jacob Pandian seems to endorse this slash-and-burn kind of move. For him "religion" is just a euphemism for supernatural irrationalities, and he advocates ending the obfuscation by forcing university departments of religion to show their hand by calling themselves "departments of supernaturalism" (Pandian 2003, p. 169). But this hostile dismissal seems foolish, first, because peak experiences convey such intense significance, second, because even nonreligious people have them. It's more reasonable to suppose that they aren't essentially religious in any conventional sense of the word, but have become associated with God-belief because they're typically expressed in religious metaphors. The experiences won't cease simply because God's existence is denied. Nor, given their importance, should they.

Moreover, it seems equally short-sighted to dismiss peak experiences by thinking of them in exclusively neurophysiological terms. Of course they're brain states at one level, and it's perfectly legitimate to examine them as such. But if we take seriously the testimony of people who have firsthand acquaintance with them, they also seem to point beyond themselves to reveal something significant about the world. To chalk up Janine's life-changing experience of regeneration as merely a case (for example) of sexual excitation is to miss its broader implication.

Although hard-line atheists like Pandian are willing to throw out peak experiences as irrationalities, most—including even the New Atheists—aren't. They acknowledge their reality as well as their significance, but insist that they can be understood within a naturalistic framework. The task for the atheist is to find a way to speak about them that avoids lapsing into traditional religious language on the one hand or reducing them to neurological descriptions on the other. One way to do this is to formulate what might be called an "atheist spirituality."

On the surface of things, there are two immediate objections to talking about an atheist spirituality. The first and most obvious is that the expression comes across as oxymoronic. Surely naturalism is a position that leaves no room for spirit. The second is that "spirituality" is one of those words in today's lexicon that seems to mean anything and nothing. So even if naturalism and spirituality are compatible, one would first have to figure out just what the latter term means.

Both of these objections are defused, however, if one thinks of "spirit" as function rather than essence. It's what animates human beings, stirs them to their depths, encourages them to wonder, to marvel, to reflect, to love, to mourn, to celebrate, and to hope. It isn't a metaphysical entity, such as a disembodied immortal soul, that transcends nature, much less a fragment or spark of the divine. Instead, "spirit" is a word that refers to the constellation of mental and emotional behaviors that attune us to experience, and "spirituality," therefore, is the cultivation of those behaviors. Philosopher Andre Comte-Sponville puts it like this:

> Spirituality is the life of the spirit. But what is the spirit? "A thing that thinks," said Descartes, "that is to say, that doubts, affirms, denies, that knows a few things, that is ignorant of many, that wills, that desires, that also imagines and perceives." And I would add: A thing that loves, that does not love, that contemplates, that remembers, that mocks or jokes. (Comte-Sponville 2007, p. 135)

Comte-Sponville goes on the say that the functions which he calls spiritual are of course dependent on brain activity. But he resists the reductionistic claim that mental events are nothing more than brain events, and does so on the basis of our lived experience of thinking, contemplating, willing, imagining, and so on. Such experiences have a "feel," if you will, that distinguishes them from their neural base. They are the emergent properties Paul Kurtz reminded us of in Chapter 2 that can't be adequately explained in terms of lower-level phenomena that give rise to them. As Comte-Sponville says, without mental events, the brain would be an organ just like any other.

Another way of putting this is to acknowledge that the kinds of experience that Comte-Sponville says make up the life of the spirit can be thought of as neuro-psychological phenomena that point beyond themselves. A traditionally religious understanding of spirituality likewise argues that certain mental states transcend themselves (with the aid of divine grace) to make contact with God. But in the context of an atheist spirituality, the movement isn't a transcendence to some deity outside of nature. Instead, it's a transcendence—a moving-beyond—of the subject's habitual self-absorption toward an appreciative attentiveness to the grandeur of the physical universe.

It's likely that something like this understanding of spirituality is what many people grope toward when they claim that they're "spiritual but not religious." They may never have articulated to themselves what they mean by the distinction, they may not have explicitly embraced a naturalist worldview, and indeed they may even be God-believers of one sort or another (pantheists, perhaps, but most likely not theists). But regardless of their proximity to atheism, they think of themselves as spiritual because they sense something in their experience that can't be adequately captured by either traditional religious idioms or straightforward empirical descriptions. Instead, it can only be gestured at with the evocative language of poetry, metaphor, and simile. Thoughtful atheists can accept this understanding of the spiritual.

TAKING MYSTERY SERIOUSLY

For nearly two decades, the Hubble Telescope has been transmitting images of nebulae, star clusters, galaxies and planets to earth. When we see these astounding pictures we're immediately overwhelmed by their beauty and majesty and left humbled and awed when we try to wrap our minds around a universe filled with such glorious things. It makes no difference whether we're scientists or laypersons. The Hubble images evoke wonderment in us.

But of course it's also possible to respond to the images in a different manner. We can use the tools of astronomy and physics to measure the distances of the galaxies, the diameters of the planets, and the ages of the stars. We can, in other words, respond to the Hubble images as data, objects of scientific scrutiny subject to the canons of quantitative analysis.

This suggests that even though there may be nothing outside nature, nature is nonetheless layered with more than one meaning or mode of interpretation. At one level, the world *stands before us* to be rationally analyzed, understood, and manipulated. But at another level, the world *reveals itself to us* in ways that defy analysis but are nonetheless charged with significance. The philosopher Gabriel Marcel described this duality of meaning in terms of the "problematic" on the one hand and the "mysterious" on the other. Marcel was no atheist. But his categories of problem and mystery are useful for the atheist who wishes to make sense of the sorts of experiences we're exploring in this chapter.

Marcel defines a problem as "something which I meet, which I find completely before me"—that is, one in which I have no pressing personal stake and to which I feel some distance (Marcel 1949, p. 117). Problems can range from anything about which we feel a non-urgent curiosity—"Is Colonel Mustard the villain?" "What's 9-down in this crossword puzzle?"—to weightier puzzles such as how to map the genome, classify a newly-discovered arachnid, or diagnose a cluster of symptoms. What they all have in common is the problem solver's relative disengagement from the puzzle he's working on; his use of a clearly defined technique for solving the problem; and the fact, based on the first two points, that he's dispensable: anyone who can manipulate the technique and maintain a certain objective distance from the puzzle can step into his place. "When I am dealing with a problem, I am trying to discover a solution that can become common property, that consequently can, at least in theory, be rediscovered by anybody at will" (Marcel 1951, p. 213). Problem solving is also adversarial. It entails laying siege to the problem at hand until its perplexity is defeated and transformed into a serviceable formula, operation, or invention. In a world that increasingly values techniques that bring in results—especially those associated with science, technology, and business—there's the risk of reducing all human experience to the problematic.

The reduction is risky because there's a dimension of human experience that's fundamentally different from the problematic, says Marcel, and it's important to respect its integrity. This is the realm of mystery. In contrast to problem, "mystery is something in which I am myself involved, and it can therefore only be thought of as a sphere where the distinction between what is in me and what is before me loses its meaning and initial validity" (p. 117). When confronted by mystery, neither the bag of techniques nor the adversarial spirit that works well when applied to problems are appropriate. Mystery isn't a problem that can be tackled and subdued. "Mysteries are not solved with techniques, and therefore cannot be answered the same way by different persons—one technique, one solution, will not apply . . . . Indeed, it is questionable if mysteries are open to 'solutions' at all" (Marcel 1949, p. 118). A problem can be solved. But a mystery can only be experienced.

The reason why the mysterious cannot be solved in the way that a problem can is because the subject doesn't have enough distance from mystery to examine it objectively. We *participate* in mystery. The usual boundaries between me and my object of interest get foggy in the face of mystery. I recognize that I'm implicated in the mystery, and so can't scrutinize it without also calling myself into question. That's why I'm totally *in*dispensable when it comes to the mysterious. No one can take my place because each of us will bring a different self to the experience. This doesn't mean, as Marcel points out, that the mysterious is relative or subjective, much less senseless, but only that it isn't susceptible to the objectification and classification appropriate to the problematic.

When I approach the Hubble images as an astrophysicist, I'm in the realm of the problematic. I analyze them with objectivity, using the same methodologies that any other astrophysicist could employ equally well. But when I respond with sheer wonderment to their beauty and grandeur, amazed that the universe can give birth to such marvels, the detached impersonality of the problematic becomes impossible because my reaction to the images immediately raises questions about how the universe can give birth to me as well. I feel myself a part of the mystery before me. The boundaries of my self expand. I and the nebulae are both citizens of a universe which is beautiful and grand and tragic, and I can't help but consider our fates as inseparable. Immersion in the mysterious won't generate the sorts of answers that cracking problems will. But what the experience of mystery does encourage is a stretching beyond one's comfortable boundaries and habitual ego-fixation (it builds me "as a subject," notes Marcel, not as an ego) and, consequently, a closer attentiveness to reality. Experiencing the mysterious, in other words, is a spiritual transcendence, but one that's perfectly compatible with naturalism (Marcel 1949, p. 114).

The astronomer Carl Sagan, famous for saying that "the universe is all that is, or ever was, or ever will be," was perfectly comfortable with recognizing and embracing mystery. "Our contemplations of the cosmos stir us," he writes. "There's a tingling in the spine, a catch in the voice, a faint sensation as if a distant memory of falling from a great height. We know that we are approaching the grandest of mysteries" (Sagan 1980, p. 4).

Albert Einstein was also familiar with the sense of touching mysteriously indescribable but immensely significant depths in the contemplation of nature.

The most beautiful experience we can have is the mysterious . . . whoever does not know it and can no longer wonder, no longer marvel, is as good as dead . . . . A knowledge of the existence of something we cannot penetrate, our perceptions of the profoundest reason and the most radiant beauty . . . It is this knowledge and this emotion that constitute true religiosity. (Jammer 1999, p. 73)

Neither Sagan nor Einstein make the popular distinction between religion and spirituality, but it's clear from what they say that they would endorse it. Neither had use for institutionalized religion and the ideology it generates. But neither was willing to forgo the spiritual insights—what Einstein calls "true religiosity" and which Sagan thinks are disclosed by contemplation of the cosmos—that theology seeks to seize and claim as its own.[1]

Even Richard Dawkins, who along with Christopher Hitchens is the most abrasive of the New Atheists in his denunciation of all things religious, shares the sense of wonder described by Sagan and Einstein. Although a tireless champion of an utterly secular outlook, he believes that his own books aspire to "touch the nerve-endings of transcendent wonder," and he allows that he may be called "religious" in the same sense that Einstein was religious. It's true that Dawkins quickly adds that he dislikes applying the label to himself because it's too loaded with superstition and supernaturalism. He also draws a clear distinction between himself and thinkers like Sagan and Einstein by insisting that mystery isn't necessarily unanswerable or unsolvable so much as presently unanswered because of gaps in our understanding of the universe (Dawkins 2006, pp. 12, 18). But his denial of mystery in the strict Marcellean sense doesn't diminish for Dawkins the thrilling beauty of the physical world.

> I believe that an orderly universe, one indifferent to human preoccupations, in which everything has an explanation even if we still have a long way to go before we find it, is a more beautiful, more wonderful place than a universe tricked out with capricious, ad hoc magic. (Shermer 2006, p. 184)

Physicist Chet Raymo, who sometimes describes himself as a "religious naturalist" and at other times as a "scientific agnostic," but who definitely rejects the God of theism, agrees with Marcel that mystery is real and irreducible to the problematic. He appeals to a striking metaphor: our knowledge of the universe is an island in a sea of mystery. For all practical purposes, the sea is infinite. Consequently, the accumulation of new knowledge which, inch by inch, adds diameter to the island, doesn't deplete the mystery. Instead, "it increases the shoreline along which we may encounter mystery" (Raymo 2008, p. 30).

It follows that, for Raymo, there will always be a necessary element of ignorance when it comes to our understanding of nature. Drawing on a term coined by the poet Gerard Manley Hopkins, Raymo suggests that "every aspect of the natural world [is] the 'visible' manifestation of an 'inscape' that is deep and mysterious beyond my knowing" (p. 21). Hopkins characterized inscape as the abiding mystery that lies hidden in every experience of reality. Beneath the visible and tactile surface of a physical object lies packets of tightly compressed energy which physicists call "quanta." But what lies beneath the quanta? What's the natural process that establishes the orderly and patterned structure of things? This is the mystery that Hopkins and Raymo believe is ultimately unanswerable. Flashes of the mystery can sometimes reveal themselves (Hopkins, for example, writes about such peak moments in contemplating the veins of a leaf or the design of a snowflake), but the flashes, to return to Raymo's own metaphor, only reveal the vast expanse of ocean surrounding our island.

The upshot is that atheists such as Sagan, Einstein, and Raymo tacitly endorse Marcel's distinction between the problematic and the mysterious. Others, like Dawkins, come close to collapsing the distinction by insisting that the universe should be viewed throughout as an only partially solved problem rather than a mystery, while at the same time acknowledging that the beauty and grandeur of even a non-mysterious universe stirs wonderment and celebration. Either position is compatible with an atheist spirituality.

CONNECTED ALL THE WAY DOWN

In his later years, Charles Darwin lamented that he'd lost his youthful enthusiasm for the arts, especially music and painting. But he never lost his ear for the poetry of language, and the final paragraph of his *Origin of Species* is as lyrical a piece of scientific writing as has ever been penned. It also expresses another important component of an atheist spirituality: the sense of interconnectedness with all of creation.

In the closing lines of *Origin*, Darwin sums up his thesis by reminding readers of just how different his understanding of species as the "lineal descendents of some few beings" is from that of adherents of special creation. They see nature populated by utterly unrelated species, each created separately by God. Darwin, on the other hand, sees creation as an "entangled bank" of thousands of species, "so different from each other" yet at the same time indissolubly "dependent on each other." The rise and fall of species can be accounted for by natural laws—particularly natural selection—that both demonstrate and emphasize their biological interrelatedness. This may have frightened and outraged Darwin's theistic contemporaries. But for Darwin,

> There is grandeur in this view of life, with its several powers, having been originally breathed into a few forms or into one; and that, whilst this planet has gone cycling on according to the fixed law of gravity, from so simple a beginning endless forms most beautiful and most wonderful have been, and are being, evolved. (Darwin 1999, pp. 399–400)

At the time Darwin wrote these words, he considered himself at best an agnostic. He'd certainly abandoned the religious belief of his youth (although even then he appears to have been more deist than theist), and had completely rejected the notion that God intervenes in the physical world either through miracles or providence. But as his final lines in the *Origin* suggest, Darwin had a sense that the universe, if indifferent and impersonal from one perspective, was also a tightly woven community in which all creatures, including humans, are kindred. That Darwin saw this as more than just a bare, descriptive fact is suggested by his discernment of beauty and grandeur in it. For him, the incredibly intricate web of relationships that comprise reality was something in which he was personally rather than only intellectually involved. As a naturalist, he spent years working at the *problem* of the origin of species, collecting data and experimenting with admirable objectivity and exactitude. But as a human, his encounter with *mystery*, sparked by the very interconnectedness that his scientific research uncovered, prompted him to reflect deeply on his own place in the universe as well as his beliefs about God, death, and ethics.

The awesome sense that the universe is a seamless garment (albeit one whose warp and woof is extremely complex), a unit ("*uni*-verse") such that humans are inseparably connected not only with the other biological inhabitants of this planet but with the very stuff of which the planet and all other celestial bodies are made, is experienced by many atheists. Theists often say that they would be crushed by a forlorn loneliness if they could be persuaded that the heavens were empty of God's presence. But an atheist spirituality holds that God's absence doesn't make the universe inhospitable because science discloses an astounding interconnectedness—one is almost tempted to say "intimacy"—that binds all of its constituents together.[2] The eternal silence of infinite space may fill Pascal with dread, as he famously wrote in his *Pensees*, and such dread is certainly an occasional possibility for the atheist as well. But it is a dread balanced by a sense of at-homeness.

Carl Sagan expresses this interconnectedness in a striking phrase. We humans are, he says, "star stuff contemplating the stars." Nothing in the universe is foreign to us, because everything has a common origin and is linked by a family tree that will probably always defy our efforts at a detailed portrait. For Sagan, this unity also means that we humans have obligations that extend to others far beyond our own species.

We've begun at last to wonder about our origins . . ., contemplating the evolution of matter, tracing that long path by which it arrived at consciousness here on the planet Earth and perhaps throughout the cosmos. Our obligation to survive and flourish is owed not just to ourselves but also to that cosmos, ancient and vast, from which we spring. (Sagan 1980, p. 345)

Although he limits his observations to earth's biosphere rather than stretching outwards to embrace the entire cosmos, E. O. Wilson, like Sagan, counsels appreciation of interconnectedness. The natural world, he writes, is "embedded in our genes and cannot be eradicated" (Wilson 2006, p. 68). We feel a deep connection with natural settings fueled by "an innate tendency to affiliate with life and life-like processes"—a tendency which Wilson calls "biophilia"[3] (p. 63). Moreover, Wilson claims that contemplating the creatures with whom we're related awakens the wonder-filled sense of mystery integral to an atheist spirituality.

We may never personally glimpse certain rare animals—wolves, ivory-billed woodpeckers, pandas, gorillas, giant squid, great white sharks, and grizzlies come to mind—but we need them as symbols. They proclaim the mystery of the world. They are jewels in the crown of the Creation. Just to know they are out there alive and well is important to the spirit, to the wholeness of our lives. If they live, then Nature lives. (p. 58)

Like Sagan, Wilson believes that an awareness of connectedness to all creation suggests a moral obligation to cherish and protect it. For Wilson, this especially means treading lightly upon the earth in such a way as to encourage the flourishing of the world's tens of thousands of bioforms. Biologist Ursula Goodenough, atheist daughter of a theologian father, agrees on both counts. Her interest in environmental preservation originates with her realization that there is a "religious fellowship" at play in the biosphere which mandates fellow-feeling and a certain moral responsibility on the part of humans. By "religious," she means to gesture at the Latin root *religio*, "to bind together again," as a reminder to us that our destiny is inseparable from that of the rest of nature. "We are connected to all creatures. Not just in food chains or ecological equilibria. We share a common ancestor . . . . We share evolutionary constraints and possibilities. We are connected all the way down" (Goodenough 1998, p. 73).

One of the most striking examples of the wonder-filled sense of interconnected unity discussed by Sagan, Wilson, and Goodenough comes from the writer and lifelong atheist Arthur Koestler. It has all the traditional earmarks of a mystical unitive experience—except that there is no God.

In 1937, while Koestler was covering the Spanish Civil War as a journalist, he was arrested by Loyalist forces, accused of being a spy, and sentenced to death. For five months he languished in solitary confinement, not knowing from day to day if he would be executed on the morrow. Deprived of visitors and books, Koestler, who'd studied engineering and mathematics as a young man, began to occupy the empty hours by scratching all the mathematical formulae he could remember on his cell wall with a piece of metal twisted from his wire mattress.

Koestler writes that Euclid's proof of the infinity of primes had always filled him with a "deep satisfaction that was aesthetic rather than intellectual." In recalling the proof and scratching it on his wall, he initially "felt the same enchantment." But then, without warning, he had a nearly visceral realization that the proof was a concrete and finite demonstration of the infinite.

The significance of this swept over me like a wave. The wave had originated in an articulate verbal insight; but this evaporated at once, leaving in its wake only a wordless essence, a fragrance of eternity, a quiver of the arrow in the blue. I must have stood there for some minutes, entranced, with a wordless awareness that 'this is perfect—perfect.' (Stace 1960, pp. 232–3)

What especially stunned Koestler was the sudden realization that the infinite, "a mystical mass shrouded in haze," could be known to a certain extent through sheer intellect rather than the "treacly ambiguities" of theology. The significance of this, he says, "swept over me like a wave," and in a flash his sense of personal identity vanished. "The I had ceased to exist" (p. 233).

Koestler admits that he cannot adequately convey through words his peak experience of disappearing into the "universal pool." The event, although profoundly significant, defied ordinary description. "It is meaningful, though not in verbal terms": a characteristic, as we've seen, of the mysterious. But despite the impossibility of adequately expressing the experience, Koestler was quite convinced of two things. First, the loss of his sense of self underscored for him "the unity and interlocking of everything that exists, an interdependence like that of gravitational fields or communicating vessels." Koestler's godless mystical experience, in other words, affirmed the unity of nature. Second, the "primary mark" of this unitive experience was "the sensation that this state is more real than any other one experienced before—that for the first time the veil has fallen and one is in touch with 'real reality,' the hidden order of things, the X-ray texture of the world, normally obscured by layers of irrelevancy" (p. 233). This is reminiscent of the experience of inscape celebrated by Hopkins and Raymo.

GRATEFUL ATTENTIVENESS

The two features of an atheist spirituality we've examined thus far, mystery and unity, bear resemblance to a couple of traditional ways in which theists look at reality: God is mysterious, unfathomable, and irreducible to verbal descriptions or analysis; and all of creation is kindred by virtue of sharing the same divine parent. This resemblance can be a source of alarm to some atheists, because it smacks to them of a clinging to religious categories that are inconsistent with a naturalist worldview. Chatter about the mystery and unity of reality is symptomatic of the self-deluded de facto believer we met in Chapter 1.

This is a reasonable concern. The supernatural worldview is so deeply embedded in our culture and historical memory that it would be astounding if even the most convinced atheist managed to expunge all vestiges of it from his way of thinking. But as we saw when exploring the natural history of religion in Chapter 5, one possible explanation of the origin of religion is that it emerged from a pre-religious sense of wonderment at the power of nature which often frightened but surely also provoked awe and a sense of the sublime. If this is the case, an argument can be made that it's not atheism which is appropriating religious categories, but religion that baptized basic human responses to nature. An atheist spirituality merely reclaims these experiences by distilling away their theological additives.

From the viewpoint of a theist, the mystery and unity of reality are occasions for grateful prayer to God the creator. Prayer is frequently thought of as petition or intercession, a pleading with God on behalf of oneself or others. But collapsing prayer into favor-begging, while common in folk religion, is seen by many theologians as an unseemly desire on the part of the faithful to transform the deity into a Santa God. They caution that petitionary prayer is but one kind of prayer. Another kind, typically seen as purer, is meditative or contemplative prayer in which the purpose isn't to plead with God but to cultivate an inner silence in order to be more receptive to the presence of the holy. This form of prayer is sometimes referred to as "alert attentiveness."[4]

Just as mystery and unity may be thought of as natural experiences co-opted by theology, so it might be argued that the attitude of alert attentiveness is prior to what the theist calls prayer. Contemplative prayer is really a radical empiricism in which the practitioner silences distracting thoughts, memories, and emotions; temporarily suspends interpretive filters; and holds herself in a state of disciplined attentiveness receptive to the inflowing of the Holy.[5] Minus the God-talk, this could easily be a description of the attitude of the atheist scientist, mathematician, or any other sensitively alert observer of the natural world. It makes sense to argue that an atheist spirituality can accommodate prayer—or, if the word "prayer" is too loaded with religious baggage, for the disciplined (and some might add "reverent") act of contemplating the Book of Nature. Thus Chet Raymo asserts "I will continue to pray, if by prayer you understand me to mean attention to the world" (Raymo 2008, p. 19).

And so I attend to the fishes in the sea, the birds of the air, the rocks beneath my feet. I attend to the DNA that spins and weaves in every one of the trillions of cells in my body. I attend to the myriad galaxies in their august spinning. I expect no response. I do not worry about dogmas or mysteries. I do hope to understand something more of myself and my place in the creation. I want to know the thing of which I am a part. And I exhalt in the stunning, inexhaustible fullness of the world with thankfulness, jubilation, praise. (Raymo 2006)

Raymo's observation that his attentiveness to the world is coupled with gratitude and praise is intriguing from an atheist point of view. (He also says that he jubilates, but this is a response with which non-believers have no problem.) The obvious questions an atheist would ask Raymo are "Gratitude *to* whom?" and "Praise *of* whom?" If there is no divine creator, then it seems pointless, or at least confusing, to be grateful (to offer thanks) for the existence of the world or to offer praises (to its designer). The world simply is.

But these reservations are needless. What Raymo is suggesting is that the object of gratitude and praise isn't a "who" but a "what." I can be grateful to a benefactor who gives me a gift. But I can also be grateful for pleasant experiences that enrich me—sunshine, the beauty of a humming bird, healthy vitality—because I know my life is fuller with than without them. I can even be grateful for unpleasant experiences if I learn a valuable life lesson from them. In none of these cases does my gratitude either presuppose or require a divine recipient. Similarly, when my alert attentiveness to the world moves me to praise, the praise is directed not to a supreme Creator but to particulars: the color of a sunset, the transparent intricacy of a protozoan, the dappled sparkle of a trout's flank. Theistic prayer addresses itself to divine holiness, and too frequently overlooks the wonder of the physical world in its striving toward deity. But when God is gone, asserts Raymo, we are freed to direct our attentiveness to every particular thing in the world from the microscopic to the telescopic level. When we do, we see that everything is holy.

RESOLVING CONTRADICTIONS

There is widespread although not unanimous agreement among atheists that it is good for humans "to celebrate," as Raymo puts it, "the unfathomable mystery of creation" (Raymo 2008, p. 4). Disagreement occurs over whether creation is actually unfathomable—as we've seen, this is a claim disputed by Dawkins—and whether it's prudent to use even quasi-religious language to express the celebratory mood. The first objection worries that talk about unfathomability taints what ought to be a purely scientific scrutiny of nature with a metaphysical bias, while the second sees a return to religious language as the camel's nose in the tent. Atheists will continue to disagree about whether there is an irreducible (but nonsupernatural) mysteriousness to nature, and the disagreement will revolve in large part on whether questions such as "Why is there something rather than nothing?" or "Why is nature patterned, orderly, and uniform?" should be taken seriously. Joy serve as salutary reminders that an atheist spirituality must carefully balance affirming the life of the spirit and remaining loyal to a naturalistic worldview.

E. O. Wilson is well aware of how difficult this balancing act is. He sees the habit of religious thinking as so deeply engrained that it will assert itself long after belief in gods has died. "The spirits our ancestors knew intimately first fled the rocks and trees, then the distant mountains. Now they are in the stars, where their final extinction is possible. *But we cannot live without them.* People need a sacred narrative." But where to find sacred narrative in a godless world? For Wilson, this question lies at the heart of "humanity's spiritual dilemma." We evolved to accept one truth—religion—but have now discovered another—science. Is there a way "to resolve the contradictions between the transcendentalist and empiricist world views" without totally dismissing either? (Wilson 1998, p. 264).

Wilson believes so. Sacred narrative as religious cosmology is no longer possible. But the "evolutionary epic, retold as poetry, is as intrinsically ennobling as any religious epic," and scientific descriptions of nature reveal "more content and grandeur than all religious cosmologies combined" (p. 265). The thing to keep in mind is that the language of science describes and explains the physical world, while the more poetic language of religion, as Paul Kurtz argues, has an entirely different function. It is eschatological and evocative, expressing hope, encouraging transcendence from fear and anxiety, and struggling to find words to communicate peak experiences. "It presents moral poetry, aesthetic inspiration, performative ceremonial rituals, which act out and dramatize the human condition and human interests, and seek to slake the thirst for meaning and purpose" (Kurtz 2003, p. 355). Note that Kurtz isn't defending a modification of Stephen Jay Gould's NOMA (non-overlapping magisteria), which, as we saw in Chapter 2, is problematic. On the contrary, he's suggesting that the poetry of religious language can be wed to scientific discoveries in order to provide an emotional and spiritual substitute for supernaturalism.

An atheist spirituality which seeks to resolve the contradictions between naturalism and supernaturalism by making use of scientific description and religious evocation can be minimalistic or quite sophisticated. On the minimalist side of the scale is something like mathematician John Allen Paulos' endorsement of "Yeahism." Paulos notes that although he's an atheist, he's always wondered whether a "proto-religion" acceptable to atheists and agnostics is possible.

> By this I mean a 'religion' that has no dogma, no narratives, and no existence claims and yet still acknowledges the essential awe and wonder of the world and perhaps affords as well an iota of serenity. The best I've been able to come up with is the 'Yeah-ist' religion, whose response to the intricacy, beauty, and mystery of the world is a simple affirmation and acceptance, 'Yeah,' and whose only prayer is the one word 'Yeah.' (Paulos 2008, p. xvi)

Paulos, like many mathematicians, has a quirky sense of humor, and it's difficult to know how seriously he means us to take his Yeahism. But joking aside, he's managed to gesture nicely at the essential sense of wonderment that motivates attempts at an atheist spirituality. Perhaps the best way to express the basic response to beauty and mystery is with a single forceful ejaculation like "yeah!" or "wow!", because doing so captures both the suddenness and forcefulness with which the experience of awe and its attendant affirmation can strike us.

But Paulos' wish to strip Yeahism of narrative and possibly even existence claims is impossible. There's a narrative already built into the proclamation "Yeah!" that affirms the natural world, celebrates it, and announces gratitude for its existence. Granted, whether Paulos' attribution of mystery to the world will be accepted as an existence claim depends on whether one accepts the ultimate unfathomability of the natural realm. But if one does, then Paulos' Yeahism contains, at least implicitly, two of the three characteristics he hoped to avoid. This doesn't show that Yeahism is fundamentally flawed, but only that there's more to even a basic response like "Yeah!" than Paulos imagines.

A less minimalistic model for resolving the contradiction is offered by author and founding editor of *Skeptic* magazine Michael Shermer. Science and spirituality (Shermer defines the latter as "a way of being in the world, a sense of one's place in the cosmos, a relationship to that which extends beyond oneself") fulfill one another because whatever elicits responses of wonderment and awe is a source of spirituality, and science "does this in spades" (Shermer 2006, pp. 158, 159). Whether it is Hubble images, evolutionary processes that work from the bottom-up under the direction of "built-in self-organizing principles of emergence and complexity," or the sheer "sensuality of discovery" that can capstone scrutiny of the natural world, science provides raw material for the transcendent (but not supernatural) narrative that we humans crave (pp 160, 161). Shermer sees the relationship between science and spirituality as so intimately complementary that he proposes a combinatory word, "sciensuality," to refer to it. Sciensuality, rather than traditional theistic narratives, is the "preeminent story of our age" through which we can explore Gauguin's three fundamental questions about who we are, whence we came, and where we're going (p. 161).

Finally, philosopher Andre Comte-Sponville offers a model of atheist spirituality that, borrowing a term from the nineteenth-century poet Jules Laforgue, he calls "immanensity." Even though Comte-Sponville believes that a godless religion is contradictory, he sees nothing inconsistent in a godless spirituality. This is because, as we saw earlier, he defines the "life of the spirit" in terms of function rather than essence, and by function he means to include the kinds of peak experiences—awe, wonder, gratitude, praise, and so on—with which we've become familiar in this chapter. The natural world alone elicits these spiritual experiences because it is all there is—in fact, it is the All. When we contemplate it, we're struck, with either awe or terror, by its immanence and its immensity (hence "immanensity").

We are in the All, and whether it is finite or not, it surpasses us (goes beyond us) in very direction; its limits, if it has any, are permanently beyond our reach. It envelops, contains and exceeds us. Is it a transcendence? Not at all, since we are inside of it. It is an inexhaustible, indefinite immanence, whose limits are both undefined and inaccessible. We are inside it—we live within the unfathomable. (Comte-Sponville 2007, p. 145)

Comte-Sponville's immanensity is especially interesting, because the immanent transcendence it defends may seem as oxymoronic as "atheist spirituality." On the one hand, the experience of the All isn't transcendent in the traditional religious sense because it doesn't go beyond the natural realm. It can't, because there's nothing to go beyond to. Nature is All there is. But on the other hand, the inexhaustibility and unfathomability of the All within which we dwell still offers opportunities for transcendence in a non-religious sense. The ocean of immanence that we're inside, when we stop to contemplate its imminence and immensity, can't but provide us with that sudden jolt that calls into question the everyday routine we take for granted.

This break in the quotidian Comte-Sponville calls an enlargement of the soul. When we grasp the fact that the universe is All, we also recognize that we, in relation to it, are "next to nothing." Coming to the realization of our own insignificance in the face of the universe "may be wounding to our ego, but it also enlarges our soul, because the ego has been put in its place at long last. It has stopped taking up all the room."

Although Comte-Sponville doesn't say it, surely part of what's involved in our ego "taking up all the room" is our projection of it into the heavens as God. But as we saw in Chapter 5, this hyper-extension of the ego is ultimately destructive of well-being. In bowing to the All of the universe, "the spirit break[s] free, at least partially, of the tiny prison of the self" (p. 148). Anxieties and fears that alienate one from the natural world can be put in perspective, thus allowing us to feel unified rather than at odds with it. Once we grasp our puniness and cease thinking of ourselves as the apex of creation, a privileged part of the cosmos that stands apart from everything else, we can finally feel at home in the world.

What a relief, when the ego gets out of the way! Nothing remains but the All, with the body, marvelously, inside of it, as if restored to the world and to itself. Nothing remains but the enormous thereness of being, nature and the universe, with no one left inside of us to be dismayed or reassured, or at least no one at this particular instant, in this particular body, to worry about dismay and reassurance, anxiety and danger. (p. 149)

It is surely something like this that Camus had in mind when he imagined Janine's extraordinary desert experience under the starry heavens.

RAPPROCHEMENT

The prospect of an atheist spirituality does more than provide nonbelievers with a "sacred" narrative that squares with their naturalism while legitimating peak experiences. It also offers a possibility for fruitful, non-acrimonious dialogue between theists and atheists that may result in some sort of rapprochement—a meeting, as E. O. Wilson evocatively puts it, "on the near side of metaphysics" (Wilson 2006, p. 4).

But for the meeting to take place, each side will have to recognize something of merit in the other. Their common ground obviously can't be either the existence of God or the legitimacy of God-belief. The bottom-line point of departure between atheist and theist is the first's denial and the second's affirmation of God. The atheist rests his nonbelief on one vision of the way reality is (naturalism), the theist on another (supernaturalism) Moreover, even though the reflective theist will concede the atheist's claim that people frequently believe in God for bad reasons, she'll insist that there are good reasons for believing as well. Nor is ethics likely to be the grounds on which rapprochement can be achieved. In Chapter 6 we saw that some atheists admit that there might be a practical use for religion-based morality if it serves to inhibit destructive behavior in believers. But it was also noted that just as many atheists—and, indeed, probably more—contend that God-belief encourages both psychological and physical destructiveness. So it's doubtful that ethics can provide the opportunity for believers and nonbelievers to meet on the near side of metaphysics.

The realm of spirituality seems a promising locus for dialogue. Even though the atheist and the theist have different explanations for peak experiences like wonder, awe, gratitude, and praise, both of them recognize how important they are to a fulfilling life. The atheist can appreciate the insight that religious traditions shed on the life of the spirit—as Comte-Sponville writes, "I have too much admiration for Pascal and Leibnitz, Bach and Tolstoy . . . to turn up my nose at the faith that inspired them"—without concurring with their God-belief (Comte-Sponville 2007, p. 77). Similarly, theists and other believers can profit from the close scrutiny and celebration of the beauty and grandeur of the natural world without adopting naturalism. In the Introduction, following Simone Weil, we saw that atheists and theists can both benefit from one another's criticisms. The complementary suggestion here is that each can also come to a more insightful self-understanding if they acknowledge that they share some common ground. Atheists and theists will never agree on the God-issue. But their disagreement is entirely compatible with deep listening, self-scrutiny, mutual respect, and an openness to new insights.

NOTES

[1] In a certain sense, it might be argued that theology, while claiming to deal with the mysterious—God—in fact typically operates as if it's attacking a problem which has a definite, comprehensible solution. This seems to have been one of Paul Tillich's objections to existential claims about God. (See Chapter 3).

[2] Along these lines, it's interesting to compare Charles Sanders Peirce's argument that a metaphysical principle of love binds the universe together (Peirce 1992).

[3] See Wilson (1984).

[4] A phrase made popular by the unknown author of the fourteenth-century mystical text *The Cloud of Unknowing.*

[5] In the Buddhist tradition, this receptivity is expressed in the wonderful simile that likens the receptive mind to a transparent and unblemished pane of glass.

WORKS CITED

Adams, Douglas (1979), *The Hitchhiker's Guide to the Galaxy*. New York: Harmony Books.

Allen, Woody (1980), *Stardust Memories*.

Anselm (2001), *Proslogion, with the Replies of Gaunilo and Anselm*, trans. Thomas Williams. Indianapolis, IN: Hackett.

Antony, Louise (2009), "Atheism as perfect piety," in Robert K. Garcia and Nathan L. King (eds), *Is Goodness without God Good Enough?* Lanham, MD: Rowman & Littlefield, pp. 67–84.

Aquinas, St. Thomas (1980), *Summa Theologiae*, Blackfriars Edition. London: Eyre & Spottiswoode.

Arnold, Matthew (1961), *Poetry and Criticism of Matthew Arnold*, A. Dwight Culler (ed.). Boston, MA: Houghton Mifflin.

Austin, J. L. (1962), *Sense and Sensibilia*. New York: Oxford University Press.

Ayer, Alfred J. (1952), *Language, Truth and Logic*. New York: Dover.

Baggini, Julian (2003), *Atheism: A Very Short Introduction*. New York: Oxford University Press.

Baggini, Julian (2004), *What's It All About? Philosophy and the Meaning of Life*. New York: Oxford University Press.

Barnes, Hazel (1967), *An Existentialist Ethics*. New York: Vintage.

Barrow, John D. and Frank J. Tipler (1988), *The Anthropic Cosmological Principle*. New York: Oxford University Press.

Bayle, Pierre ([1682]1708), *Miscellaneous Reflections, Occasion'd by the Comet Which Appear'd in December, 1680*. London: J. Morphew.

Beattie, Tina (2007), *The New Atheists: The Twilight of Reason and the War On Religion*. Maryknoll, NY: Orbis Books.

Beit-Hallahmi, Benjamin (2007), "Atheists: A psychological profile," in Michael Martin (ed.), *The Cambridge Companion to Atheism*. New York: Cambridge University Press, pp. 300–17.

Bradlaugh, Charles (1980), "A plea for atheism," in Gordon Stein (ed.), *An Anthology of Atheism and Rationalism*. Buffalo, NY: Prometheus, Books, pp. 7–19.

Buckley, Michael J. (1987), *At the Origins of Modern Atheism*. New Haven, CT: Yale University Press.

Bulhof, Else, and Laurens ten Kate (2000), *Flight of the Gods: Philosophical Perspectives on Negative Theology*. New York: Fordham University Press.

Burrill, Donald R. (ed.), (1967), *The Cosmological Arguments*. New York: Anchor.

Bury, J. B. (1913), *A History of Freedom of Thought*. New York: Henry Holt.

Camus, Albert (1955), *The Myth of Sisyphus and Other Essays*, trans. Justin O'Brien. New York: Vintage.

Camus, Albert (1958), *Exile and the Kingdom*, trans. Justin O'Brien. New York: Vintage.

Carlin, George (2009), "I've been worshipping the sun . . .", freeTHOUGHTpedia, http://freethoughtpedia.com/wiki/George_Carlin (accessed December 15, 2009).

Cartwright, Nancy (2008), *The Dappled World: A Study of the Boundaries of Science*. Cambridge: Cambridge University Press.

Cicero (1972), *The Nature of the Gods*, trans. Horace C. P. McGregor. London: Harmondsworth.

Clifford, W. K. (1999), *The Ethics of Belief and Other Essays*. Amherst, NY: Prometheus Books.

Comte, Auguste (2009), *The Positive Philosophy of Auguste Comte*, trans. Harriet Martineau. 2 vols. New York: Cambridge University Press.

Comte-Sponville, Andre (2007), *The Little Book of Atheist Spirituality*, trans. Nancy Huston. New York: Viking.

Cottingham, John (2006), *On the Meaning of Life*. London: Routledge.

Craig, William Lane (1995), *Theism, Atheism, and Big Bang Cosmology*. New York: Oxford University Press.

Craig, William Lane (2000a), "The absurdity of life without god," in E. D. Klemke (ed.), *The Meaning of Life*. New York: Oxford University Press, pp. 40–56.

Craig, William Lane (2000b), *The Kalam Cosmological Argument*. Eugene, OR: Wipf & Stock.

Craig, William Lane (2001), *The Cosmological Argument from Plato to Leitnitz*. Eugene, OR: Wipf & Stock.

Critias (2001), *The Sisyphus Fragment*, trans. R. G. Bury; revised by J. Garrett. www.wku.edu/~jan.garrett/302/critias.htm (accessed March 2009).

Darwin, Charles (1958), *The Autobiography of Charles Darwin*. Nora Barlow (ed.). New York: W. W. Norton.

Darwin, Charles (1993), *The Correspondence of Charles Darwin*, Volume 8. Sydney Frederick Burckhardt, Janet Browne, Duncan M. Porter, and Marsha Richmond (eds). Cambridge: Cambridge University Press.

Darwin, Charles ([1859]1999), *The Origin of Species*. New York: Bantam.

Davies, Brian (1993), *An Introduction to the Philosophy of Religion*. (2nd edn). Oxford: Oxford University Press.

Davies, Paul (1994), "The unreasonable effectiveness of science," in John Marks Templeton (ed.), *Evidence of Purpose: Scientists Discover the Creator*. New York: Continuum, pp. 44–56.

Dawkins, Richard (2001), "Eulogy for Richard Adams." www.edge.org/documents/adams_index.html (accessed May 10, 2009).

Dawkins, Richard (2003), "You can't have it both ways: Irreconcilable differences?", in *Science and Religion: Are They Compatible?*, Paul Kurtz (ed.). Amherst, NY: Prometheus Books, pp. 205–9.

Dawkins, Richard (2006), *The God Delusion*. Boston: Houghton Mifflin.

Day, Vox (2008), *The Irrational Atheist*. Dallas, TX: BenBella Books.

Dennett, Daniel (1984), *Elbow Room*. Cambridge, MA: MIT Press.

Dennett, Daniel (1995), *Darwin's Dangerous Idea: Evolution and the Meaning of Life*. New York: Simon and Schuster.

Dennett, Daniel (2005), Interview in "The Atheist Tapes." Disc 1.

Dennett, Daniel (2006), *Breaking the Spell: Religion as a Natural Phenomenon*. New York: Penguin.

Dennett, Daniel (2007), "Atheism and evolution," in Michael Martin (ed.), *The Cambridge Companion to Atheism*. Cambridge: Cambridge University Press, pp. 135–48.

Dombrowski, Daniel A. (2006), *Rethinking the Ontological Argument: A Neoclassical Theistic Response*. New York: Cambridge University Press.

Dostoyevsky, Fyodor (1980), *The Brothers Karamazov*, trans. Constance Garnett. New York: Signet.

Dostoyevsky, Fyodor (2009), *Notes from Underground,* trans. Boris Jakim. Grand Rapids, MI: William B. Eerdmans.

Durkheim, Emile (2008), *The Elementary Forms of Religious Life*, Mark Cladis (ed.). New York: Oxford University Press.

Epicurus (1940), "Letter to Menoeceus," in Whitney J. Oates (ed.), *The Stoic and Epicurean Philosophers*. New York: Random House, pp. 30–4.

Fales, Evan (2007), "Naturalism and physicalism," in Michael Martin (ed.), *The Cambridge Companion to Atheism*. Cambridge: Cambridge University Press, pp. 118–34.

Feuerbach, Ludwig (2004), *The Essence of Christianity*, trans. Alexander Loos. Amherst, NY: Prometheus Books.

Fine, Jonathan (2008), "Contrasting religious and secular terrorism," in *Middle Eastern Quarterly* 15 (1), 59–69.

Flew, Anthony (1955), 'Theology and Falsification,' in Anthony Flew and Alasdair MacIntyre (eds), *New Essays in Philosophical Theology*. New York: Macmillan, pp. 96–9.

Flew, Antony (1966), *God and Philosophy*. London: Hutchinson.

Flew, Antony (1976), *The Presumption of Atheism*. London: Pemberton.

Flew, Antony (2007), *There Is a God*. New York: HarperCollins.

Flew, Antony and Alasdair MacIntyre (eds) (1955), *New Essays in Philosophical Theology*. New York: Macmillan.

Franklin, Benjamin (1963), *Papers of Benjamin Franklin*, Volume 7. Leonard W. Labaree et al. (eds). New Haven, CT: Yale University Press.

Franklin, Benjamin (1995), *Papers of Benjamin Franklin*, Volume 31. Barbara B. Oberg (ed.). New Haven, CT: Yale University Press.

Frazer, James (1998), *The Golden Bough: A Study in Magic and Religion* (abridged edn) New York: Oxford University Press.

Frege, Gottlob (1980), *The Foundations of Arithmetic*, trans. J. L. Austin. Oxford: Oxford University Press.

Freud, Sigmund (1961), *The Future of an Illusion*, in *The Standard Edition of the Complete Psychological Works of Sigmund Freud*, James Strachey (ed.). Volume 21. London: Hogarth Press.

Freud, Sigmund (1963), *Psychoanalysis and Faith*, trans Eric Mosbacher. New York: Basic Books.

Gaskin, J. C. A. (1988), *Varieties of Unbelief from Epicurus to Sartre*. New York: Prentice-Hall.

Gillies, Donald (1998), "The Duhem thesis and the Quine thesis," in Martin Curd and J. A. Cover (eds), *Philosophy of Science: The Central Issues*. New York: Norton, pp. 302–19.

Gingerich, Owen (2006), *God's Universe*. Cambridge, MA: The Belknap Press of Harvard University Press.

Goetz, Stewart and Charles Taliaferro (2008), *Naturalism*. Grand Rapids, MI: William B. Eerdmans.

Goodenough,. Ursula (1998), *The Sacred Depths of Nature*. New York: Oxford University Press.

Gould, Stephen Jay (1999), *Rock of Ages: Science and Religion in the Fullness of Life*. New York: Ballantine.

Gould, Stephen Jay (2003), "Nonoverlapping magisteria," in Paul Kurtz (ed.), *Science and Religion: Are They Compatible?*. Amherst, NY: Prometheus Books, pp. 191–203.

Greeley, Andrew (2003), *Religion in Europe at the End of the Second Millennium*. New Brunswick, NJ: Transaction.

Grey, William (2000), "Gasking's proof." *Analysis* 60 (4), 368–70.

Grim, Patrick (1979), "Plantinga's god and other monstrosities." *Religious Studies* 15, 91–7.

Hamer, Dean (2004), *The God Gene: How Faith is Hardwired into Our Genes*. New York: Doubleday.

Harbour, Daniel (2001), *An Intelligent Person's Guide to Atheism*. London: Duckworth.

Harris, Sam (2004), *The End of Faith: Religion, Terror, and the Future of Reason*. New York, NY: W. W. Norton.

Harris, Sam (2006), *Letter to a Christian Nation*. New York: Alfred A. Knopf.

Hartshorne, Charles (1965), *Anselm's Discovery: A Re-examination of the Ontological Argument for God's Existence*. LaSalle, IL: Open Court Press.

Hartshorne, Charles (1983), *Omnipotence and Other Theological Mistakes*. Albany, NY: State University of New York Press.

Haught, John (2000), *God After Darwin: A Theology of Evolution*. Boulder, CO: Westview.

Haught, John (2008), *God and the New Atheism*. Louisville, KY: Westminster John Knox Press.

Hecht, Jennifer Michael (2003), *Doubt: A History*. San Francisco: Harper.

Hedges, Chris (2008), *I Don't Believe in Atheists*. New York, NY: Free Press.

Heidegger, Martin (1962), *Being and Time*, trans. John Macquarrie and Edward Robinson. New York: Harper.

Herrick, Jim (2005), *Humanism: An Introduction*. Amherst, NY: Prometheus Books.

Hick, John (ed.) (1964), *The Existence of God*. New York: Collier.

Hick, John (1966), *Faith and Knowledge* (2nd edn). London: Fontana.

Hick, John (1971), *Arguments for the Existence of God*. London: Herder & Herder.

Hick, John (2007), *Evil and the God of Love* (rev. edn) London: Palgrave Macmillan.

Hick, John and Arthur C. McGill (eds), (2009), *The Many-Faced Argument: Studies on the Ontological Argument for the Existence of God*. Eugene, OR: Wipf & Stock.

Hitchens, Christopher (2007), *God Is Not Great: How Religion Poisons Everything*. New York, NY: Twelve.

Hobbes, Thomas ([1651]1904), *Leviathan*. Cambridge: Cambridge University Press.

Howard-Snyder, Daniel and Paul Moser (eds) (2001), *Divine Hiddenness: New Essays*. New York: Cambridge University Press.

Hume, David ([1748]1955), *An Inquiry Concerning Human Understanding*. New York: Liberal Arts Press.

Hume, David ([1757]1956), *The Natural History of Religion*. Stanford, CA: Stanford University Press.

Hume, David ([1740]1972), *A Treatise of Human Nature*, Bks 2 and 3. Pall S. Ardal (ed.). London: Fontana/Collins.

Hume, David ([1779]1998), *Dialogues Concerning Natural Religion, with Of the Immortality of the Soul, Of Suicide, Of Miracles* (2nd edn). Indianapolis, IN: Hackett.

Hyman, Gavin (2007), 'Atheism in modern history,' in Michael Martin (ed.), *The Cambridge Companion to Atheism*. Cambridge: Cambridge University Press, pp. 27–46.

Irvine, William (1956), *Apes, Angels and Victorians*. London: Weidenfeld & Nicolson.

Jacoby, Susan (2004), *Freethinkers: A History of American Secularism*. New York: Henry Holt.

James, William (1911), *The Will to Believe and Other Essays in Popular Philosophy*. London: Longman, Greens, and Co.

James, William (1994), *The Varieties of Religious Experience*. New York: Modern Library.

Jammer, Max (1999), *Einstein and Religion: Physics and Theology*. Princeton, NJ: Princeton University Press.

Jefferson, Thomas (2002), *The Political Writings of Thomas Jefferson*, Merrill D. Peterson (ed.). Chapel Hill, NC: University of North Carolina Press.

Johnson, B. C. (1983), *The Atheist Debater's Handbook*. Amherst, NY: Prometheus Books.

Joshi, S. T. (2000), *Atheism: A Reader*. Amherst, NY: Prometheus Books.

Kant, Immanuel (1909), *Critique of Practical Reason*, trans. Thomas Kingsmill Abbott. London: Longman's, Green, and Company.

Kant, Immanuel (1965), *Critique of Pure Reason*, trans. Norman Kemp. New York: St. Martin's Press.

Kierkegaard, Soren ([1844]1974), *Philosophical Fragments*, trans David Swenson & Howard V. Hong. Princeton: Princeton University Press.

Kuhn, Thomas S. (1996), *The Structure of Scientific Revolutions*. Chicago: University of Chicago Press.

Kurtz, Paul (1988), *Forbidden Fruit: The Ethics of Humanism*. Buffalo, NY: Prometheus Books.

Kurtz, Paul (2003), "Afterthoughts," in Paul Kurtz (ed.), *Science and Religion: Are They Compatible?*. Amherst, NY: Prometheus Books.

Kurtz, Paul (2007), *What Is Secular Humanism?* Amherst, NY: Prometheus Books.

Lecky, W. E. H. (1955), *The Rise and Influence of Rationalism in Europe*. New York: George Braziller.

Lewis, C. S. (2001), *The Problem of Pain*. San Francisco: HarperOne.

Lewis, Daniel Day (1959), *What Present-Day Theologians are Thinking*. New York: Harper & Row.

Lucretius (1940), *On the Nature of Things*, in Whitney J. Oates (ed.), *The Stoic and Epicurean Philosophers*. New York: Random House

MacIntyre, Alasdair (1957), *Metaphysical Beliefs*. London: SCM Press.

Mackie, J. L. (1988), *The Miracle of Theism*. Oxford: Oxford University Press.

Macquarrie, John (1967), *God-Talk: An Examination of the Language and Logic of Theology*. New York: Harper and Row.

Malcolm, Norman (1965), "Anselm's ontological arguments," in Alvin Plantinga (ed.), *The Ontological Argument*. Garden City, NY: Doubleday, pp. 136–59.

Malinowski, Bronislaw (1992), *Magic, Science, and Religion, and Other Essays*. Long Grove, IL: Waveland Press.

Marcel, Gabriel (1949), *Being and Having*, trans. Katharine Farrer. Westminster, UK: Dacre Press.

Marcel, Gabriel (1951), *The Mystery of Being*. Volume 1: *Reflection and Mystery*, trans. G. S. Fraser. London: Harvill Press.

Marion, Jean-Luc (1995), *God Without Being*, trans. Thomas A. Carlson. Chicago: University of Chicago Press.

Martin, Michael (1990), *Atheism: A Philosophical Justification*. Philadelphia, PA: Temple University Press.

Martin, Michael and Ricki Monnier (2003), *The Impossibility of God*. Amherst, NY: Prometheus Books.

Marx, Karl (1982), *Critique of Hegel's 'Philosophy of Right,'* trans. Joseph O'Malley. Cambridge: Cambridge University Press.

McClellan, David (1976), *Karl Marx*. New York: Viking Press.

McGinn, Colin (2005), Interview in "The Atheist Tapes." Disc 1.

McGrath, Alister (2007), *The Dawkins Delusion: Atheist Fundamentalism and the Denial of the Divine*. London: SPCK.

Mill, John Stuart (1924), *Autobiography*. London: Oxford University Press.

Miller, J. Hillis (1963), *The Disappearance of God*. Cambridge, MA: The Belknap Press of Harvard University Press.

Montaigne, Michel ([1588]1993), "On the lame," in *The Complete Essays*, trans. M.A. Screech. New York: Penguin, pp. 1160–1172.

Muller, Max (2002), *The Essential Max Muller: On Language, Mythology, and Religion*, Jon R. Stone (ed.). New York: Palgrave Macmillan.

Nagel, Thomas (2000), "The meaning of life," in E. D. Klemke (ed.), *The Meaning of Life*. New York: Oxford University Press, pp. 5–7.

Nagel, Thomas (2001), *The Last Word*. New York: Oxford University Press.

Nahm, Milton C. (1964), *Selections from Early Greek Philosophy*. New York: Appleton-Century-Crofts.

National Academy of Sciences (1998), "Teaching about evolution and the nature of science." www.nap.edu/catalog/5787.html (accessed June 2009).

Niebuhr, Reinhold (ed.) (1969), *Marx and Engels on Religion*. New York: Schocken Books.

Nielsen, Kai (1971), *Contemporary Critiques of Religion*. New York: Herder & Herder.

Nielsen, Kai (1990), *Ethics Without God* (rev. edn). Amherst, NY: Prometheus Books.

Nielsen, Kai (1997), "Naturalistic explanations of theistic belief," in Phillip Quinn and Charles Taliaferro (eds), *A Companion to Philosophy of Religion*. Malden, MA: Blackwell, pp. 402–16.

Nielsen, Kai (2000), "Death and the meaning of life," in E. D. Klemke (ed.), *The Meaning of Life*. New York: Oxford University Press, pp. 153–9.

Nielsen, Kai (2001), *Naturalism and Religion*. Amherst, NY: Prometheus Books.

Nietzsche, Friedrich (1974), *The Gay Science*, trans. Walter Kaufmann. New York: Vintage.

Noelle, David C. (2003), "Searching for god in the machine," in Paul Kurtz (ed.), *Science and Religion: Are They Compatible?* Amherst, NY: Prometheus Books.

Norman, Richard (2005), *On Humanism*. London: Routledge.

Nowacki, Mark R. (2007), *The Kalam Cosmological Argument for God*. Amherst, NY: Prometheus Books.

Onfrey, Michel (2008), *Atheist Manifesto*, trans. Jeremy Leggatt. New York: Arcade Publishing.

Oppy, Graham (2007), *Ontological Arguments and Belief in God*. New York: Cambridge University Press.

Paley, William (1802), *Natural Theology; or, Evidence of the Existence and Attributes of the Deity* (12th edn). London: J. Faulder.

Pals, Daniel L. (1996), *Seven Theories of Religion*. New York: Oxford University Press.

Pandian, Jacob (2003), "The dangerous quest for cooperation between science and religion," in Paul Kurtz (ed.), *Science and Religion: Are They Compatible?* Amherst, NY: Prometheus Books, pp. 161–9.

Pascal (1958), *Pensees*, trans. W. F. Trotter. New York: E. P. Dutton.

Paulos, John Allen (2008), *Irreligion: A Mathematician Explains Why the Arguments for God Just Don't Add Up*. New York: Hill and Wang.

Peirce, C. S. (1992), "Evolutionary love," in Nathan Houser and Christian J. W. Kloesel (eds), *The Essential Peirce: Selected Philosophical Writings*. Volume 1. 1867–1893. Bloomington, IN: Indiana University Press, pp. 352–371.

Plantinga, Alvin (ed.) (1965), *The Ontological Argument from St. Anselm to Contemporary Philosophers.* New York: Anchor Books.

Plantinga, Alvin (1977), *God, Freedom, and Evil.* Grand Rapids, MI: William B. Eerdmans.

Plantinga, Alvin (1999), "Reformed epistemology," in Phillip Quinn and Charles Taliaferro (eds), *A Companion to Philosophy Of Religion.* Malden, MA: Blackwell, pp. 383–9.

Plantinga, Alvin (2000), *Warranted Christian Belief.* New York: Oxford University Press.

Quine, W. V. and J. S. Ullian (1978), *The Web of Belief.* New York: McGraw-Hill.

Radcliffe-Brown, A. R. (1976), *Structure and Function in Primitive Society.* London: Routledge & Kegan.

Rashdall, Hastings (1963), "God and the moral consciousness," in William Alston (ed.), *Religious Belief and Philosophical Thought.* New York: Harcourt, Brace and World.

Raymo, Chet (2006), "On prayer," in ScienceMusings.com (16 April). www.sciencemusings.com/2006/04/on-prayer.html. (accessed February 2, 2009).

Raymo, Chet (2008), *When God is Gone, Everything is Holy.* Notre Dame, IN: Sorin Books.

Rees, Martin (2001), *Just Six Numbers: The Deep Forces that Shape the Universe.* New York: Basic Books.

Reichenbach, Bruce (1982), *Evil and a Good God.* New York: Fordham University Press.

Rorty, Richard (1989), *Contingency, Irony, and Solidarity.* Cambridge: Cambridge University Press.

Rowe, William (1998), *The Cosmological Argument.* New York: Fordham University Press.

Russell, Bertrand (1957), *Why I Am Not a Christian and Other Essays.* New York: Simon and Schuster.

Russell, Bertrand and F. C. Copleston (1964), 'A debate on the existence of God,' in John Hick (ed.), *The Existence of God.* New York: Collier, pp. 167–91.

Sagan, Carl (1980), *Cosmos.* New York: Random House.

Sartre, Jean-Paul (1969), *Being and Nothingness,* trans. Hazel Barnes. London: Routledge.

Sartre, Jean-Paul (1977), *Existentialism is a Humanism,* trans. Philip Mairet. Brooklyn, NY: Haskell House.

Schellenberg, J. L. (2006), *Divine Hiddenness and Human Reason.* Ithaca, NY: Cornell University Press.

Schumacher, E. F. (1999), *Small Is Beautiful: Economics as if People Mattered.* Point Roberts, WA: Hartley & Marks.

Scriven, Michael (1966), *Primary Philosophy.* New York: McGraw-Hill.

Searle, John (2004), *Mind: A Brief Introduction.* New York: Oxford University Press.

Sellers, Roy Wood (1922), *Evolutionary Naturalism.* Chicago: Open Court.

Shermer, Michael (2006), *Why Darwin Matters.* New York: Henry Holt & Co.

WORKS CITED

Shotwell, Daniel A. (2003), "From the anthropic principle to the supernatural," in *Science and Religion: Are they Compatible?*, Paul Kurtz (ed.). Amherst, NY: Prometheus Books, pp. 47–9.

Slack, Gordy (2007), *The Battle Over the Meaning of Everything: Evolution, Intelligent Design, and a School Board in Dover, PA*. San Francisco: Jossey-Bass.

Solomon, Robert (2002), *Spirituality for the Skeptic: The Thoughtful Love of Life*. New York: Oxford University Press.

Sorel, Tom (1994), *Scientism: Philosophy and the Infatuation with Science*. New York: Routledge.

Stace, Walter (1960), *The Teachings of the Mystics*. New York: New American Library.

Stark, Rodney and William Sims Bainbridge (1996), *A Theory of Religion*. Piscataway, NJ: Rutgers University Press.

Stroud, Barry (2004), "The charm of naturalism," in Mario De Caro and David Macarthur (eds), *Naturalism in Question*. Cambridge, MA: Harvard University Press, pp. 21–35.

Swinburne, Richard (1977), *The Coherence of Theism*. London: Oxford University Press.

Swinburne, Richard (1991), *The Existence of God*. Oxford: Clarendon Press.

Swinburne, Richard (1998), "Argument from the fine-tuning of the universe," in John Leslie (ed.), *Modern Cosmology and Philosophy*. Amherst, NY: Prometheus, pp. 160–79.

Thrower, James (1979), *The Alternative Tradition: A Study of Unbelief in the Ancient World*. The Hague: Mouton de Gruyter.

Thrower, James (2000), *Western Atheism: A Short History*. Amherst, NY: Prometheus.

Tillich, Paul (1973), *Systematic Theology*, Volume 1. Chicago: University of Chicago Press.

Tolstoy, Leo (2003), *The Death of Ivan Ilych and Other Stories,* trans. Hugh McLean. New York: Signet.

Troyat, Henri (1965), *Tolstoy*, trans. Nancy Amphoux. New York: Dell.

Tylor, E. B. (1903), *Primitive Culture*. (4th edn) London: John Murray.

van Doren, Carl (2007), "Why I am an unbeliever," in *The Portable Atheist*, Christopher Hitchens (ed.). Philadelphia, PA: Da Capo Press, pp. 138–42.

Varghese, Roy Abraham (2007), "Preface," in Antony Flew, *There Is a God: How the World's Most Notorious Atheist Changed His Mind*. New York, NY: HarperCollins.

Weil, Simone (1952), *Gravity and Grace*, trans. Arthur Wills. New York: G. P. Putnam's Sons.

Weinberg, Steven (1977), *The First Three Minutes*. New York: Basic Books.

Weinberg, Steven (2001), "A universe with no designer," in *Cosmic Questions Annals of the New York Academy of Sciences*, 950, 169–174.

Weinberg, Steven (2003), "A designer universe?' in Paul Kurtz (ed.), *Science and Religion: Are They Compatible?* Amherst, NY: Prometheus Books, pp. 31–40.

Whitehead, Alfred North (1933), *Adventures of Ideas*. Cambridge: Cambridge University Press.

Wiesel, Elie (1982), *Night*. trans. Stella Rodway. New York: Bantam.

Wilde, Oscar ([1890]2008), *The Picture of Dorian Gray*. New York: Oxford University Press.

Wilson, A. N. (1999), *God's Funeral*. New York: Ballantine.

Wilson, E. O. (1978), *On Human Nature*. New York: Bantam.

Wilson, E. O. (1984), *Biophilia*. Cambridge, MA: Harvard University Press.

Wilson, E. O. (1998), *Consilience*. New York: Alfred A. Knopf.

Wilson, E. O. (2006), *Creation: An Appeal to Save Life on Earth*. New York: W. W. Norton.

Wilson, Eric (2008), *Against Happiness: In Praise of Melancholy*. New York: Farrar, Straus and Giroux.

Wittgenstein, Ludwig ([1921]2001), *Tractatus Logico-Philosophicus*, trans. David Pears & Brian McGinnis. New York: Routledge.

Wolf, Gary (2006), "The church of the non-believers," in *Wired* 14/11, 1–7. www.wired.com/wired/archive/14.11/atheism.html. (accessed November 13, 2007).

Zuckerman, Phil (2007), "Atheism: Contemporary numbers and patterns," in Michael Martin (ed.), *The Companion to Atheism*. New York, NY: Cambridge University Press.

INDEX